IMAGES
of America

LOUISVILLE'S HISTORIC BLACK NEIGHBORHOODS

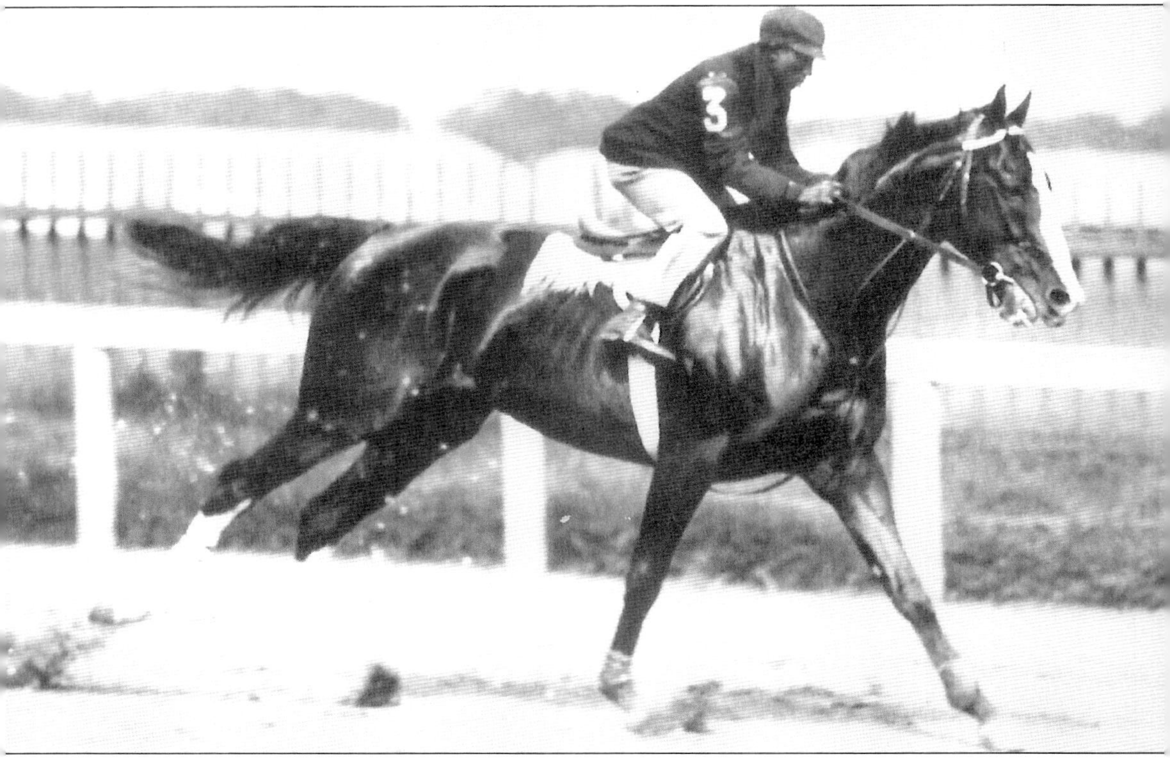

JAMES "JIMMY" WINKFIELD RIDING ALAN-A-DALE, 1902. Jimmy Winkfield was the winning jockey in the Kentucky Derby in both 1901 and 1902. "In the first Kentucky Derby, in 1875, 13 out of 15 jockeys were black," writes Lisa K. Winkler in "The Kentucky Derby's Forgotten Jockeys," on *Smithsonian* magazine's website. Then, Jim Crow laws and segregation drove them out of the league. In 1902, Winkfield was the last black jockey to win the Kentucky Derby, and "by 1921, they had disappeared from the Kentucky track and would not return until Marlon St. Julien rode in the 2000 race," notes Winkler. Fifteen of the first 28 Derby winners were black, and these African American jockeys who dominated the world of racing are a legacy nearly forgotten. (Photograph courtesy of the University of Louisville Photographic Archives Special Collection, Ekstrom Library.)

ON THE COVER: This 1928 image shows the Louisville Free Public Library Western Colored Library children's room at the library at 604 South Tenth Street. African American children are sitting at tables or standing by bookshelves; books are all around. In 1905, this was the first public library in the nation opened for African Americans and fully staffed by African American educators. On October 28, 1908, the newly constructed Carnegie library opened at its current location. The original site of the African American library was at 1123 West Chestnut Street. Pioneering African American librarian Thomas F. Blue focused on serving the community by educating African Americans in the science of librarianship. His apprentice program lasted into the 1930s and attracted students from across the South. This library was added to the National Register of Historic Places in 1975. (Photograph courtesy of the Louisville Free Public Library, Western Branch.)

IMAGES
of America

LOUISVILLE'S HISTORIC BLACK NEIGHBORHOODS

Beatrice S. Brown, PhD

ARCADIA
PUBLISHING

ISBN 978-0-7385-9185-8

Published by Arcadia Publishing
Charleston, South Carolina

Printed in the United States of America

Library of Congress Control Number: 2011944037

For all general information, please contact Arcadia Publishing:
Telephone 843-853-2070
Fax 843-853-0044
E-mail sales@arcadiapublishing.com
For customer service and orders:
Toll-Free 1-888-313-2665

Visit us on the Internet at www.arcadiapublishing.com

I dedicate this book to my late parents' rich legacy—Thomas and Irene Brown—and to all those who are hungry for truth and clarity.

To the African American children and children everywhere, who deserve the right to hear, read, and share their historic legacies with confidence and self-esteem. The images in Louisville's Historic Black Neighborhoods *display a story of durability and resilience, a "black diamond" of light and encouragement to all who dare to journey through its pages. Let's celebrate!*

Contents

Acknowledgments

I am most humbled for the sincere help and guidance in this very important project. Assisting me when needed, Kerry Hunter, librarian at the Louisville Free Public Library Western Branch, literally opened the archives room and allowed me to spend extensive time researching. Rev. Dr. Wilbur S. Browning Sr., senior pastor of the Centennial Olivet Baptist Church, shared photographs of the church and its origin; and Markham French, director of Plymouth Community Renewal Center, formerly Plymouth Settlement House, took the time to share such historical heritage. Thanks go to "Little David" Anderson, former religious program director and commercial production manager at WLOU, who was very generous in sharing prominent photographic images; and to Bill Carner, Pam Yeager, and Amy Purcell at the University of Louisville Photographic Archives Special Collection, Ekstrom Library. Unless otherwise noted, all images are the courtesy of this library. Also, special thanks go to the Smithsonian Institution; Bradley Swearingen, caretaker of the historic Berrytown Cemetery Inc.; and Ray "Dittle" Smith, Churchill Downs' black horseman and groomer, for sharing his photographs. Special thanks also go to Essie Sitgraves, wife of Carl Hamilton Sitgraves, an African American horse trainer and owner, for sharing authentic images from the Sitgraves Archives.

I also wish to thank my acquisitions editors at Arcadia Publishing, Elizabeth Gurley and Elizabeth Bray, for their expert guidance when needed. Special thanks also go to the Louisville Free Public Library, Main Branch Reference Division. Sources of information include the *Encyclopedia of Louisville* (2001 edition), the 1906 *Caron's Directory of the City of Louisville*, Kentucky Historical Society, and *The Village of Anchorage* by Samuel W. Thomas (first edition, 2004).

I am also very grateful to have been allowed to take photographs of historic churches, communities, centers, and businesses throughout Louisville. Thanks go to Albert E. Meyzeek Middle School (formerly Jackson Junior High), The Villages of Park DuValle, Newburg Community Center, and Parkland's Historic District Queen Anne Victorian homes. Thanks go to the following historic churches: Fifth Street Baptist Church (formerly First Baptist African Mission/First Colored Baptist Church), Green Street Baptist Church (formerly Second Baptist Church/Second Colored Baptist Church), Walnut Street Baptist Church (formerly First Baptist Church, the mother church to First Baptist African Mission), Coke Memorial United Methodist Church, Little Flock Missionary Baptist Church, Lampton Street Baptist Church, Zion Baptist Church, Centennial Olivet Baptist Church, and New Hope Baptist Church. These 19th-century churches held the torch as beacons of light and hope, standing in the gap for African American slaves and emancipated men and women in the Louisville area.

INTRODUCTION

The images in *Louisville's Historic Black Neighborhoods* unveil the complexity of life and the tenacity of people. These African Americans faced hostile challenges of racism and Jim Crow laws attempting to prevent them from excelling, yet their hope in the faith of their God and the commitment to press forward gave them courage and unmovable determination. They endured hardships and inhumane treatment designed to hinder and sway them towards staying in their place of inequality, injustice, and lack. Aware of their uphill battles, they continued steadfastly to meet rejection and immoral and hypocritical concepts of the time. *Louisville's Historic Black Neighborhoods* reveals triumph and unfolding victories over obstacles. Emancipated slaves, freed men, and women of color after the American Civil War, and during the Reconstruction era, purchased acres and developed their own communities and resting places for their loved ones. They bought land and leased shotgun cottages and lots from whites to begin their newly emancipated lives.

Smoketown is the only neighborhood in the city of Louisville that has continuously been home to free African Americans. By 1866, Smoketown was settled by these freemen; by 1871, the first public building in the community, the Eastern Colored School, was erected. Many in Smoketown worked in tobacco warehouses as cutters, processors, and haulers. This community had one of city's first African American public schools, which was founded in 1874. Smoketown is the only post–Civil War neighborhood settled mainly by African Americans that remains in the city of Louisville. By the 1950 census, 10,653 people lived in Smoketown and other historic black neighborhoods such as Petersburg and Newburg, Parkland, California, Russell, Berrytown, Griffytown, and Black Hill in Old Louisville, which began to thrive.

As these new neighborhoods sprang up populating this city, another historic event was being born. In 1875, the first Kentucky Derby was held, and 13 of the 15 jockeys were African American. That black horsemen, jockeys, groomers, trainers, and horse owners were most prominent in the Kentucky Derby is a nearly forgotten legacy. South Louisville holds this legacy.

Black Hill, an African American community in Old Louisville, was along Levering Street, where residents, who occupied over 100 bungalow homes, worked at Rib Tyler Company and in private homes of the wealthy, from whom they were isolated. These African Americans attended to their employers by cooking their meals, stabling their horses, and raising their children. These servants also attended to lawns and nurseries. At the end of World War I, Rev. William Washington was the first pastor of the New Hope Baptist Church, founded in 1872 in the Black Hill community. The church nourished Black Hill residents both in spirit, soul, and body. New Hope Baptist Church is presently located at 1026 Dixie Highway.

The California neighborhood was initially called Henderson and was settled by German immigrants around 1849. After the American Civil War and during the Reconstruction period, African Americans settled in the area.

Parkland was once a town named Homestead, Kentucky. It was surveyed in 1871 and was incorporated in 1874. In 1884, the name was changed to Parkland. On March 27, 1890, a tornado literally destroyed Parkland, and many homes were lost. In 1894, Parkland was annexed by Louisville and by the turn of the century had become a section of the larger city. White wealthy residents of central Parkland occupied 34th to 26th Streets from west to east and Woodland to Broadway Streets from north to south. Beyond these boundaries, homes were occupied by African Americans. The Joseph Seaman Cotter Homes, named after the prominent African American educator, civic leader, and prolific author, were a vital resource for African American families. Those African Americans who were financially stable bought homes in the surrounding areas of central Parkland.

The Central Business District was the heartbeat of Louisville and a very thriving area of businesses and social and entertainment activities.

The historic Berrytown Cemetery became the focal point for the Berrytown community when Alfred Berry (1840–1920)—for whom the community is named—purchased five acres in 1874. Other freedmen and freedwomen joined in to buy land as well. Kidd Williams purchased eight acres; Sally Carter, five acres; and William Butler, five acres—for a total of 23 acres. More than 300 burials at the site include the Berry family, other early settlers, and several military casualties. Since 1984, Berrytown Cemetery has been owned and operated by a corporation formed by area residents. It continues to exemplify the traditions of African American community building. Berrytown Cemetery is in the area of Old Henry and Berrytown Roads, off English Station Road.

Griffytown was established in 1879 and is located along the Old Harrods Creek Road. In 1879, Dan Griffy, an African American, purchased the land he previously lived on as a slave.

Petersburg was named after the freedman Peter Laws, who built a log cabin in the area of Indian Trail and Petersburg Roads after the Civil War, around 1865. Eliza Curtis Hundley Tevis and her husband, Henry, were early settlers of the Petersburg community. Eliza was born a slave but gained freedom in 1833. She and Henry purchased 40 acres in 1851 in Wet Woods. Tevis's 40 acres and Laws's 40 acres were joined together to form a rural African American community called Petersburg. Petersburg's Forest Home Cemetery evolved from an old slave burial ground and is the final resting place of Eliza Curtis Hundley Tevis (1802–1884) and other early settlers of the Petersburg community. The cemetery is located near the site of the Tevis home and is one of the oldest dedicated African American burial grounds in Kentucky.

Russell neighborhood was named after the renowned African American educator Harvey Clarence Russell, a Bloomfield, Kentucky, native. African Americans began moving in the area around the 1870s.

The historic Louisville Cemetery established in 1886 became the resting place for many African American inner-city residents from Smoketown, Russell, Black Hill, California, and Parkland. The cemetery is located at 1339 Popular Level Road.

African Americans in Louisville made the most of a bittersweet lifestyle and carved out a better society for all to live in. Pursuing their hunger for education and a better quality of life allowed them to build strong communities, churches, schools, and lodges. They had a solid commitment to become ideal citizens and role models for their communities and their country. Their accelerated determination led them to attend colleges and universities and to tread in arenas where no person of color had ventured. After achieving their educational goals, many returned to their communities to strengthen families and children. Louisville's African Americans taught their children sound principles and good morals of honesty and hard work, stressing the philosophy that education, initiative, and sound principles would take them far. This city embraces such an astounding history, and this book relives its magnificent and rich narrative.

One

Smoketown

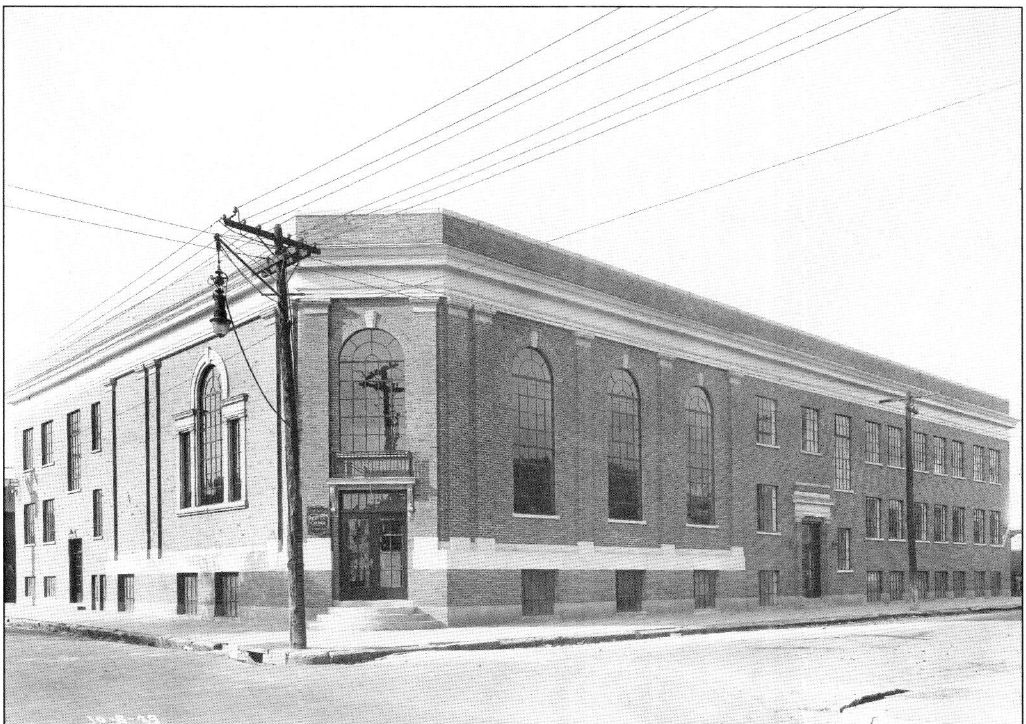

Grace Presbyterian Colored Mission, Louisville, Kentucky, October 8, 1929. Grace Hope Presbyterian Church, a low, brick building located at Hancock and Roselane Streets, served the African American Smoketown-Jackson community and continues to do so today. The Grace Hope Presbyterian Church was established in 1908, and its current address is 702 East Breckinridge Street. This historically black community began to flourish following the end of slavery in 1865, when thousands of African Americans moved to Louisville.

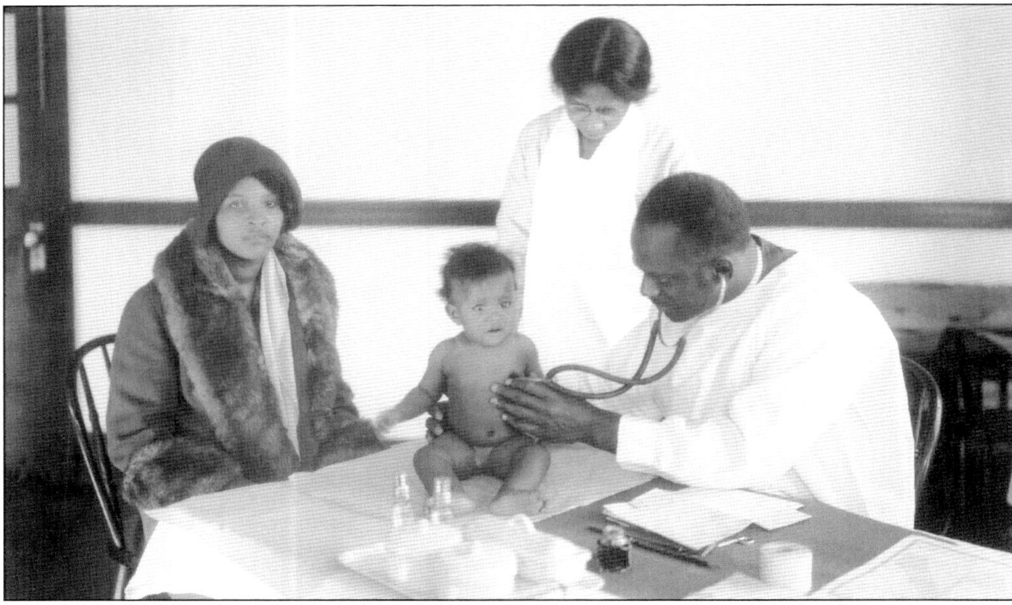

THE CLINIC AT PRESBYTERIAN COLORED MISSION, 1930. In this photograph, an unidentified doctor examines a baby while a nurse and a woman, who is probably the child's mother, look on. Located at 760 Hancock Street, the Presbyterian Colored Mission, initially named Hope Mission Station, was founded in 1898 by Rev. John Little. Its purpose was to be a help station for African Americans after the Civil War, offering resources and needed services.

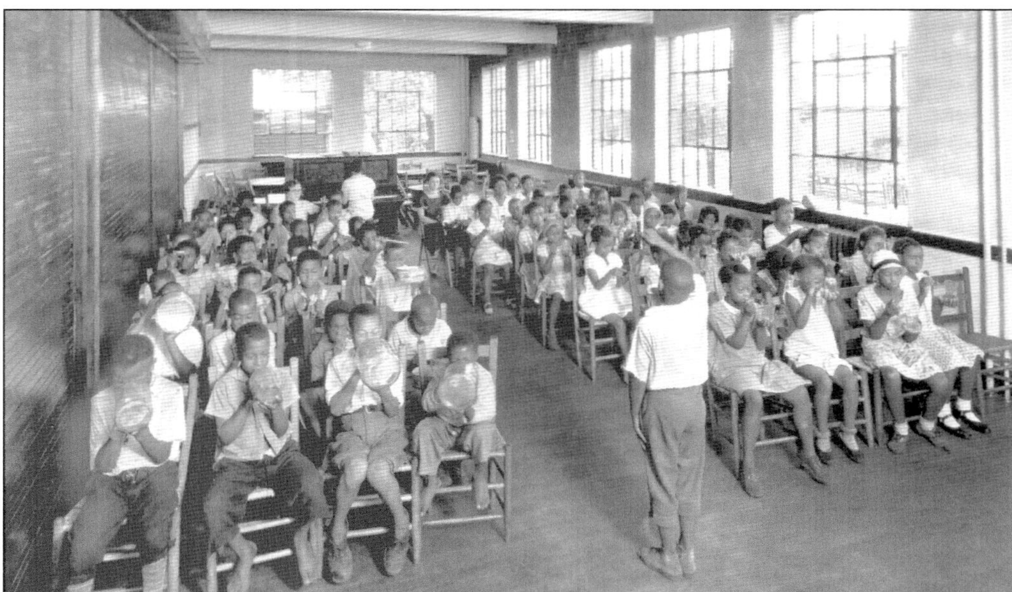

PRESBYTERIAN COLORED MISSION SUMMER SCHOOL, LOUISVILLE, KENTUCKY, 1932. A child stands at the front of the room with a baton in one hand appearing to act as the conductor. Rows of other African American children sit with various musical instruments, including jugs, drums, and glasses partially filled with water. An adult is playing piano at the back of the room, while two other white women sit nearby. Grace Hope Mission was established in 1898.

Refugees at Presbyterian Colored Mission, 1937. A vibrant resource in Smoketown, the Presbyterian Colored Mission was located at 314 South Hancock Street. In the view, two men and two women sit among beds and makeshift room dividers. The mission assisted in the well-being of its residents by offering temporary housing and feeding programs as well as through vocational and educational training.

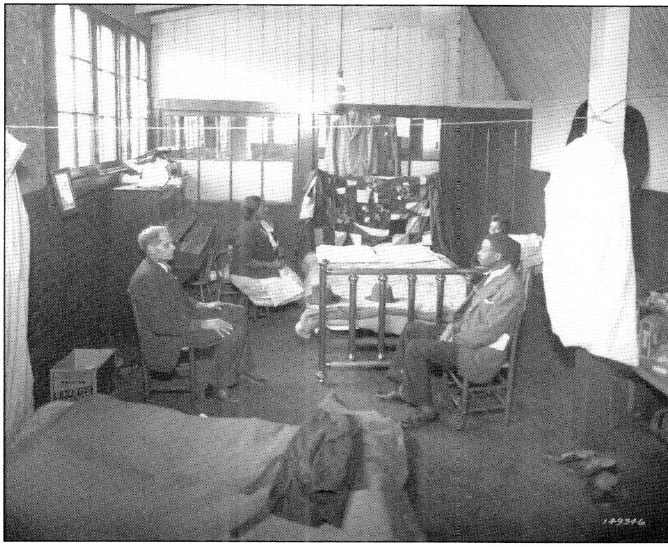

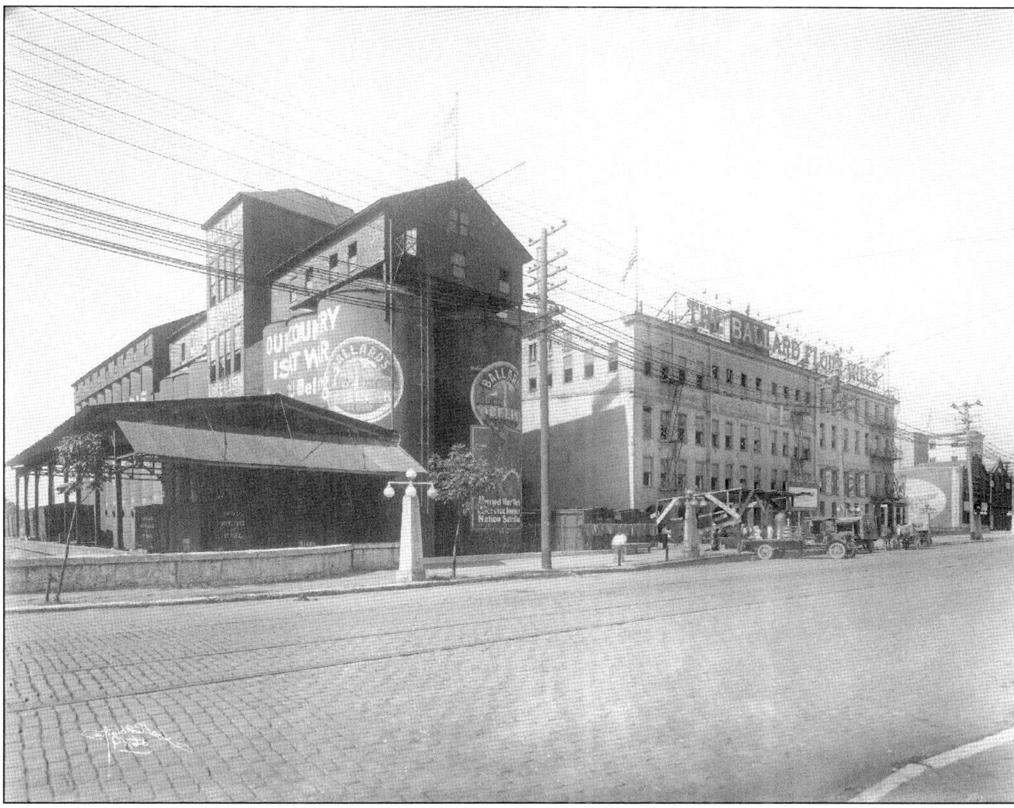

Ballard & Ballard Mills Receiving Grain Factory, Louisville, Kentucky, 1919. Ballard & Ballard Mills was located at 912 East Broadway. These flour mills had rounded grain towers to hold the grain. Between the tower and the neighboring brick building is a covered area where a truck has backed in to unload grain. Farther down in the view, two mules are attached to a cart.

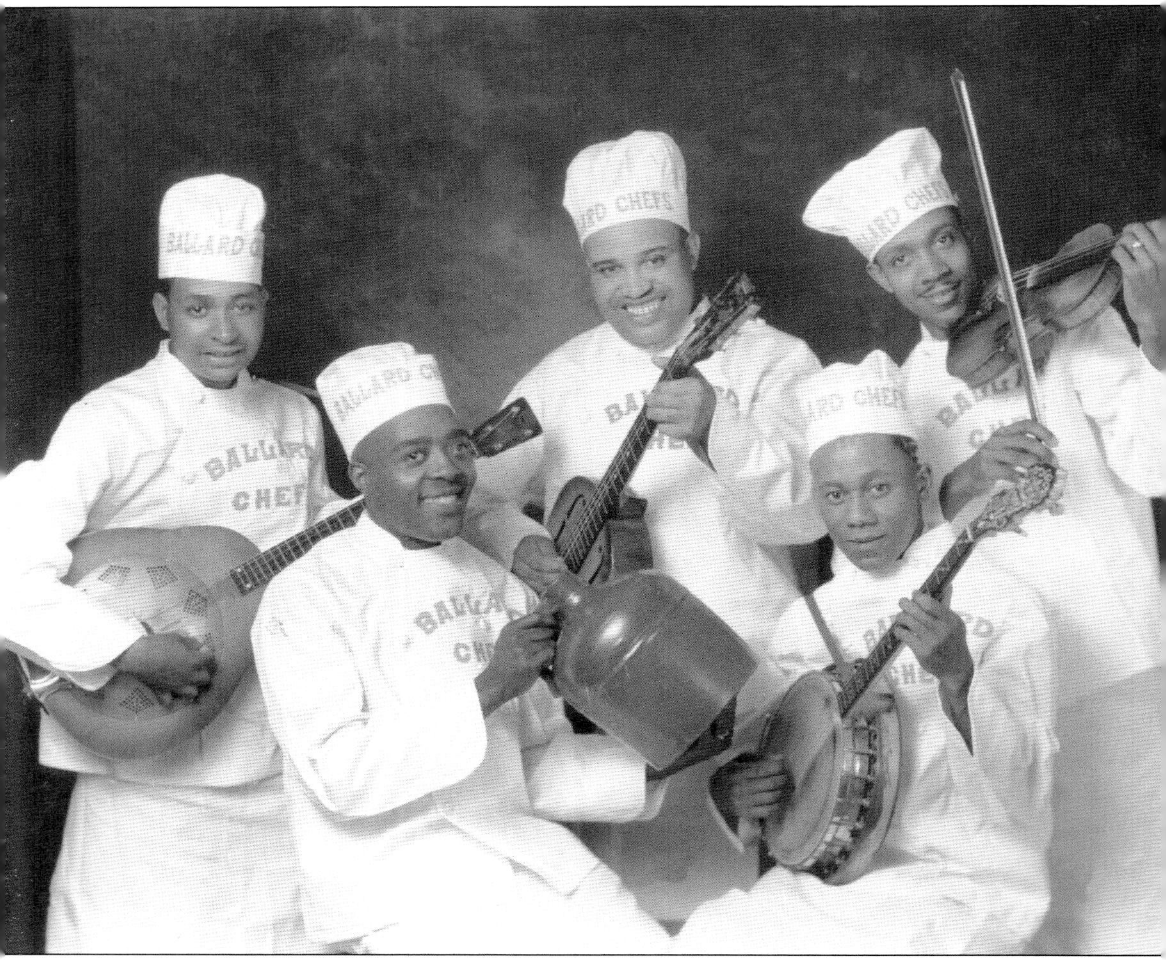

BALLARD CHEFS JUG BAND, SEPTEMBER 13, 1932. The Ballard Chefs, members of a jug band known by that name, pose in chef's garb with their instruments. One plays a violin, while others play the mandolin, guitar, banjo, and the jug. This type of music was well accepted throughout Louisville and surrounding towns. Crowds gathered at grocery stores, outdoor events, halls, and luncheons. Whites and blacks enjoyed the unique sound of the jug with its rhythmic airy bass sound as the banjo's tangy strings overlapped the fiddle and guitars, a unique and vibrant combination. It is without a doubt that these musicians worked at the Ballard and Ballard Grain Mills Factory. Ballard and Ballard sponsored the group (and the men's outfits depict this) as a unique way to advertise the company while showing off the splendid talents of its employees.

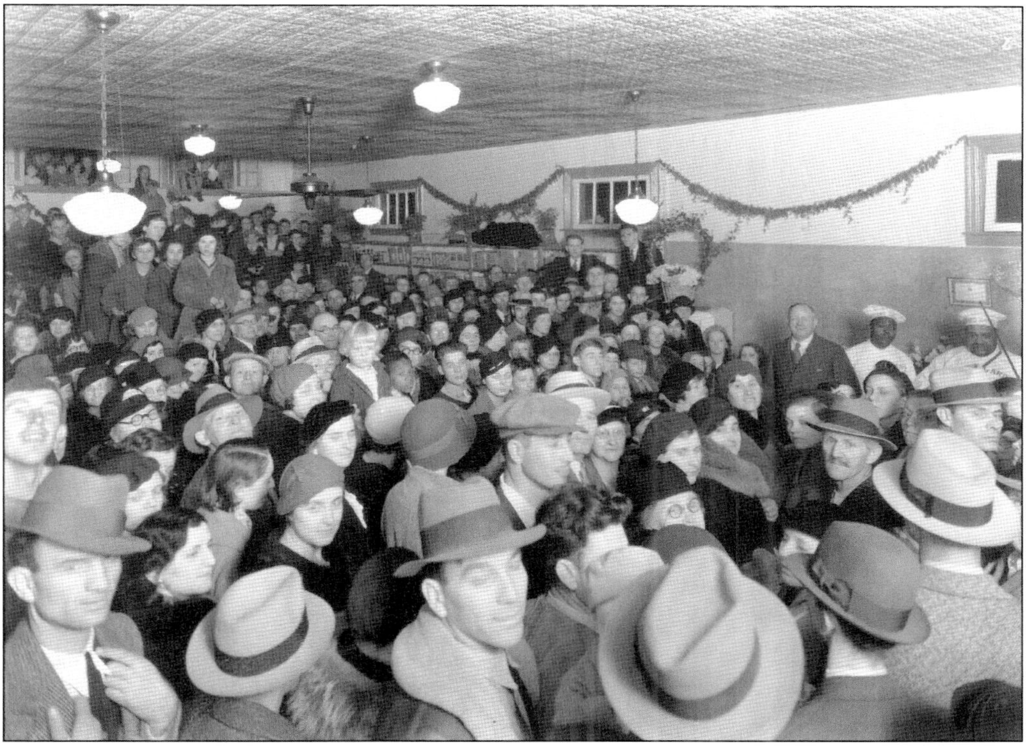

Ballard Chefs Performance at Mason Grocery & Supply Co., 1933. This interior view of a Ballard Chefs performance at Mason Grocery and Supply Co. in Middletown, Kentucky, shows the demand for the musicians. White admirers gathered to hear the Chefs are still wearing their outdoor coats and hats as children peer through the back windows. The anticipation of a grand performance is apparent in the room.

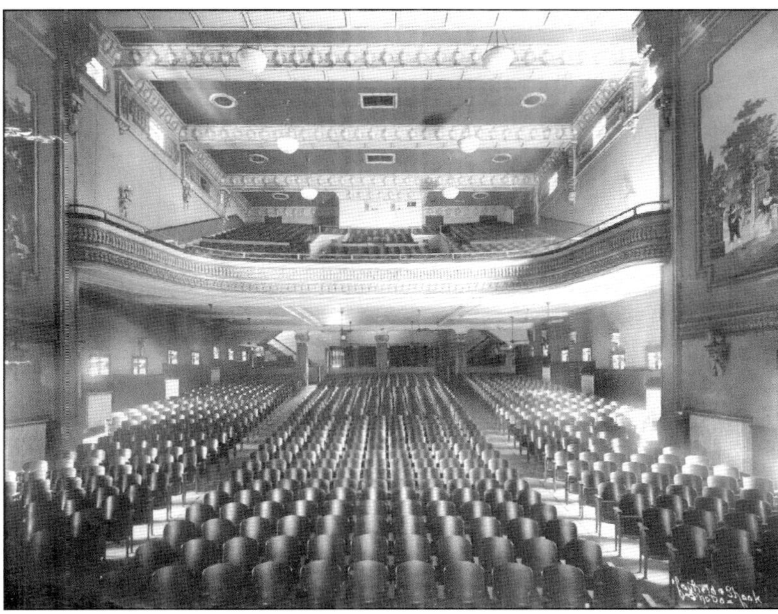

East Broadway Theatre, 1915. This interior view of the East Broadway Theatre was taken on or near the stage looking out into the rows and rows of seats. The theater included a balcony section and murals along the sidewalls.

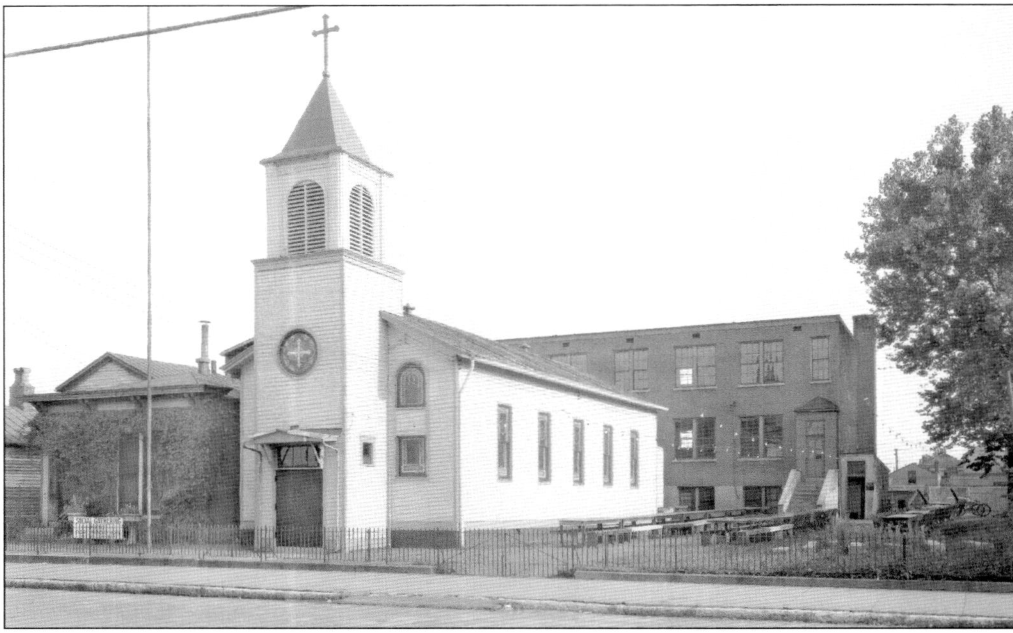

EXTERIOR VIEW OF ST. PETER CLAVER CHURCH, 1946. This white building with a steeple was located at 526 Lampton Street. It was an African American Catholic church in the Smoketown neighborhood. The church offered several resources to accommodate the needs of the poor.

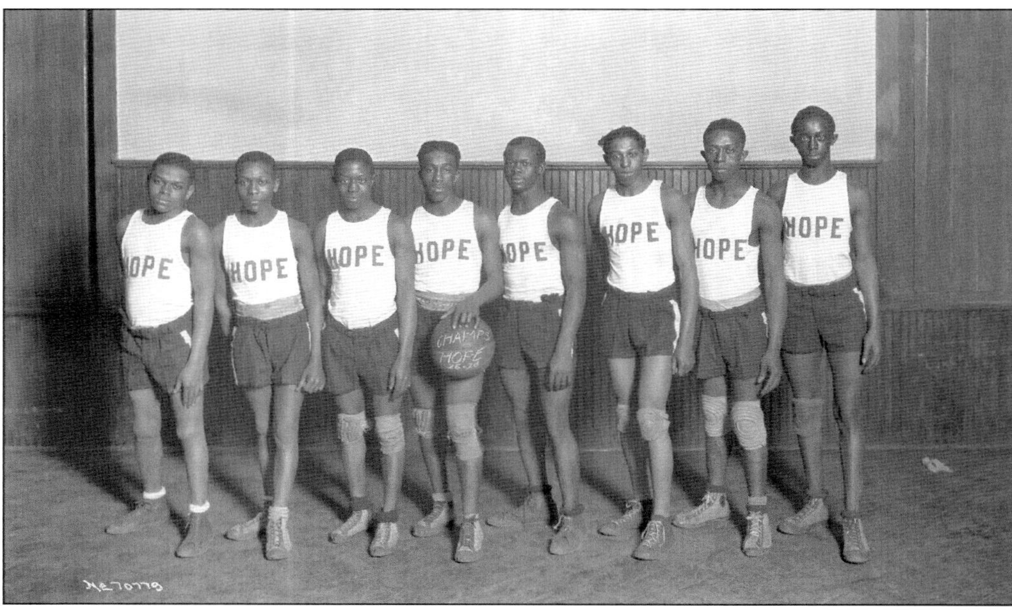

THE BASKETBALL TEAM OF HOPE MISSION, 1926. Later named Presbyterian Community Center, Grace Hope Mission helped African American boys in the Smoketown-Jackson neighborhood gain self-worth, pride, and an esteem of accomplishment. With both educational and recreational benefits, it was a place of acceptance. The center has been a beacon of hope to the residents of Smoketown-Jackson.

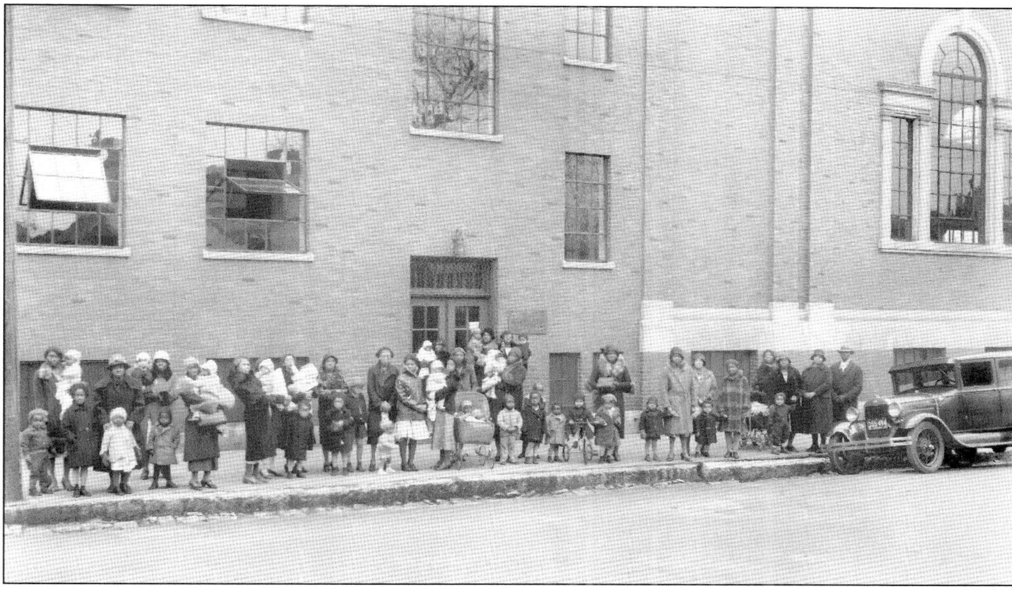

WOMEN AND CHILDREN WAIT IN FRONT OF PRESBYTERIAN COLORED MISSION, 1933. Located at 760 South Hancock Street, the Presbyterian Colored Mission assisted in the welfare of the Smoketown neighborhood. Here, African Americans wait to receive assistance during the Great Depression. Food, clothing, employment, and vocational training resources as well as temporary housing were offered by the mission founded by Rev. John Little.

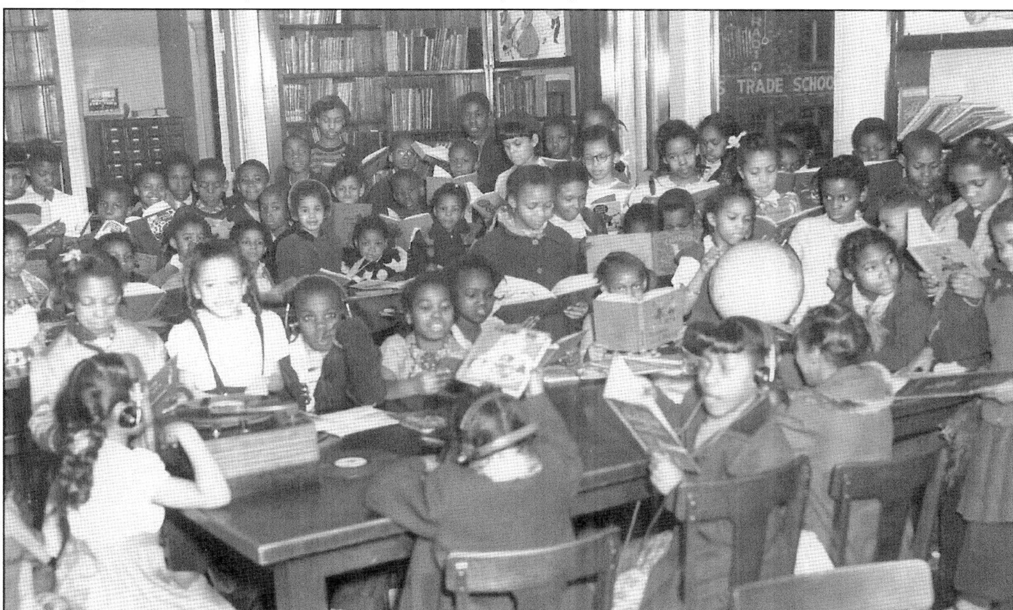

WAITING FOR STORY HOUR, 1930s. The Eastern Colored Branch Library, located at 600 Lampton Street, provided education through storytelling. Children learned about other lands and people who contributed to the world. Rev. Thomas F. Blue, a librarian, opened the library, a branch of the main Louisville Free Public Library at 301 York Street, to meet the needs of the Smoketown community. The Eastern Colored Branch Library opened on January 28, 1914.

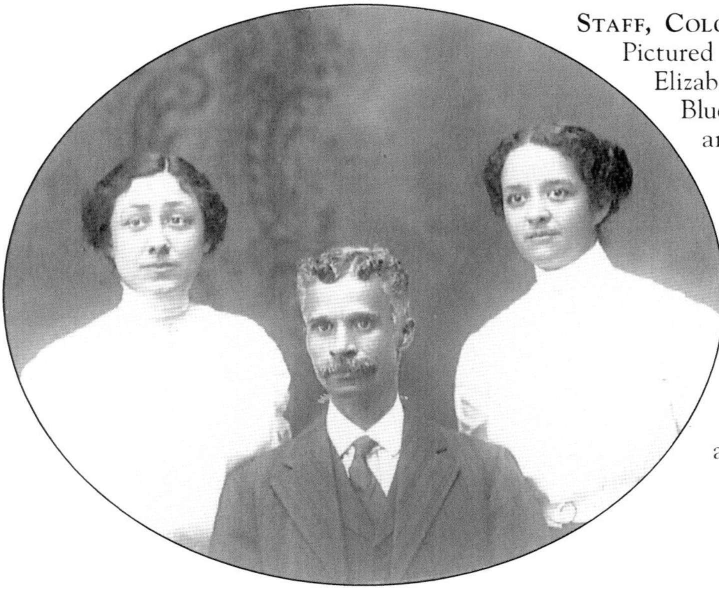

STAFF, COLORED DEPARTMENT, 1914. Pictured here are, from left to right, Elizabeth Finney, Rev. Thomas F. Blue, manager of both Western and Eastern Branches, and Rachel Harris, assistant in charge of children's work. Reverend Blue, a visionary, endeavored to strengthen African American families through education utilizing reading as a tool for expanding knowledge. Children gathered in crowds for story hours and group readings.

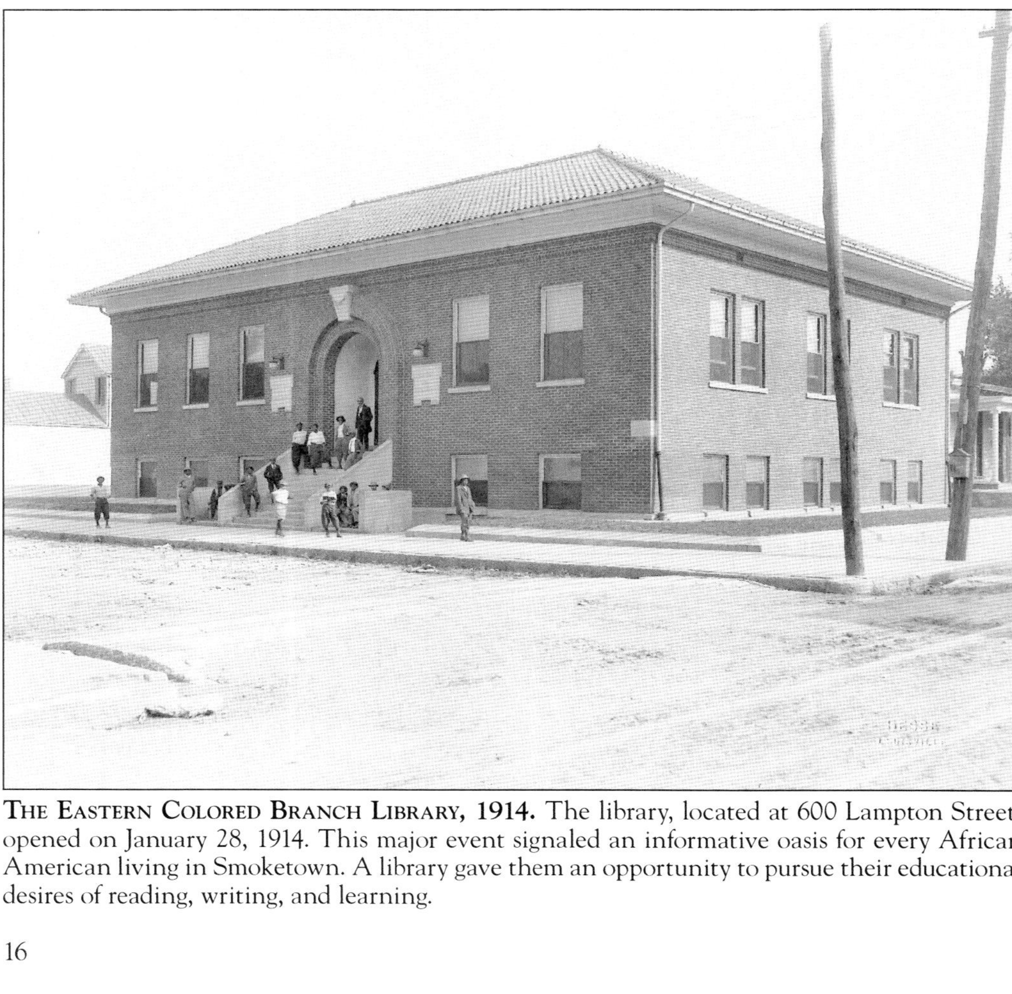

THE EASTERN COLORED BRANCH LIBRARY, 1914. The library, located at 600 Lampton Street, opened on January 28, 1914. This major event signaled an informative oasis for every African American living in Smoketown. A library gave them an opportunity to pursue their educational desires of reading, writing, and learning.

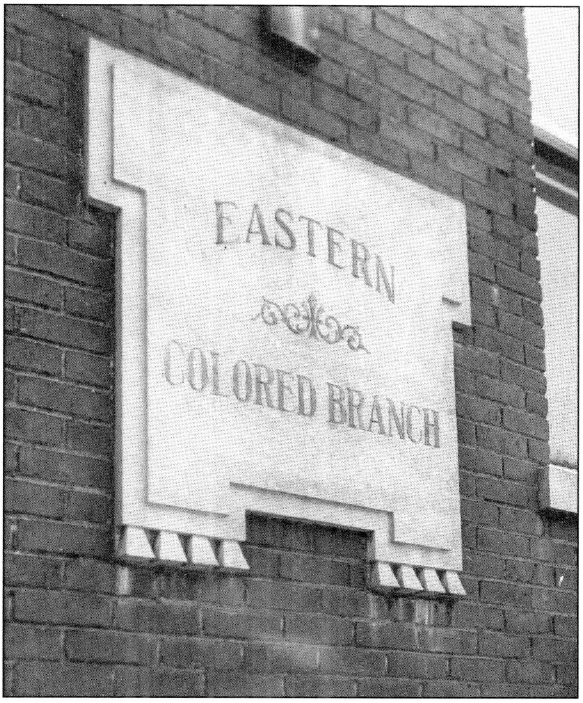

The Eastern Colored Branch Banner, 1914. This sign was outside the front entrance of the building. The opening of the library was a pivotal moment in the Smoketown community: citizens now had a library filled with African American as well as mainstream literature. It was a place for locals to read and study about their history and those who had made that history.

Grand Piano and 1937 Flood. Located at the Eastern Colored Branch, this grand piano was ruined by the 1937 flood in Louisville. The deluge devastated structures throughout Louisville. Families' homes and businesses were completely or partially destroyed. Many books and other materials at the library were ruined as well.

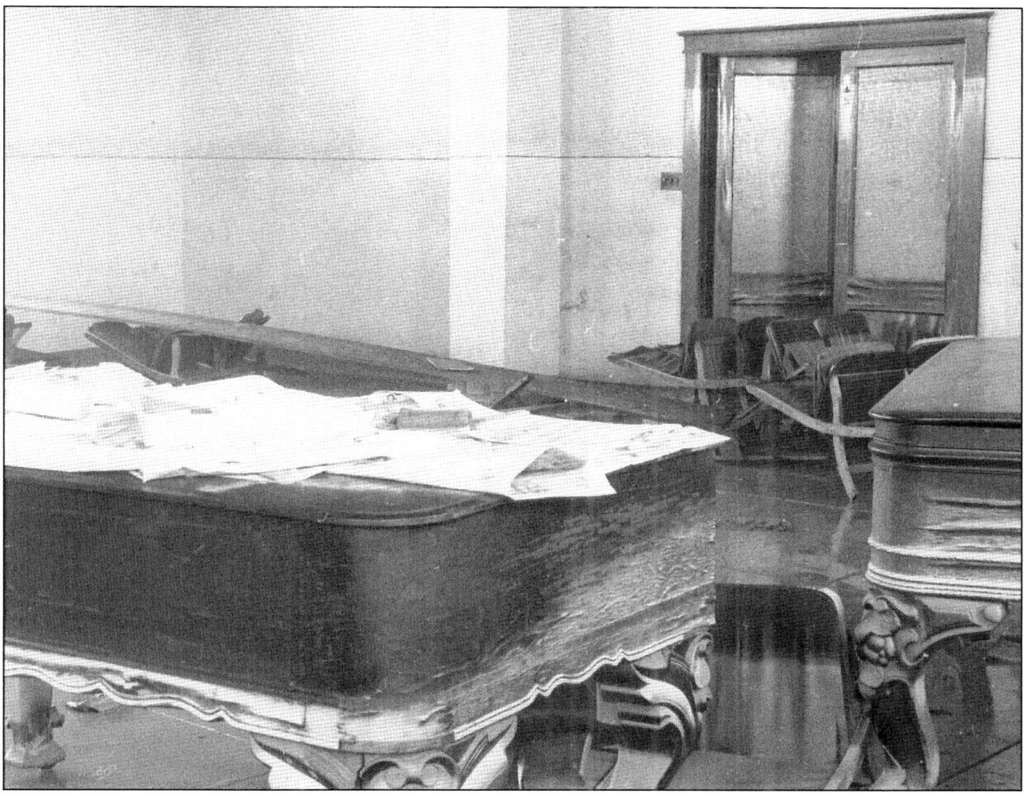

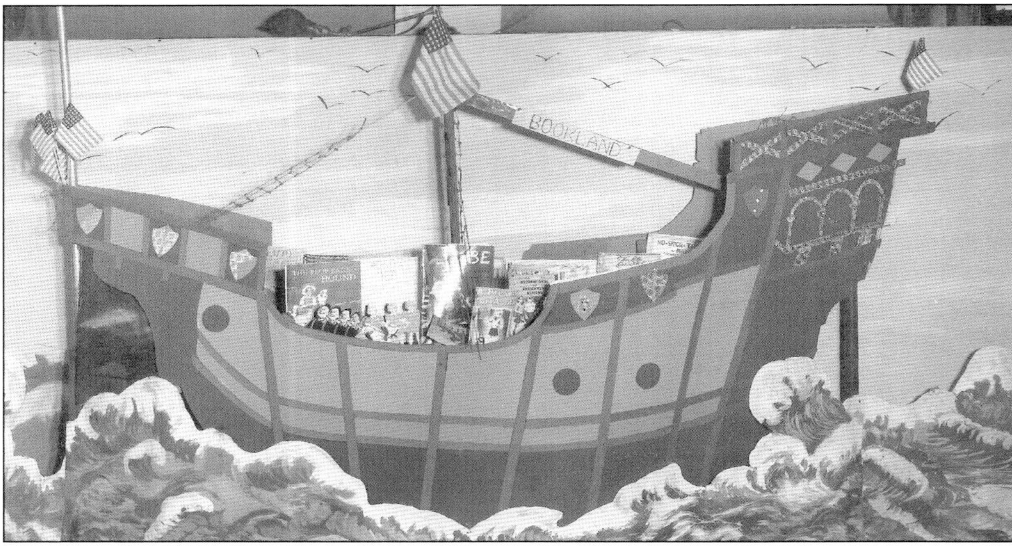

Weekly Book Display, 1940. This photograph shows the weekly book display at the Eastern Colored Branch. Children in the Smoketown community met at the Eastern Library for reading on a specific topic each week. The book display was a vital component in encouraging children to learn outside their own community, to travel intellectually to other lands and other cultures. This empowering effort made the children excited about learning and reading.

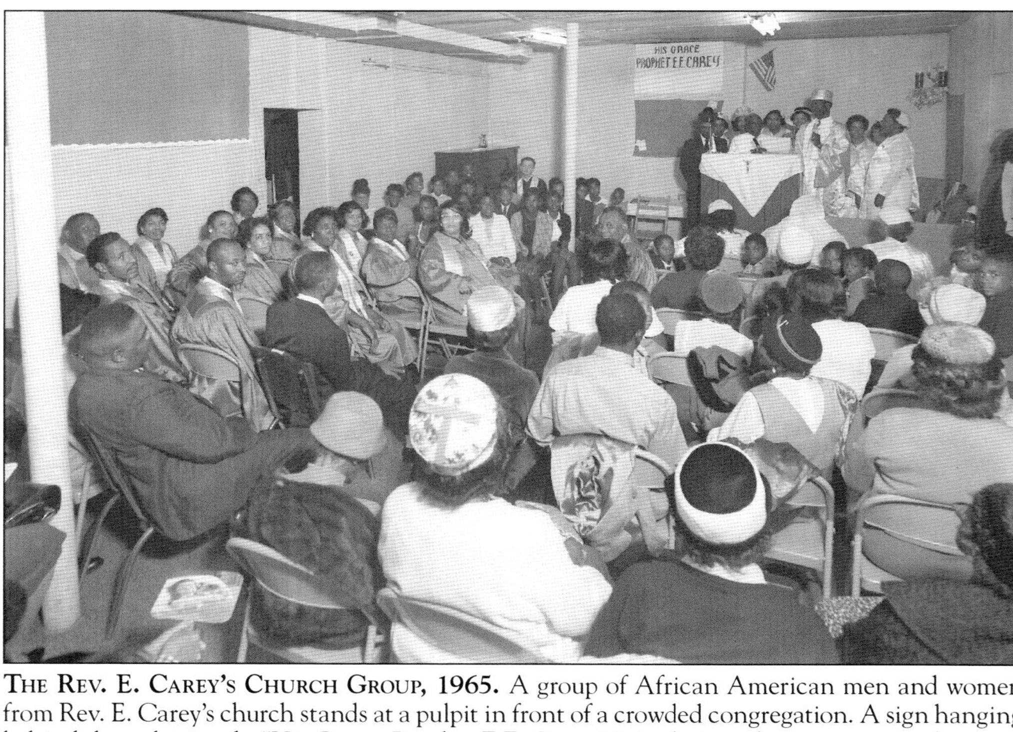

The Rev. E. Carey's Church Group, 1965. A group of African American men and women from Rev. E. Carey's church stands at a pulpit in front of a crowded congregation. A sign hanging behind the pulpit reads, "His Grace, Prophet E.E. Carey." It is obvious the congregation honored him as its spiritual leader.

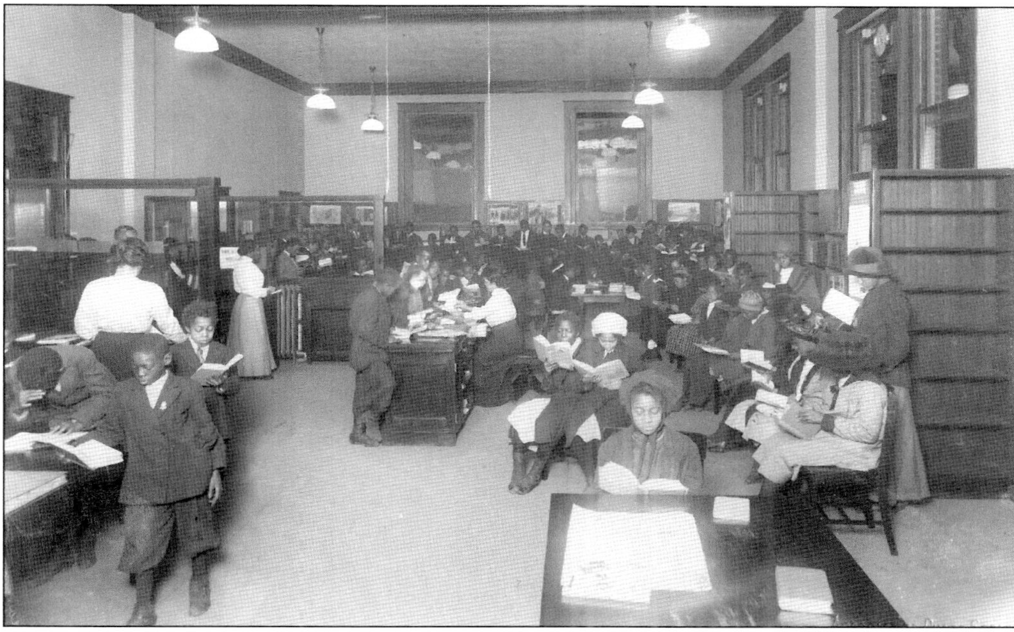

THE CHILDREN'S AREA OF THE EASTERN COLORED BRANCH, 1935. The young male at left stands in deep concentration, absorbed in the contents of a book. The little girl in the foreground is intrigued with her book as she sits at the table. Other children of various ages are immersed in the adventures of reading as they sit quietly in the library.

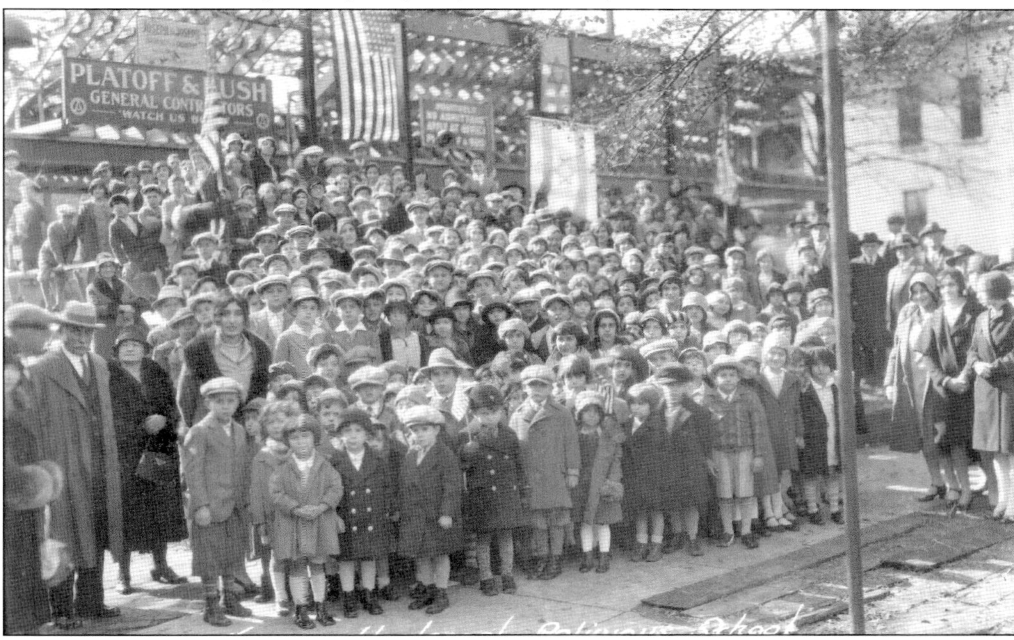

THE KENESETH ISRAEL RELIGIOUS SCHOOL'S CORNERSTONE CEREMONY, 1924. The school's cornerstone exercises were held on November 4, 1928, at 232 East Jacob Street in the Smoketown-Jackson community. An American flag and a Star of David flag hang in the background. Smoketown-Jackson was a community of diversity, a multicultural neighborhood of many faiths.

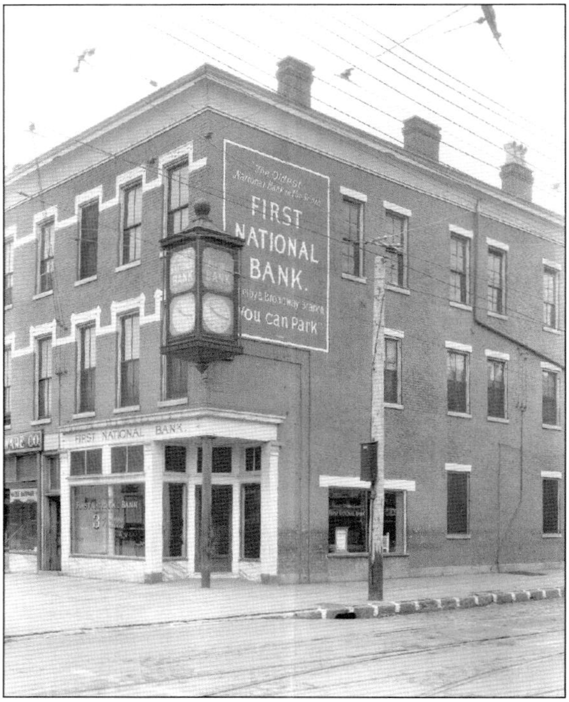

THE FIRST NATIONAL BANK, 1930. The First National Bank was located at 743 East Broadway (Shelby Street and Broadway). It was a brick, stone, and marble building. A sign proclaims it is "the Oldest National Bank in the South." Many businesses in the Smoketown community were among the bank's customers.

JACOB STREET TABERNACLE ORGAN DEDICATION SERVICE. In 1943, Rev. E.H. Curry was the pastor of this church located at 971 South Preston Street, formerly known as the Curry Chapel. Members of a predominantly African American congregation sit in pews facing the altar. Three rows from the rear on the right side, a young white man looks on as the organ dedication proceeds.

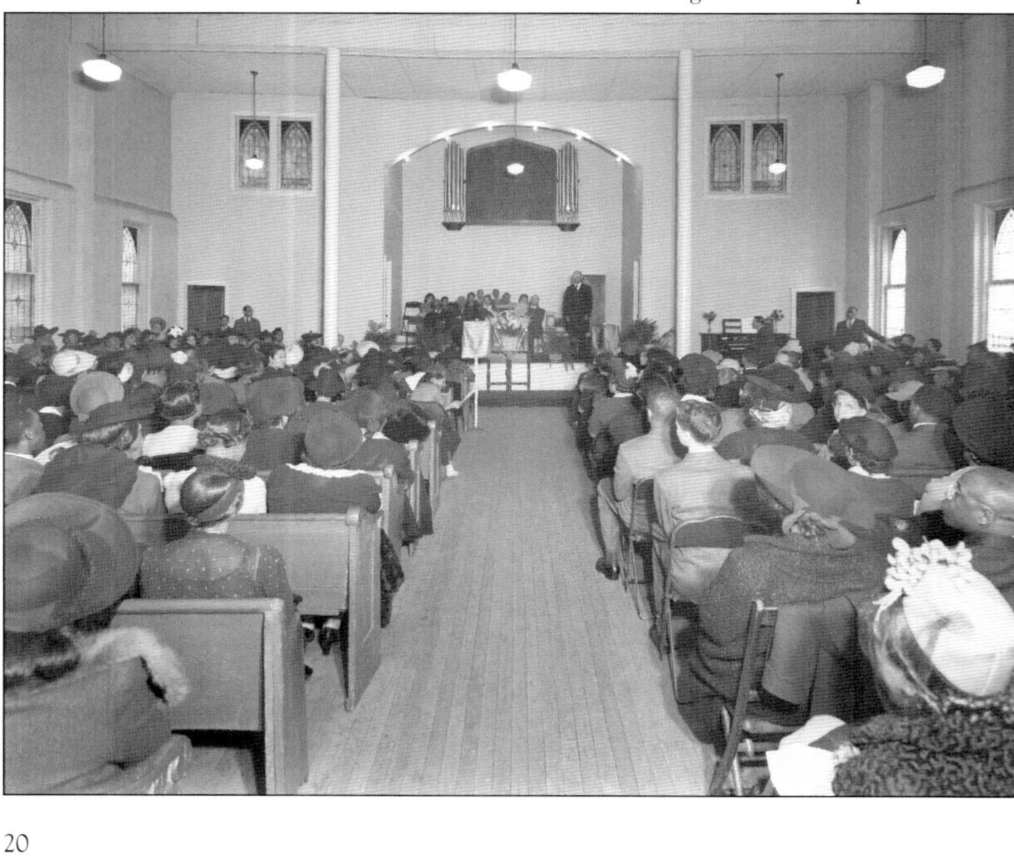

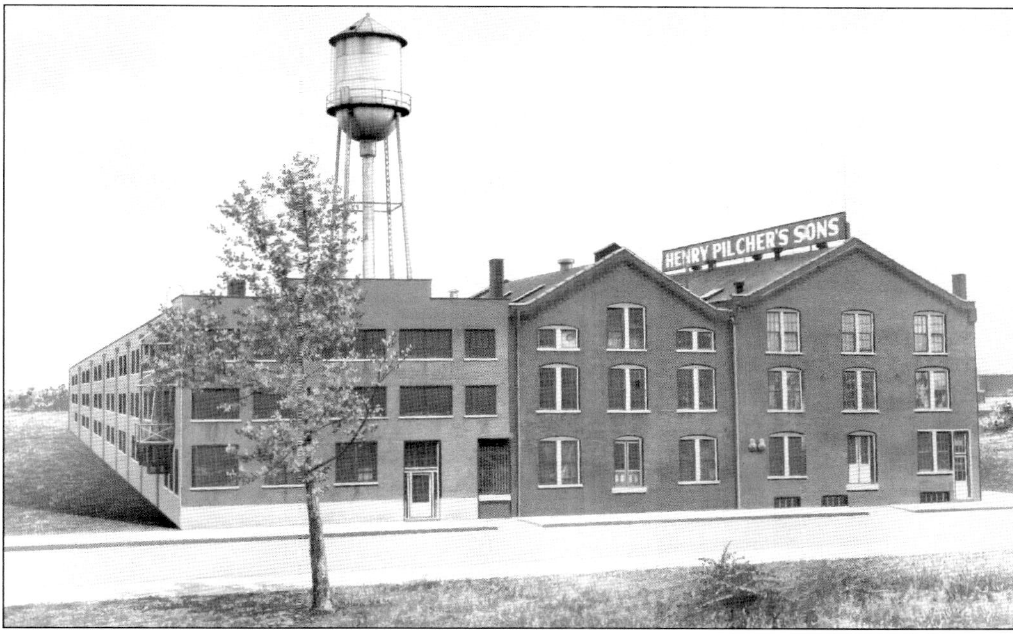

HENRY PILCHER AND SONS FACTORY, 1946. Organ builder Henry Pilcher (1798–1880) was born in Canterbury, England. He came to the United States in 1832. The address of the factory was 908 Mason Avenue, in Louisville's Smoketown-Jackson business community.

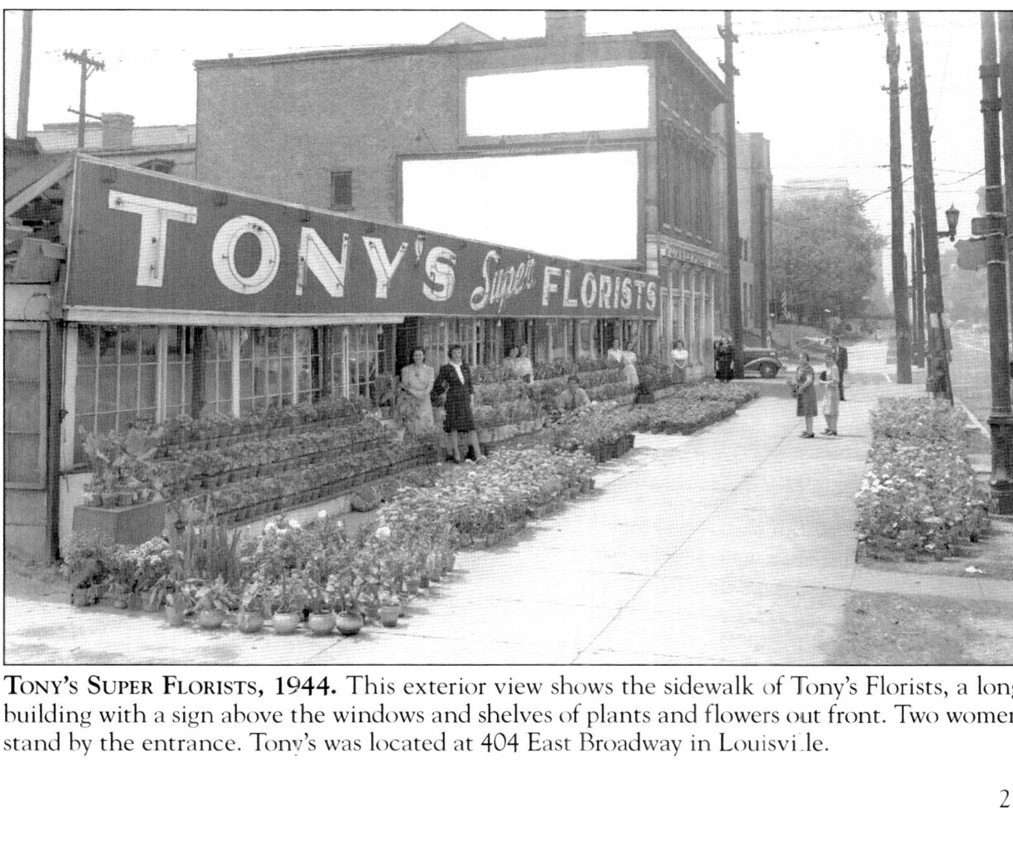

TONY'S SUPER FLORISTS, 1944. This exterior view shows the sidewalk of Tony's Florists, a long building with a sign above the windows and shelves of plants and flowers out front. Two women stand by the entrance. Tony's was located at 404 East Broadway in Louisville.

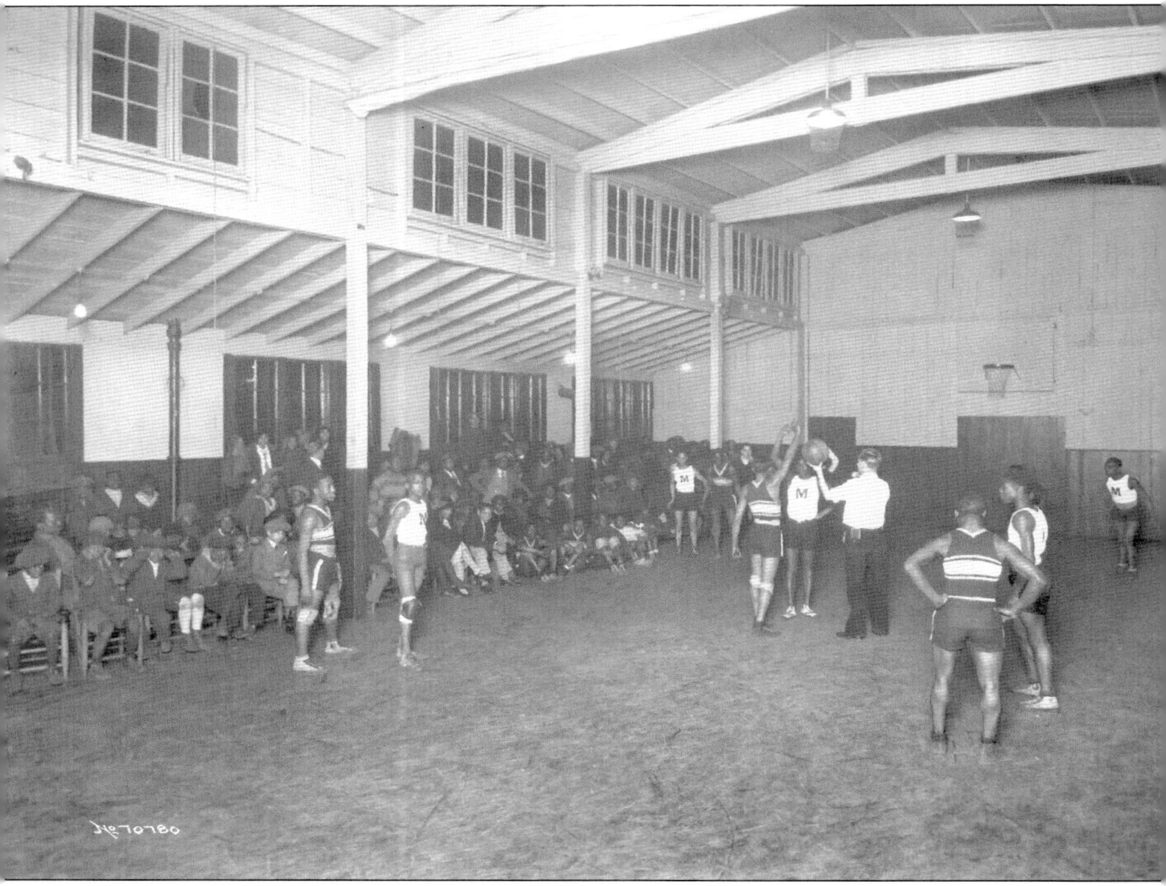

Hope Mission Basketball Game, Louisville, Kentucky, 1926. A referee holds a basketball up between two young African American men. Each has an arm raised in anticipation of the ball being released. The two teams have distinctive uniforms: one uniform is made up of a white tank top with the letter M on it and dark shorts; the other team's uniform has a horizontally striped tank top and dark shorts with vertical stripes down the side. Some players wear kneepads. An audience sits on chairs or on the ground along the sidelines. Many of the spectators are well-dressed, with men in suits and women in dresses and hats. Founded in 1898 by seminarians as Hope Mission Station, a summer Sunday school for African American children, the center evolved into a settlement house for the Smoketown neighborhood of Louisville and was joined in its tasks by Grace Mission.

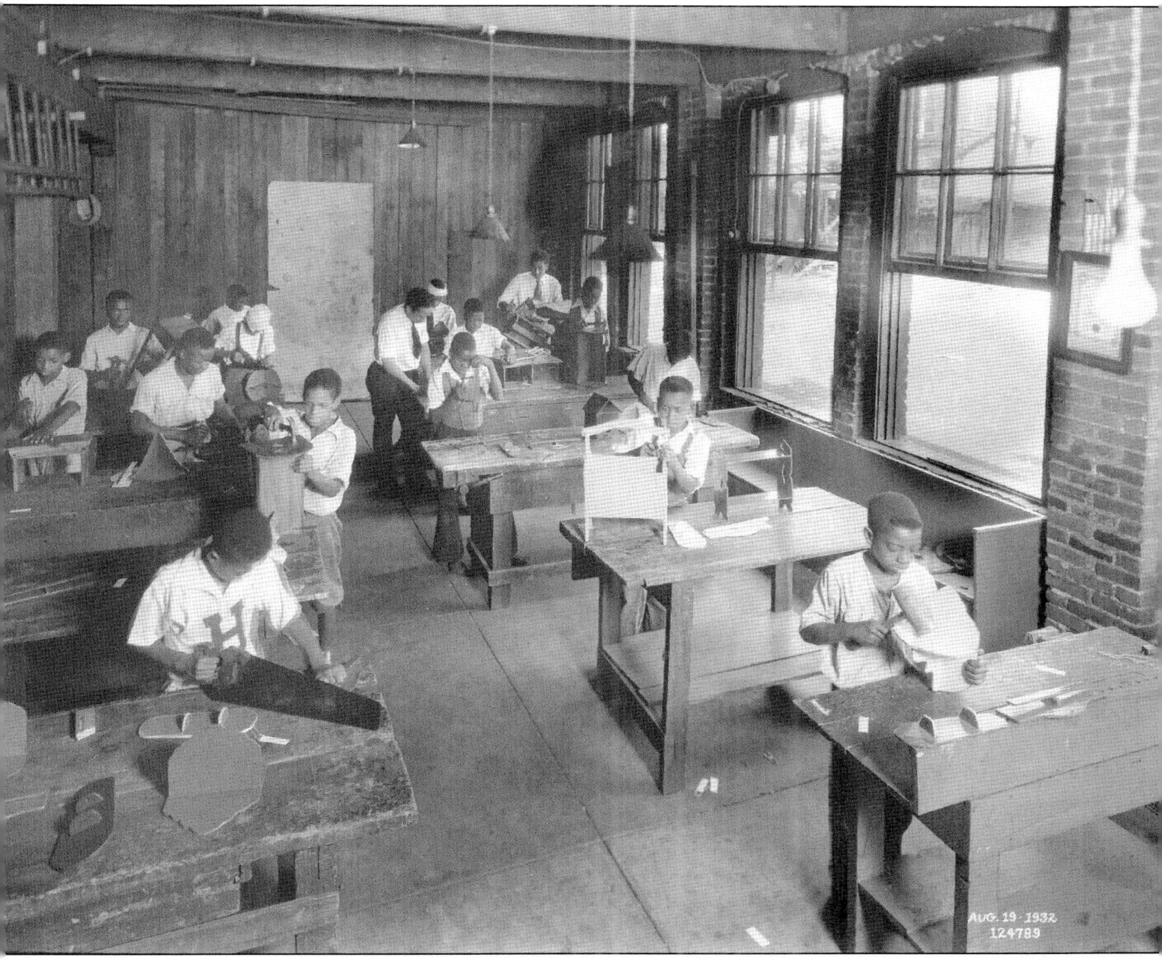

PRESBYTERIAN COLORED MISSION CARPENTRY CLASS, 1932. Young African American boys work in a carpentry lab at the Presbyterian Colored Mission in Louisville. They use saws, hammers, mallets, and other woodworking tools as a man in dark slacks, a white shirt, and dark tie helps them. Financial support came from sponsoring churches, friends, and the community chest. In 1955, the mission's name was changed to the John Little Presbyterian Center, in honor of the center's founder and director for 50 years, Rev. John Little (1874–1948). In 1965, the name was changed again, to the Presbyterian Community Center. Records contain annual reports, minutes, audit reports, programs, brochures, scrapbooks, and photographs, together with correspondence, reports, and a historical sketch of the mission. The University of Louisville Archives collection also includes a biographical sketch of Reverend Little. The collection provides rich documentation of the center's activities and its role as an outpost in the federal government's war on poverty.

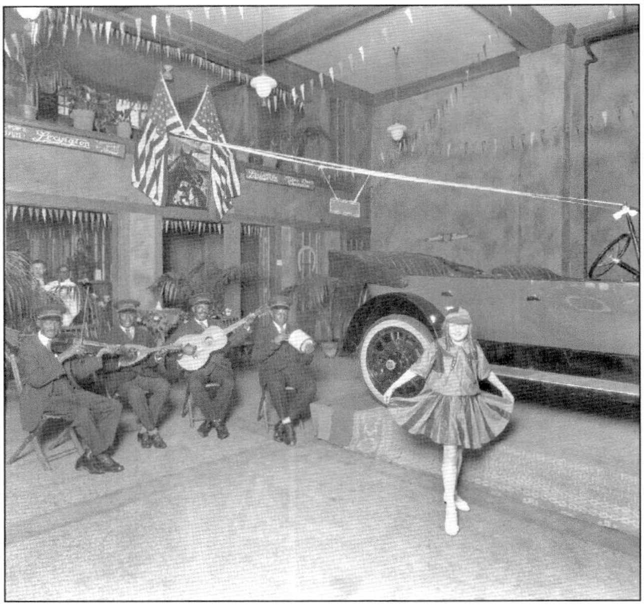

Jazz Band, 1921. This photograph was taken at 2600 West Broadway in Louisville. A girl in a knee-length skirt, top, and cap of what looks like silk curtsies next to a convertible car on a stage. Four African American musicians wearing hats reading "Jazz Band" play, from left to right, a violin, a mandolin, a guitar, and a jug as others look on. Two American flags, some plants, and pennants decorate the upper part of the room. Between the two flags is a photograph of a horse. A sign by the flags reads, "More power—less fuel! Lexington Minute Man Six. Comfort, Safety, Style, Economy. April 27, 1921."

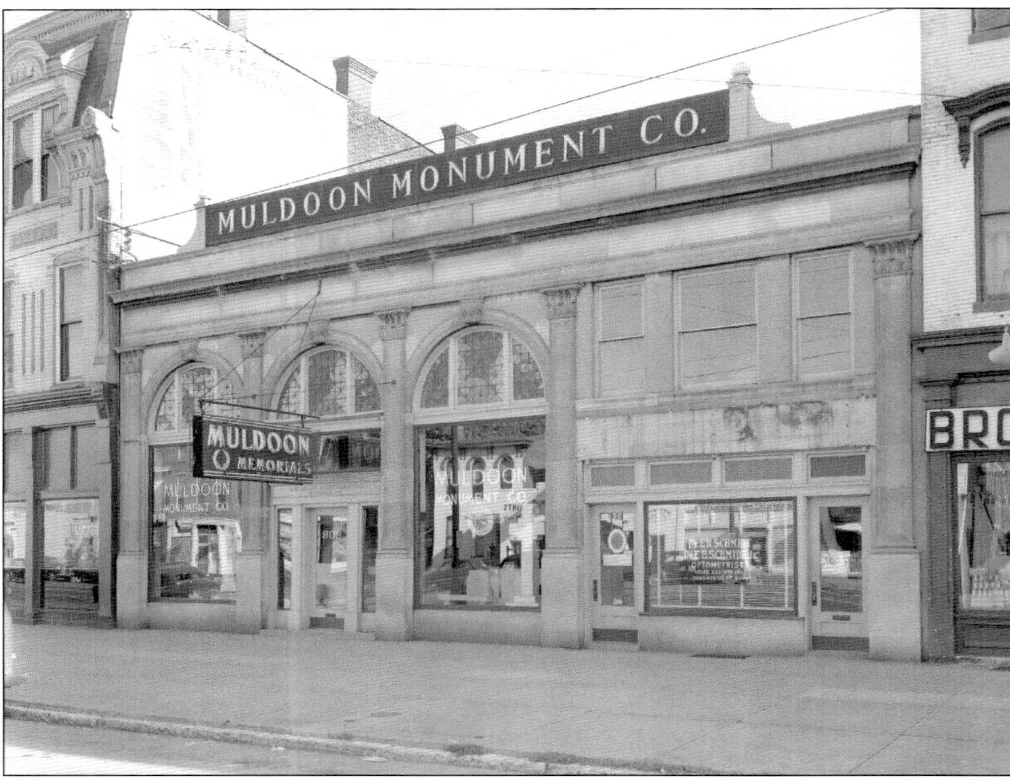

Muldoon Monument Company, September 15, 1951. Col. Michael Muldoon founded the company in 1854. It handcrafted granite memorials and mausoleums. Muldoon Monument is Kentucky's oldest and largest memorial provider assisting families to make one of life's most permanent decisions. The company was located in the Smoketown-Jackson business community.

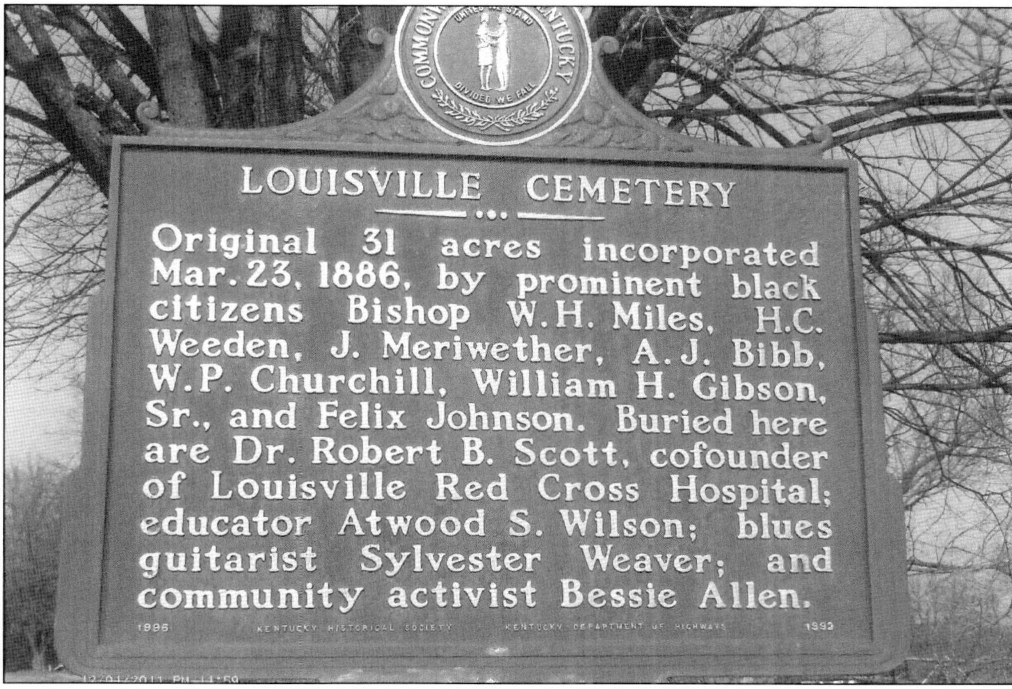

Louisville Cemetery Marker. On March 23, 1886, prominent black citizens bishop W.H. Miles, H.C. Weeden, J. Meriwether, A.J. Bibb, W.P. Churchill, William H. Gibson Sr., and Felix Johnson incorporated 31 acres as a cemetery. Those buried here include Dr. Robert B. Scott, cofounder of Louisville Red Cross Hospital; educator Atwood S. Wilson; blues guitarist Sylvester Weaver; and community activist Bessie Allen. Once at 903 Poplar Road, its current address is 1339 Poplar Road. (Photograph courtesy of the author.)

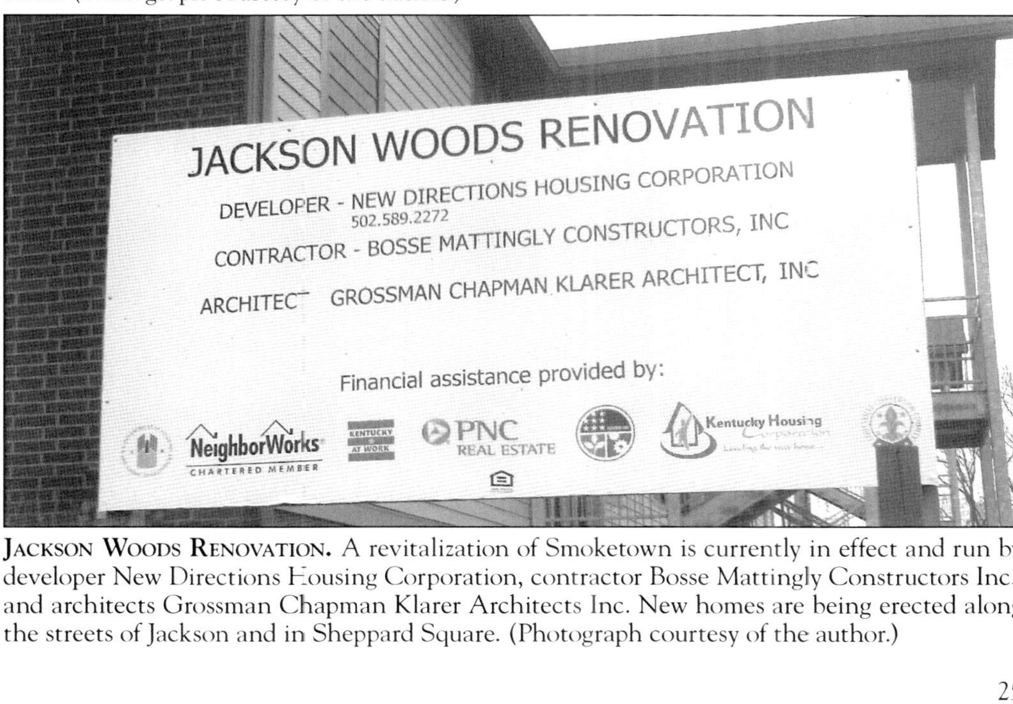

Jackson Woods Renovation. A revitalization of Smoketown is currently in effect and run by developer New Directions Housing Corporation, contractor Bosse Mattingly Constructors Inc., and architects Grossman Chapman Klarer Architects Inc. New homes are being erected along the streets of Jackson and in Sheppard Square. (Photograph courtesy of the author.)

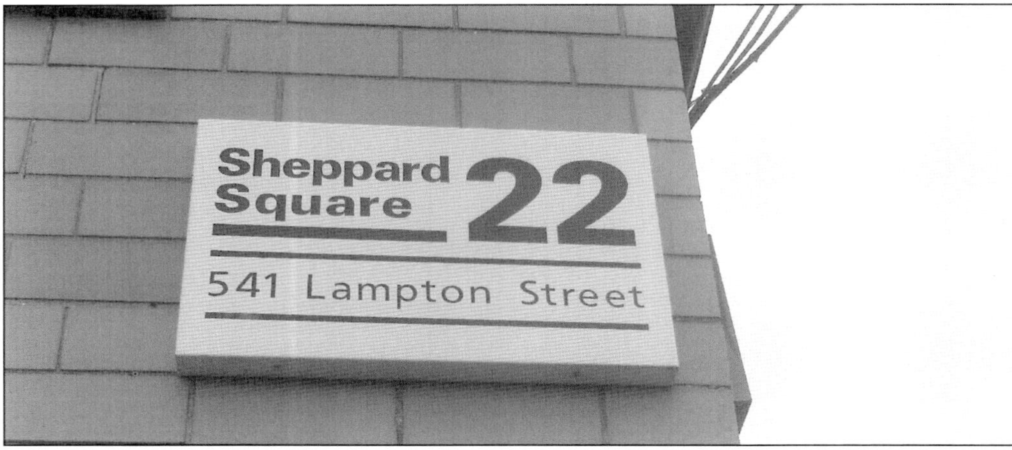

SHEPPARD SQUARE APARTMENTS. At 541 Lampton Street, residents are presently relocating for the massive revitalization of Sheppard Square Apartments Complex. They were built for low-income urban families and were named after the renowned Rev. William H. Sheppard, honoring his work in the Smoketown community. Born in 1865 in Waynesboro, Virginia, Sheppard attended Hampton and Stillman Institutes. Sent to the Belgian Congo in 1890, he served as a missionary in Africa until 1910. (Photograph courtesy of the author.)

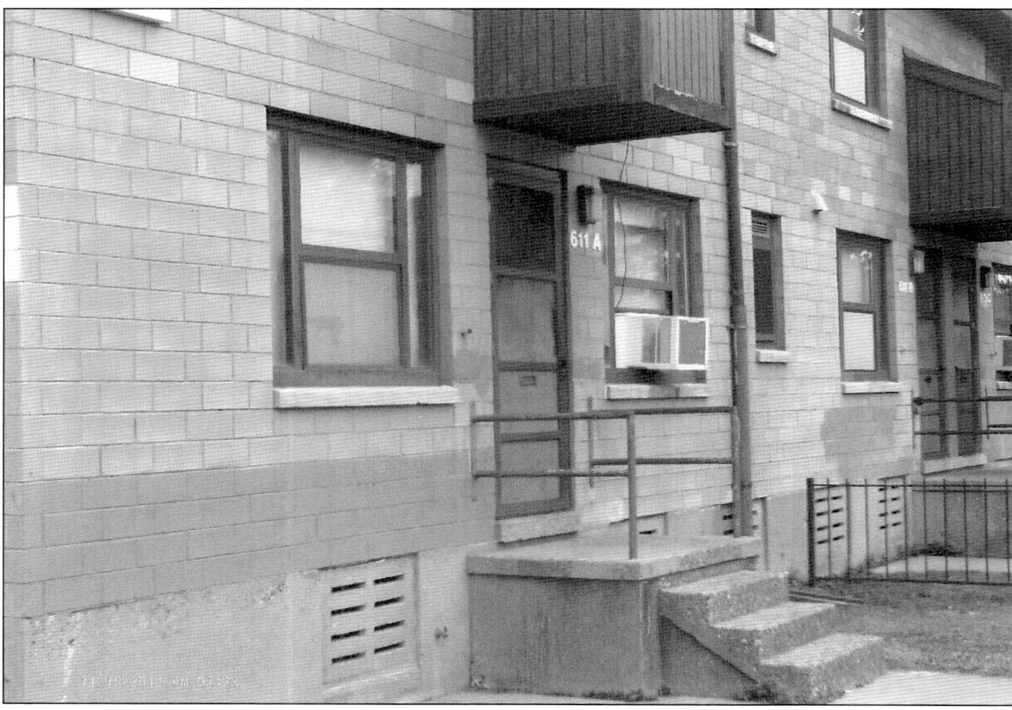

SHEPPARD SQUARE BARRACKS STRUCTURE APARTMENTS. The Sheppard Square Projects were built in 1943 to accommodate the dense Smoketown population. These barracks structures have serviced the community for over 68 years. In June 2011, a Hope VI Grant Award of $22 million was granted by the Department of Housing and Urban Development (HUD) to the Louisville Metro Housing Authority for the Smoketown Revitalization Project. Soon, new homes will be built for the community. (Photograph courtesy of the author.)

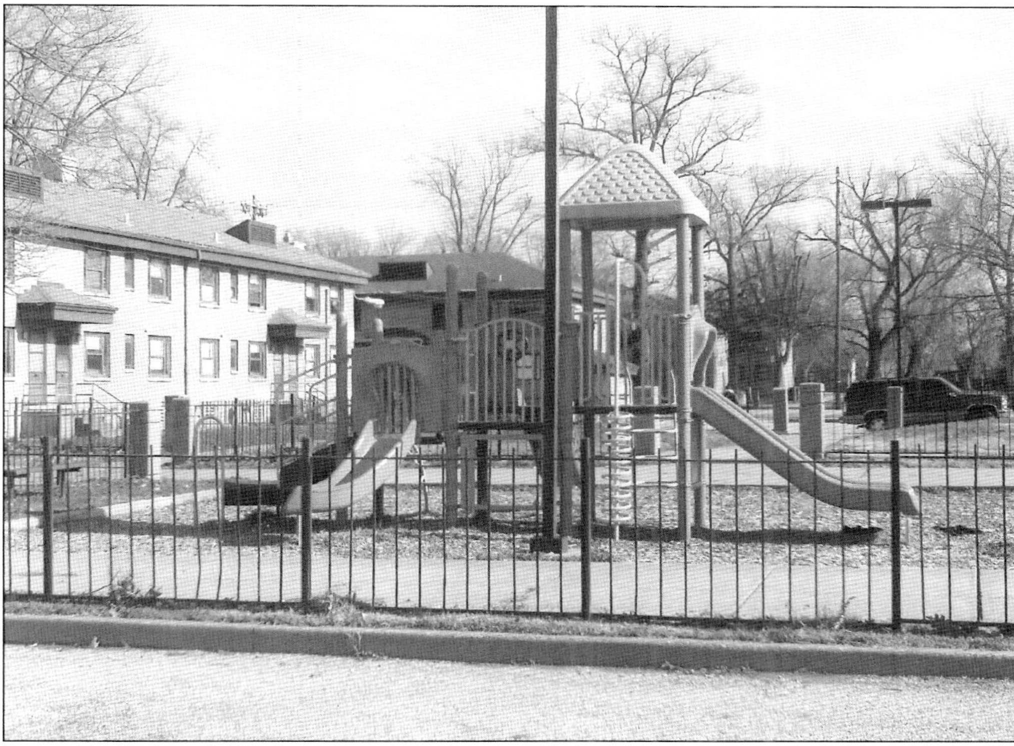

SHEPPARD SQUARE PLAYGROUND AT ROSELANE COURT. Sheppard Square Complex was named after the Rev. William H. Sheppard, pastor of Grace Presbyterian Church in Louisville from 1912 until his death in 1927. He was one of the city's most respected African American leaders and was known for his work in the Smoketown community. Sheppard Park (1924) and Sheppard Square Housing Project (1942) are also named in his honor. (Photograph courtesy of the author.)

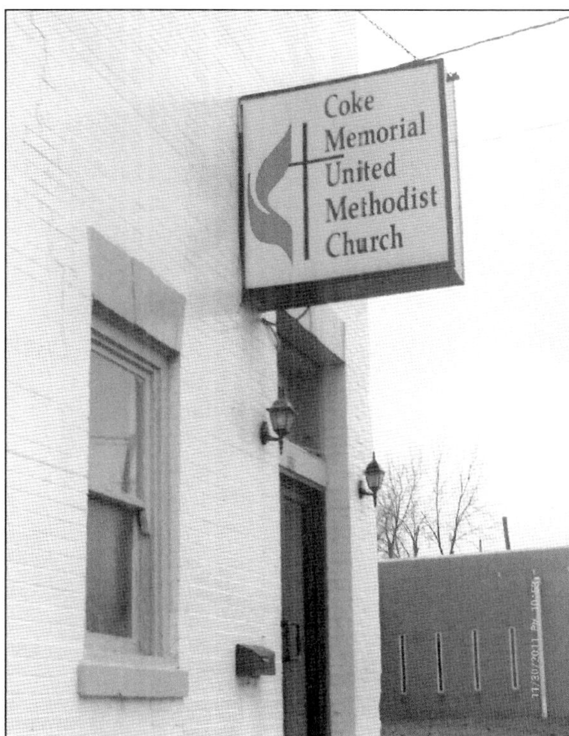

COKE MEMORIAL UNITED METHODIST CHURCH. Coke Memorial is one of Smoketown-Jackson's historical churches established 1872. Located at 428 East Breckinridge Street, Coke Memorial was a vital pillar for the early African American settlers, giving both spiritual and necessary aid. (Photograph courtesy of the author.)

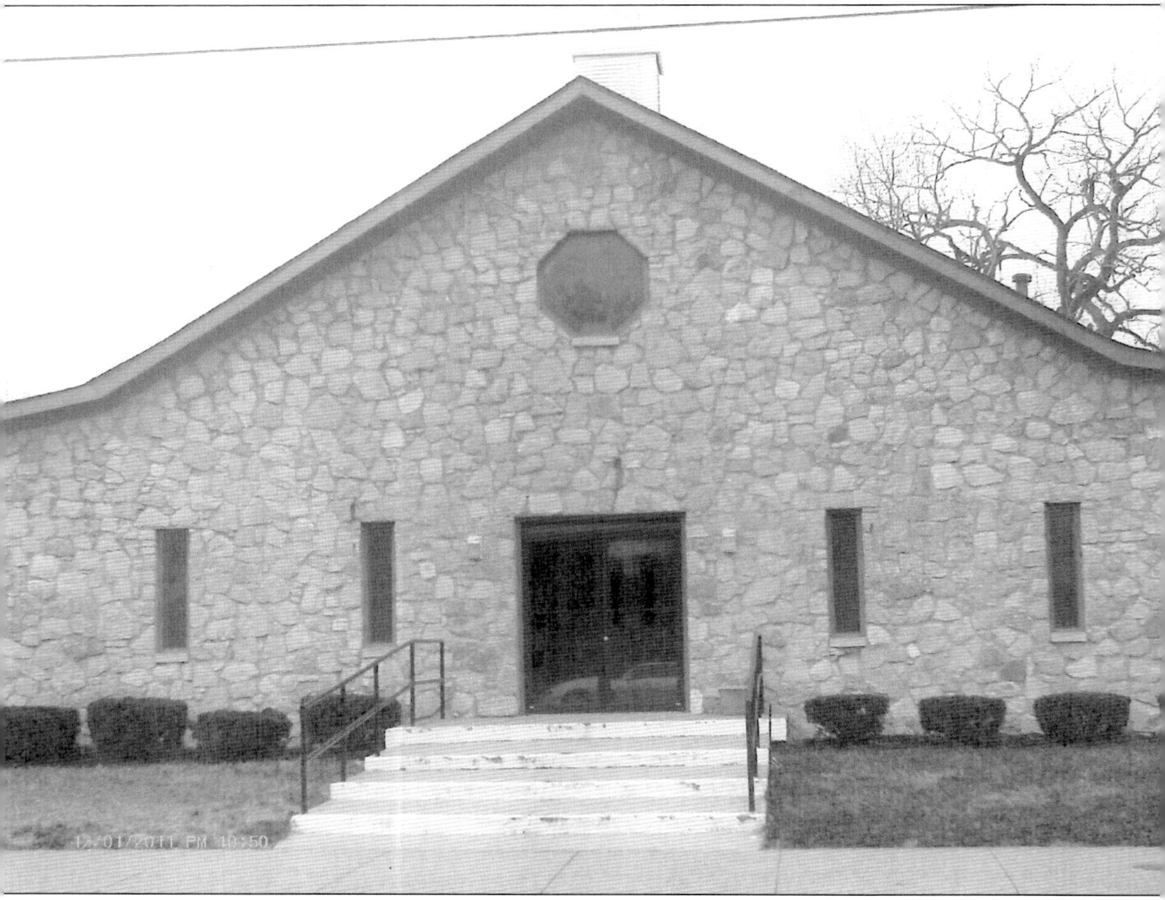

Little Flock Missionary Baptist Church. Little Flock is one of Smoketown's historic churches. Established in 1867, it became a pillar of strength for freedmen and freedwomen. Its first pastor was Rev. Charles Oldham. The first church was located on Second Street between Magnolia and Burnett Streets. Little Flock continues to nurture the surrounding community from its present location at 1030 South Hancock Street under the senior pastoral leadership of Rev. Bernard Crayton. (Photograph courtesy of the author.)

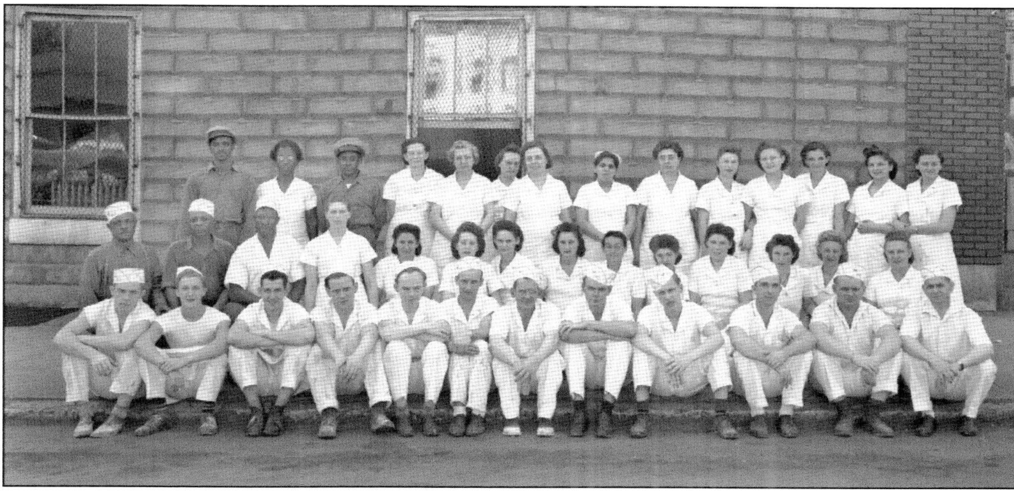

Blue Bird Pie Company. This photograph taken on June 11, 1946, shows three rows of employees, including four African American men and one African American woman, in front of the stone exterior of Blue Bird Pie Company. Most of the employees wear white cook uniforms, while a few other workers wear darker uniforms. Blue Bird Pie Company prepared, packed, and distributed its products from 434 East Broadway.

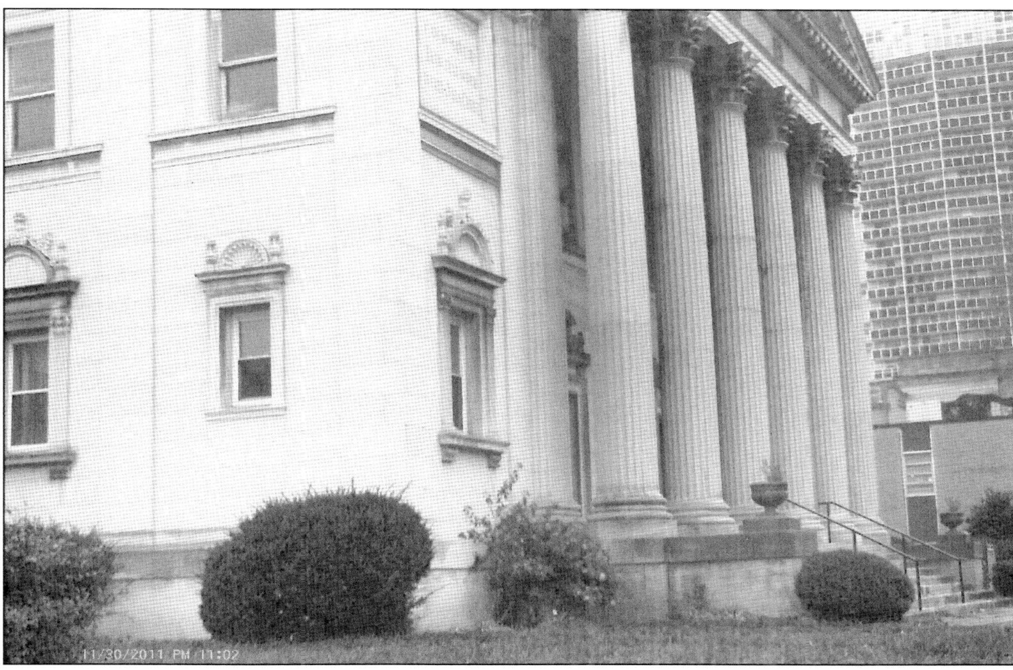

Lampton Street Baptist Church. The current Classical Revival–style church is located at 850 South Fourth Street in Old Louisville, but its historic original site was at 910 Hancock Street in Smoketown. The church was established in 1866, one year after the emancipation of slaves in the United States. Lampton Street became a beacon of hope and through its Out Reach Ministries continues to bring hope and restoration to those in need. Rev. Dr. James Miller presides as the senior pastor. (Photograph courtesy of the author.)

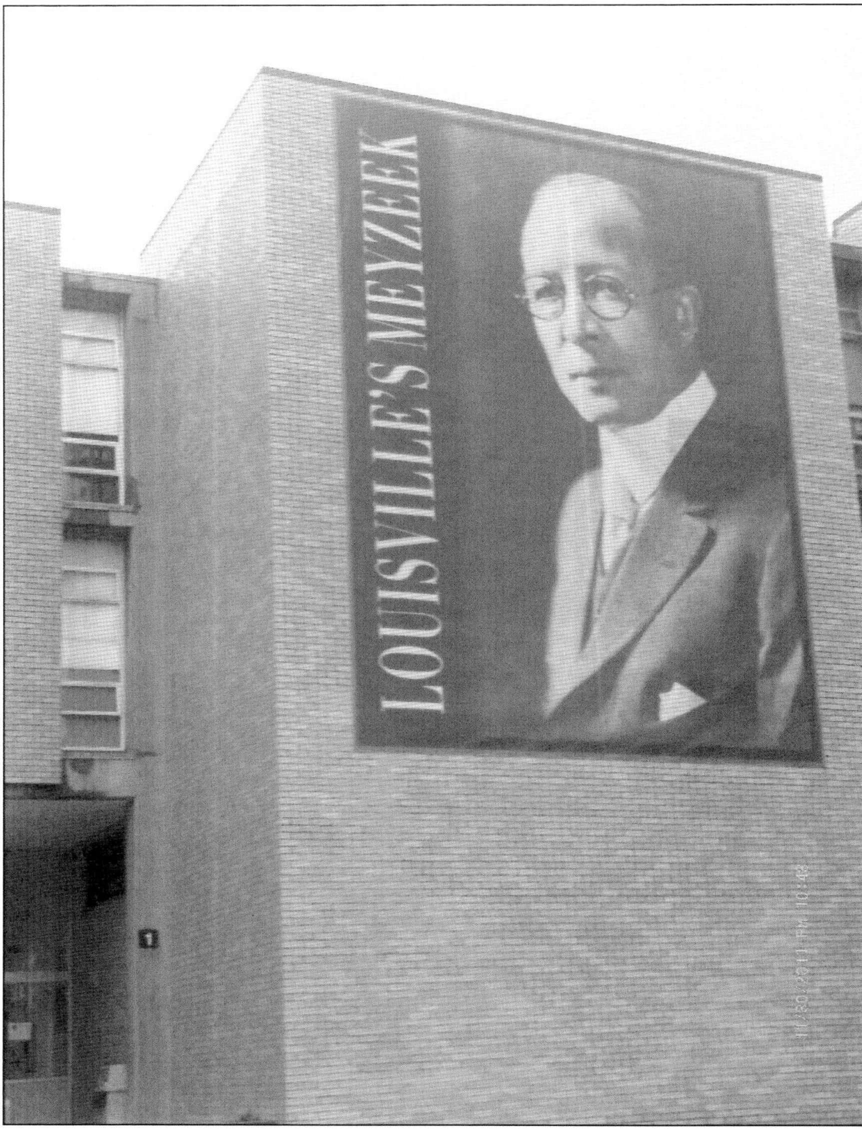

Albert E. Meyzeek Middle School. Originally named Jackson Junior High in 1967, the school was renamed in 1977 in honor of Albert Ernest Meyzeek, a civil rights activist and educator who served as the school's principal for a number of years. He was one of the founders of the Louisville Urban League and served as it chairman for 29 years. Meyzeek also served on the state board of education from 1948 to 1956. The school's website notes that "Meyzeek Middle School is located in the heart of Smoketown, a historic community of downtown Louisville. The rich academic tradition at 828 South Jackson Street extends historically through multiple generations. Prior to the merger of Jefferson County's segregated school systems, the campus hosted Booker T. Washington Elementary School and Jackson Junior High School. These institutions were the prestigious schools for African Americans. Many of today's civic leaders are their alumni. Over time, the two buildings were combined into a larger Jackson Junior High School. In the early 1970s, Jefferson County Public Schools adopted the middle school model." (Photograph courtesy of the author.)

Two

BLACK HILL–OLD LOUISVILLE, CALIFORNIA, PARKLAND

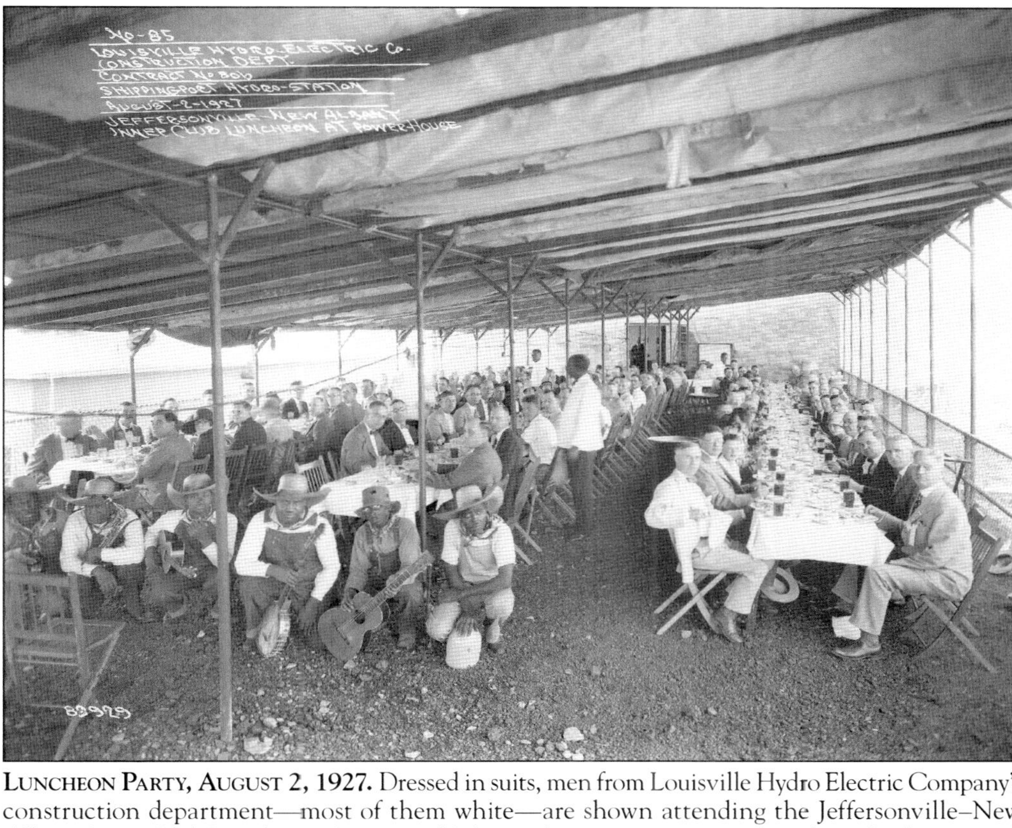

LUNCHEON PARTY, AUGUST 2, 1927. Dressed in suits, men from Louisville Hydro Electric Company's construction department—most of them white—are shown attending the Jeffersonville–New Albany Inner Club Luncheon. A group of African American musicians kneels in the foreground. They wear overalls and straw hats, and each has an instrument; a jug, two guitars, a banjo, and a saxophone are visible.

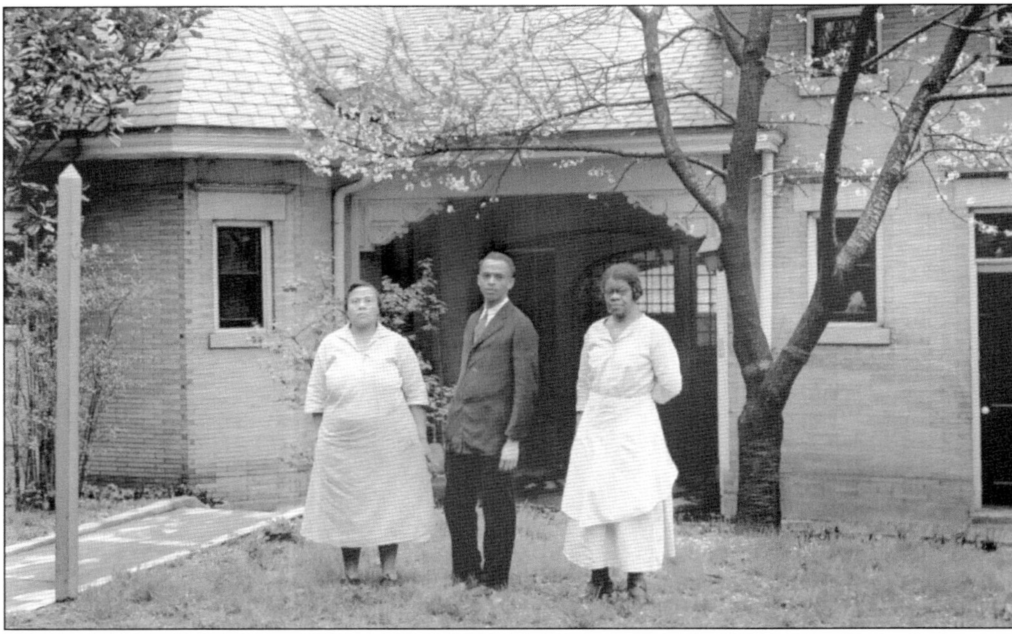

Servants Outside Home of Col. Charles Christopher Mengel, 1932. This photograph shows three servants posing by the Mengel home, located at 1325 South Third Street. Both women have aprons tied on over their dresses. The man is wearing a dark suit, a white shirt, and a tie. The servants may have resided in Black Hill.

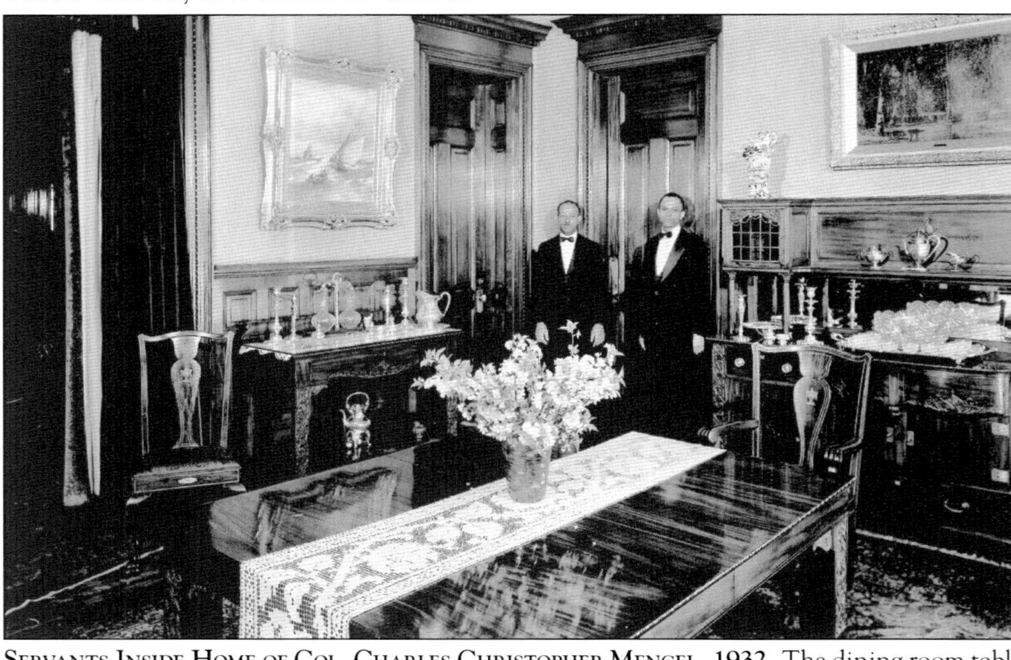

Servants Inside Home of Col. Charles Christopher Mengel, 1932. The dining room table has a white runner and a vase of flowers on it. Two servants in black suits, white shirts, and black bow ties stand in the corner of the room by two doors. To one side of the room, some decanters, candlesticks, and a pitcher sit on a table. Most likely, these servants resided in Black Hill.

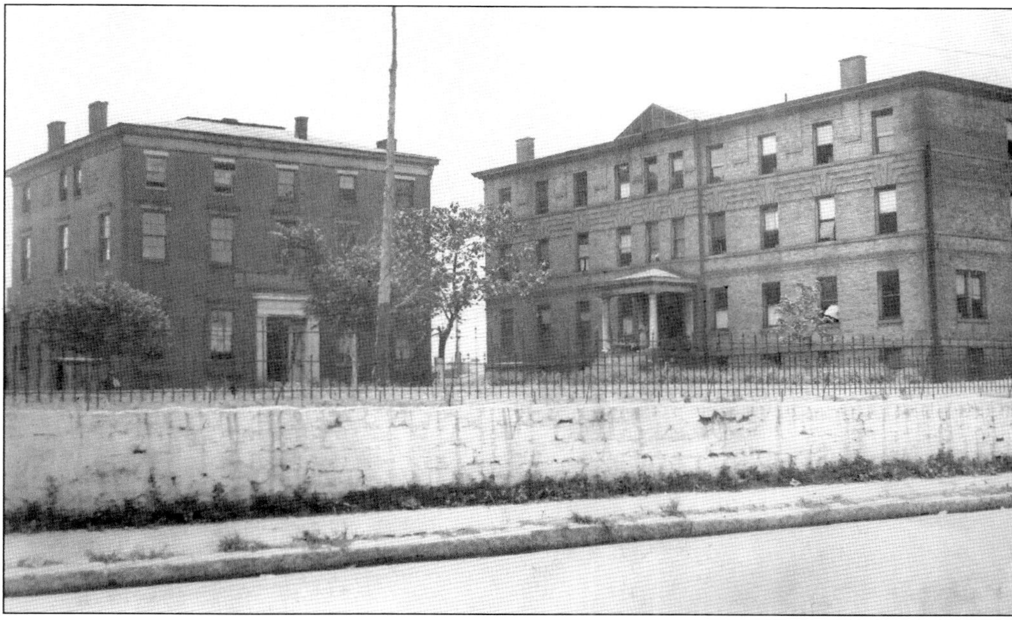

SIMMONS UNIVERSITY, 1930. This is an August 4, 1930, view of Simmons University, located at Seventh and Kentucky Streets in the California neighborhood. The college was founded in the 1870s to provide educations to African American students. The name was changed from Simmons Bible College to Simmons University in 1919. In 1982, when the college's mission changed to a focus on Christian service and studies, it was renamed Simmons Bible College. It is now known as Simmons College of Kentucky. William J. Simmons was a former slave who became president of the college in 1880.

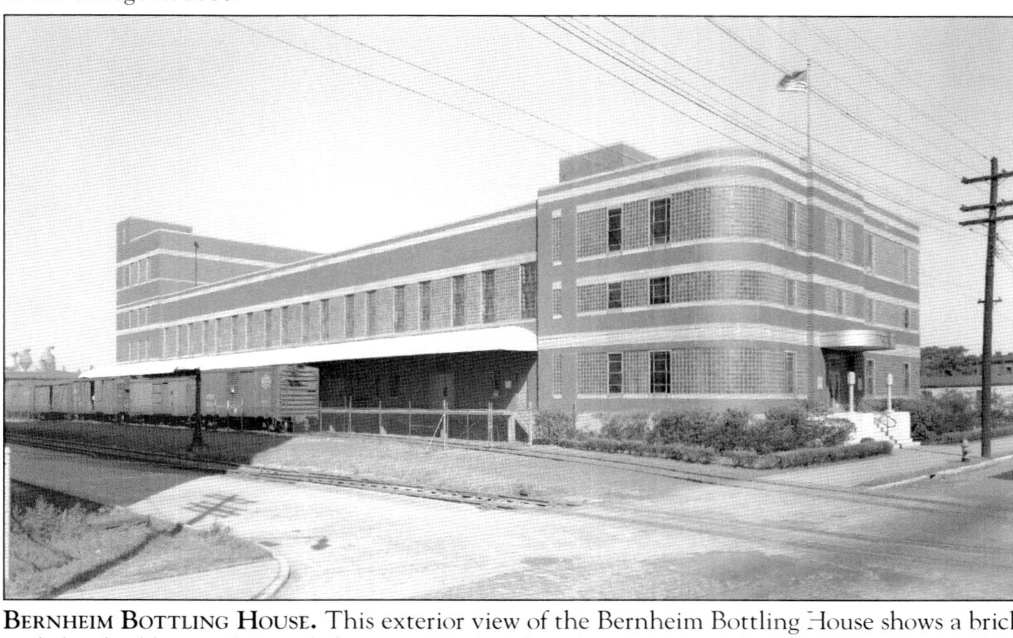

BERNHEIM BOTTLING HOUSE. This exterior view of the Bernheim Bottling House shows a brick and glass building with rounded corners. Railroad tracks run next to the structure. The distilling industry was prominent in the California neighborhood around 1940.

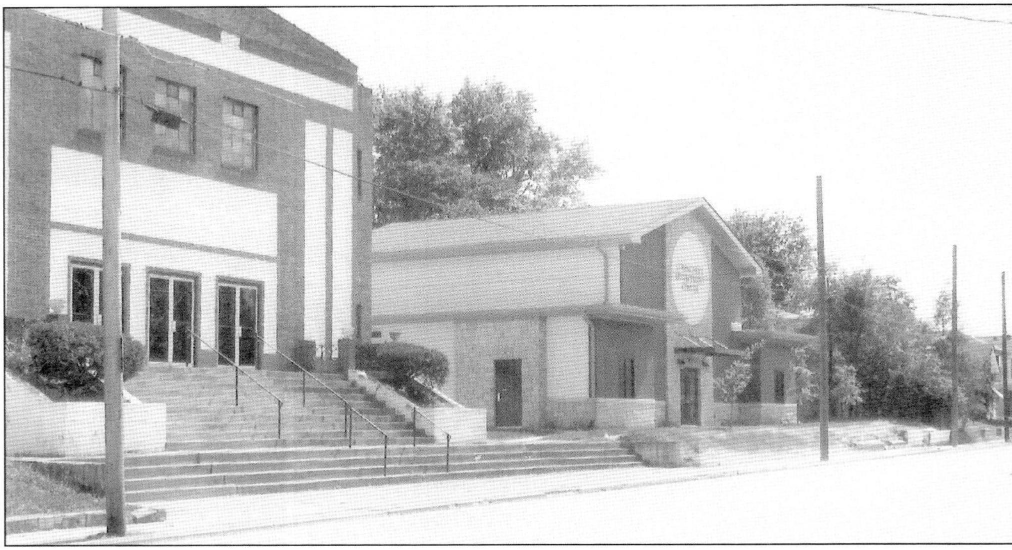

Centennial Olivet Baptist Church and Community Development Center, 2010. Around 1807, Lee Smith and Calvin Shipp, two devout deacons of the York Street Baptist Church, now known as the Calvary Baptist Church, learned of a Sunday school being held in the residence of Washington and Margaret Harris. The couple gathered people in their home to teach them to read and learn about God. It is from this humble gathering that Smith and Shipp organized the Harvey Street Baptist Church, which was later renamed Centennial Olivet. This church is in the California neighborhood.

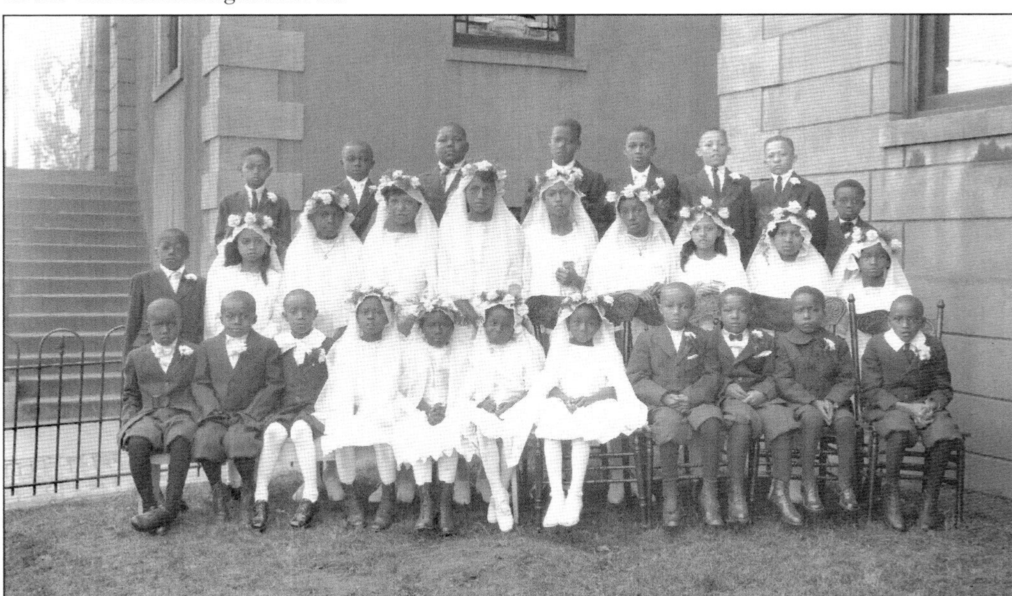

St. Augustine Communion of African American Children, 1921. In front of St. Augustine's Roman Catholic Church, located at 1304 West Broadway, three rows of children pose for a photograph commemorating their first communion. The children range in ages from around seven to 12 years old. The boys wear dark suits with white shirts and corsages, and the girls wear white dresses, with headscarves and wreaths of flowers on their heads.

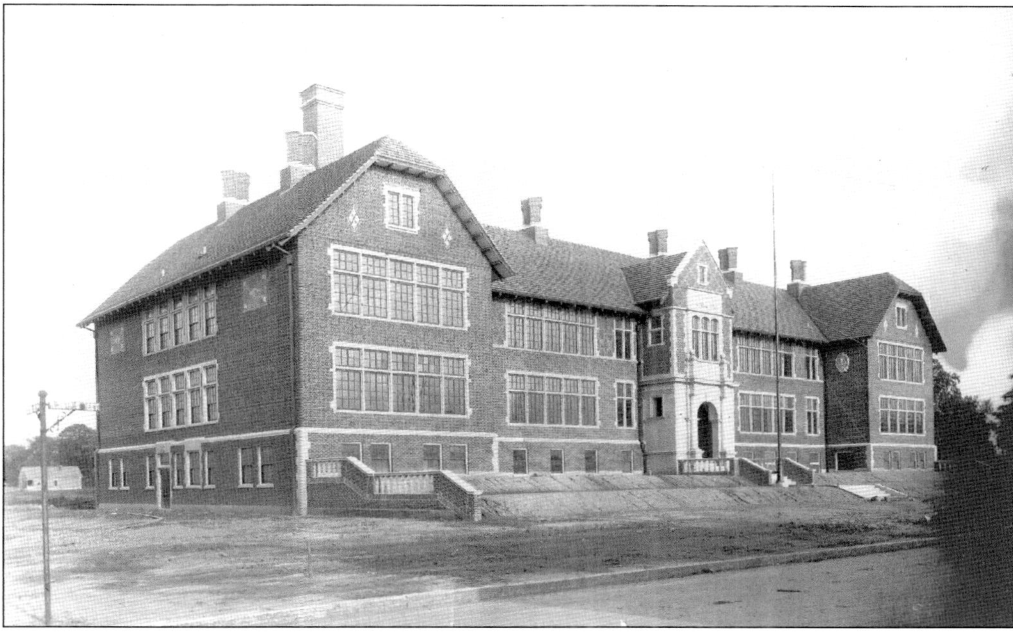

ALBERT S. BRANDEIS ELEMENTARY SCHOOL, 1921. Albert S. Brandeis Elementary School is located at Twenty-sixth and Date Streets in the California neighborhood. The two-story brick building has projecting front and side sections; the side sections have roofs forming triangular peaks towards the front. The front vestibule has a domed entrance. An embankment with brick retaining walls runs up to the front of the building. The school is now located at 2817 West Kentucky Street.

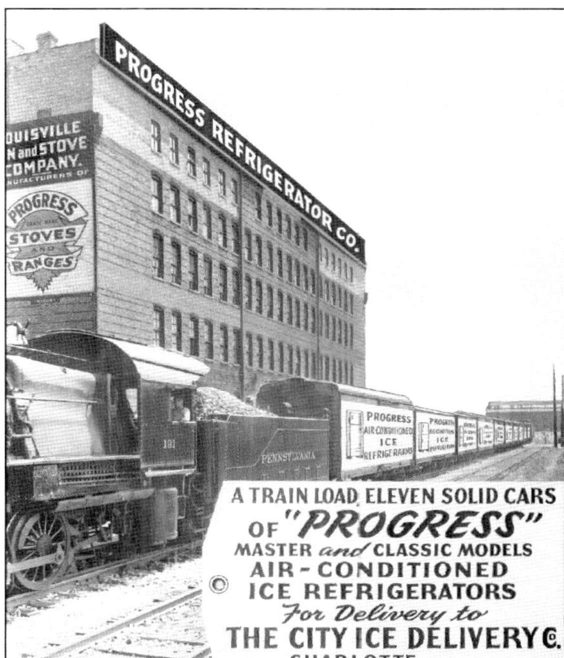

PROGRESS REFRIGERATOR CO., 1940. Shown here is the Louisville Tin and Stove Company, "manufacturers of Progress stoves and ranges." Signs for Progress air-conditioned ice refrigerators are on the sides of some of the railcars. The advertisement reads, "A train load, eleven solid cars of 'Progress' master and classic models air-conditioned ice refrigerators for delivery to the City Ice Delivery Co. Charlotte, North Carolina." The Louisville manufacturer was located at 737 South Thirteenth Street, in the California neighborhood.

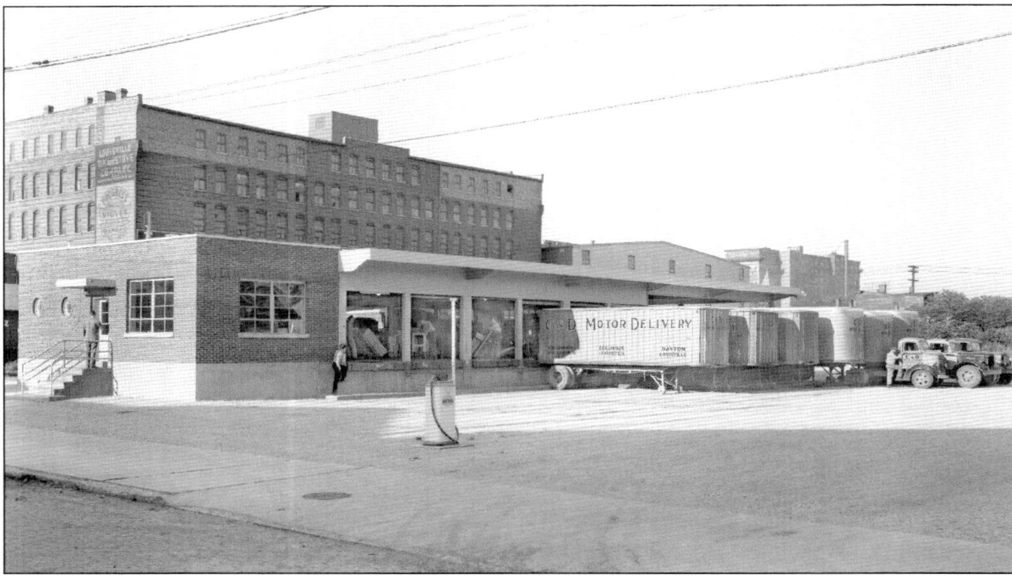

C&D Motor Company, May, 23, 1946. Freight trucks are backed into the C&D terminal's loading dock. A large brick building is in the background. Truck trailers read "C&D Motor Delivery." C&D was on Thirteenth Street in the California neighborhood.

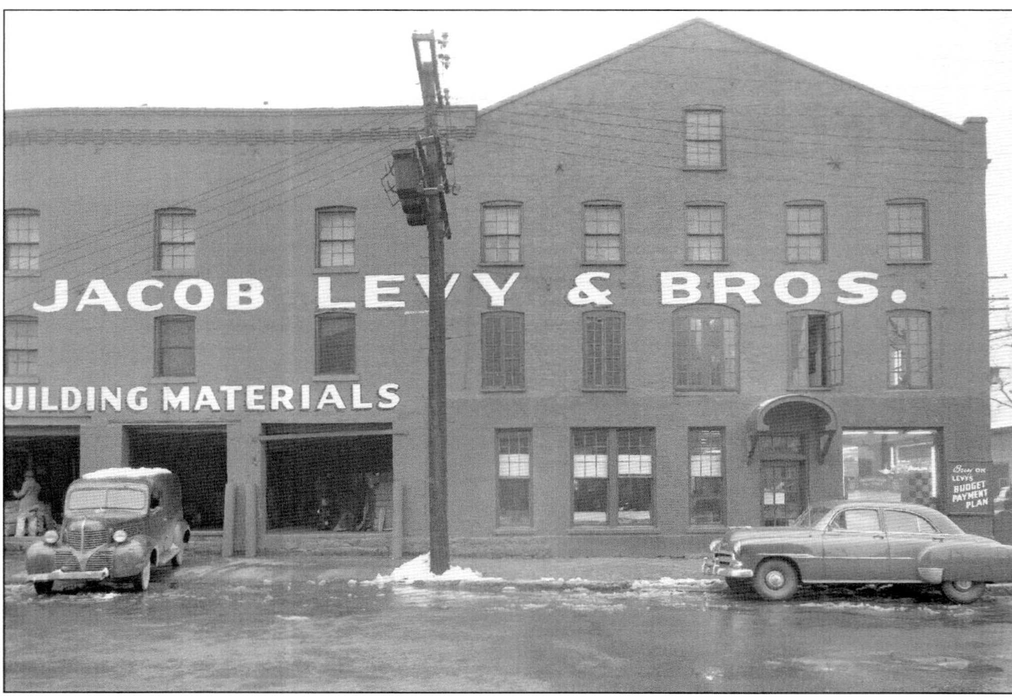

Jacob Levy and Bros., 1953. The Lumber and Millwood Building, located on Twelfth Street in the California neighborhood, housed a store selling tools, hardware, outdoor equipment, and worktables. Today, Jacob Levy & Bros. continues the legacy by offering outdoor equipment, lawn mowers, and lawn tools at a new location.

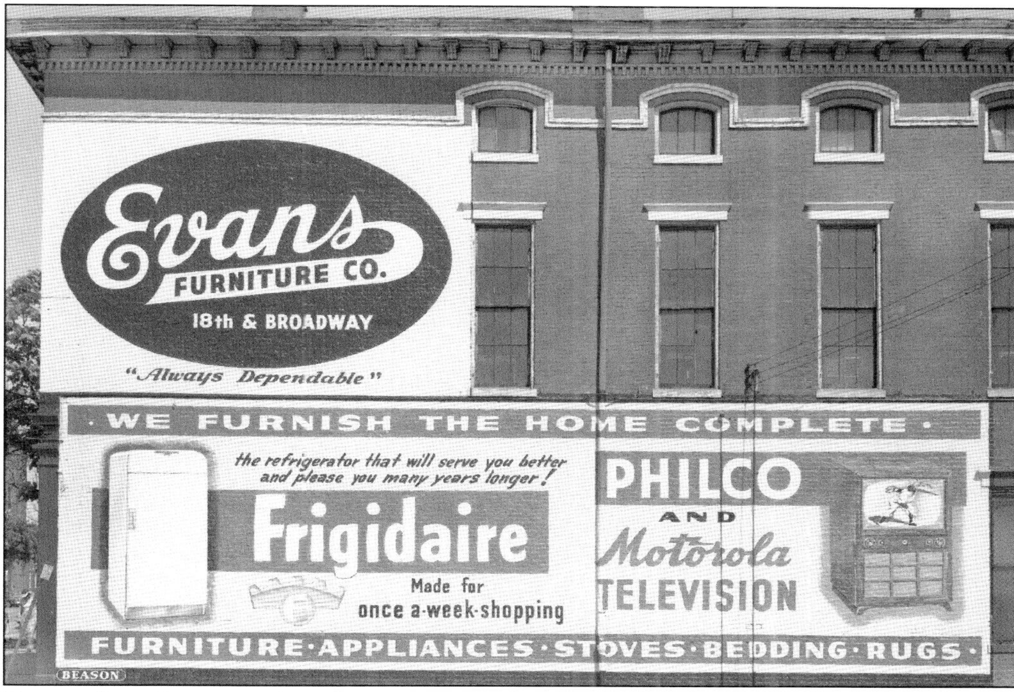

Beason Sign Company, June 14, 1951. These signs painted on the structure advertise Evans Furniture Company, located at Eighteenth Street and Broadway. The ad notes Evans Furniture's complete line of appliances, including Frigidaire refrigerators, as well as stoves, bedding, rugs, and Philco and Motorola televisions. At the bottom of the sign, in the lower left corner, Beason's name is displayed. The sign is very visible and eye-catching.

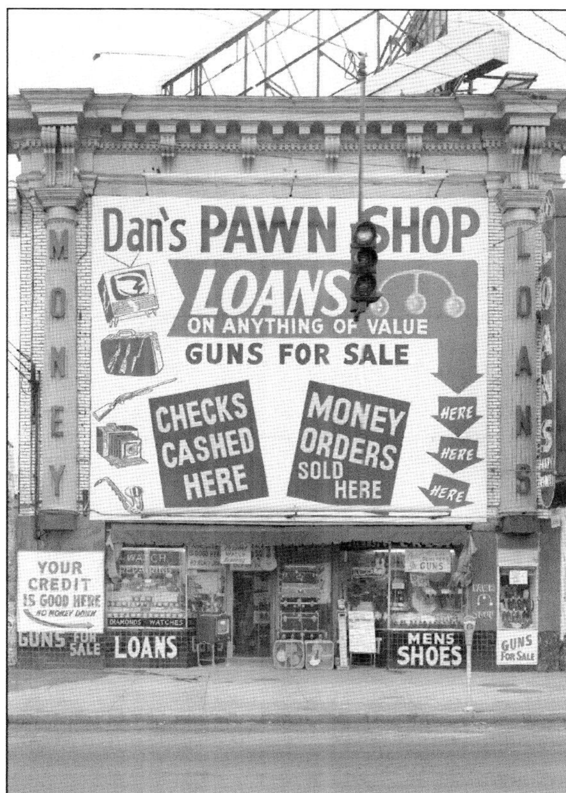

Dan's Pawn Shop, May 27, 1964. The Broadway location in the California neighborhood provided check cashing services, money order purchases, and shoes, jewelry, and many other items for sale. Dan's Pawn Shop continues to hold its legacy as a dealer and pawnbroker loaning money on anything of value. Its motto is "Get the cash you want and the respect you deserve. Bring us your broken or unwanted gold!" Dan's Pawn Shop is currently located at 5609 Preston Highway.

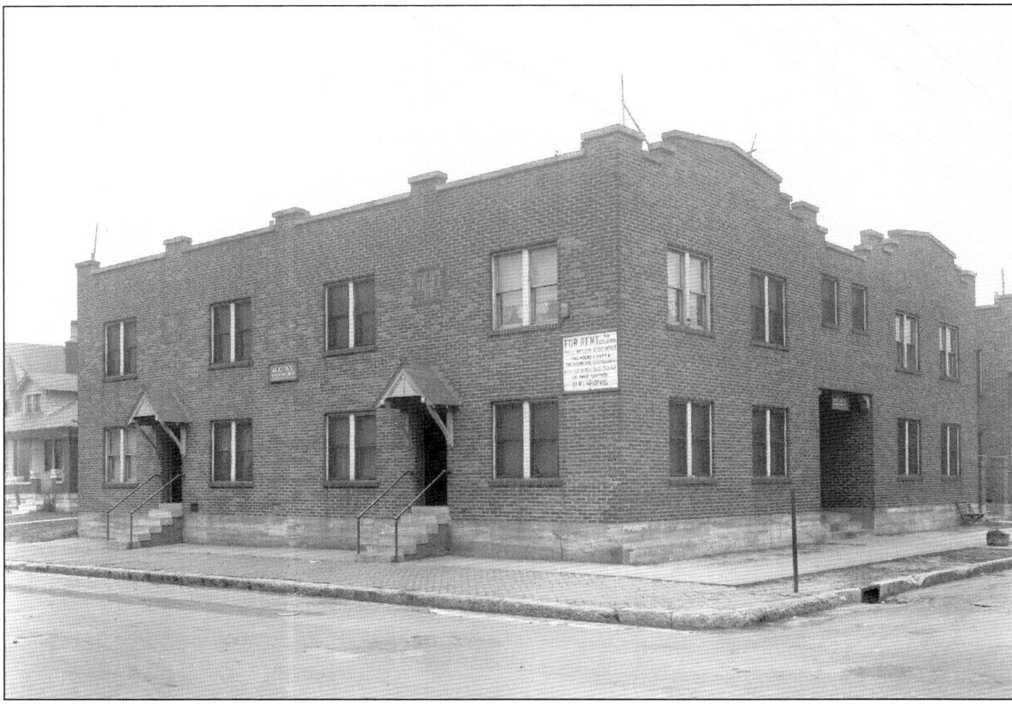

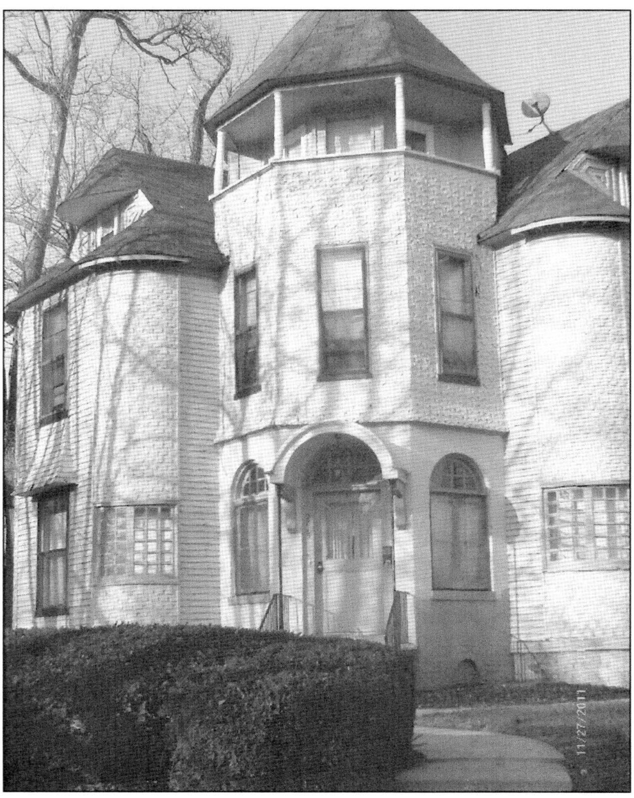

RUBY APARTMENTS, LOUISVILLE, KENTUCKY, 1934. These apartments can be found at 1127 South Seventeenth Street in the California neighborhood. The brick apartment building is located in a residential area. A small sign identifies the Ruby Apartments, while another sign reads, "For Rent to Colored. These modern apartments / Two rooms & bath & / Two rooms, kitchenette & bath / Electric lights, hot water, Clow gas steam heat / Gas range furnished / Apply 411 M.E. Taylor Bldg. City 3699."

PARKLAND HISTORIC HOME, 1900. This Queen Anne structure sits at 2815 Virginia Avenue. It was built by L.D. Bailey in 1900. The Queen Anne style became popular in the Late Victorian era, from 1880 to 1910. This style replaced the previous architecture of buildings.

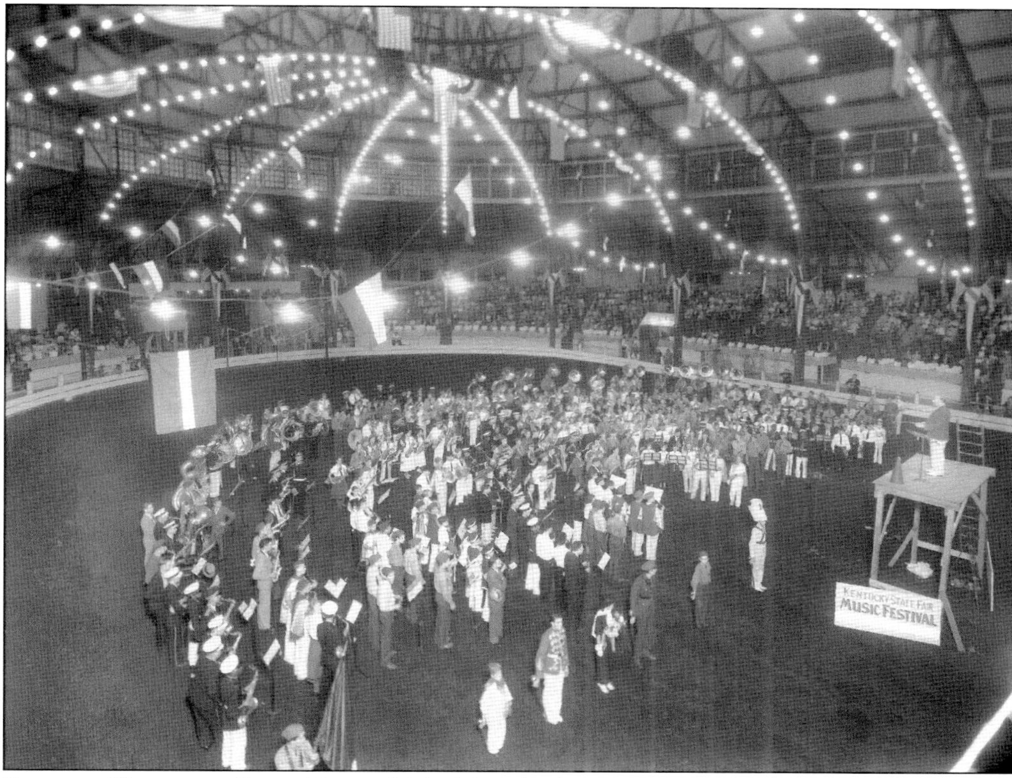

Band at Kentucky State Fair, 1934. A band takes center stage at the Kentucky State Fair Music Festival in the Parkland neighborhood. The group stands in concentric semicircles facing a band director on a wooden stand. A crowd watches from raised bleachers as numerous lights and flags hang from the ceiling, giving the event a festive flair.

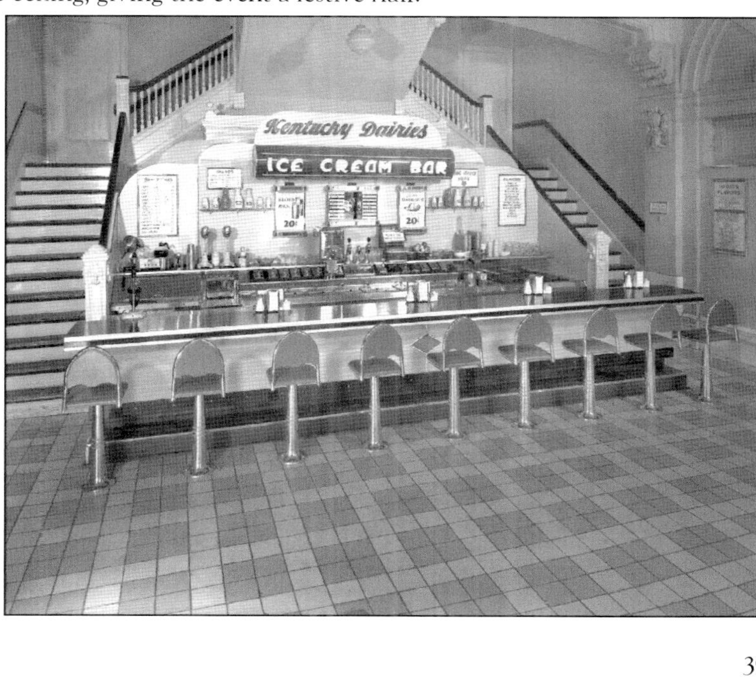

Kentucky Dairies Bar, May 21, 1940. The Kentucky Dairies Ice Cream Bar could be found at 1223 South Twenty-eighth Street in the Parkland neighborhood. The ice cream counter with bar stools set up between two stairways can be seen here. Ice cream equipment and menus hang on the wall. The sign reads "Kentucky Dairies Ice Cream Bar."

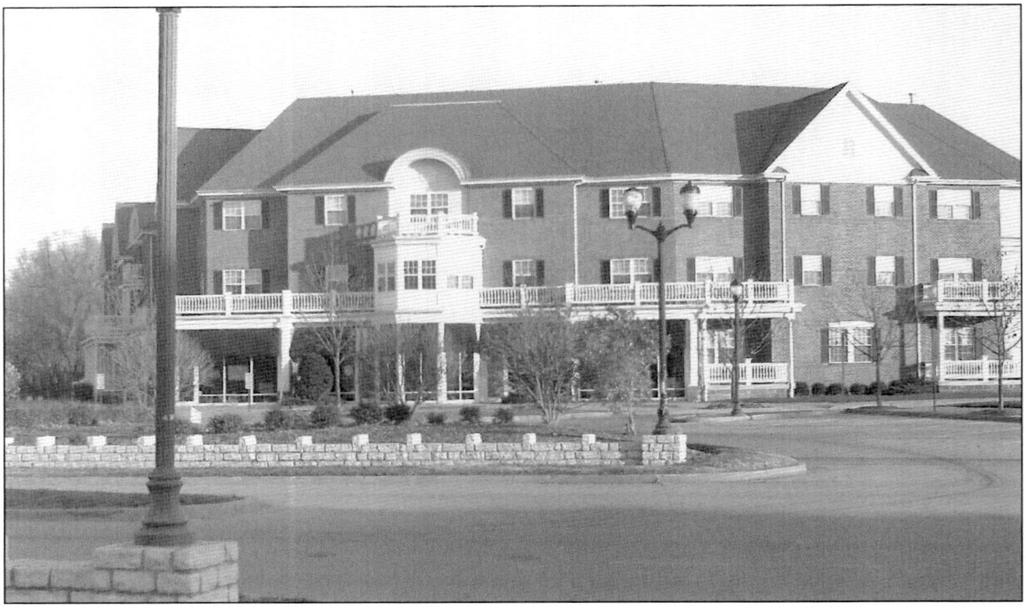

The Villages of Park DuValle. This revitalized community is now quiet and eloquent, exhibiting beautiful homes with well-kept lawns. In the early 1900s, this neighborhood was a part of Black Parkland, sometimes called "Little Africa," located in the Southwick–Cotter Homes area. It was southwest of central Parkland and extended as far west as Thirty-seventh Street. The first unit of the Villages of Park DuValle was erected in 1999. (Photograph courtesy of the author.)

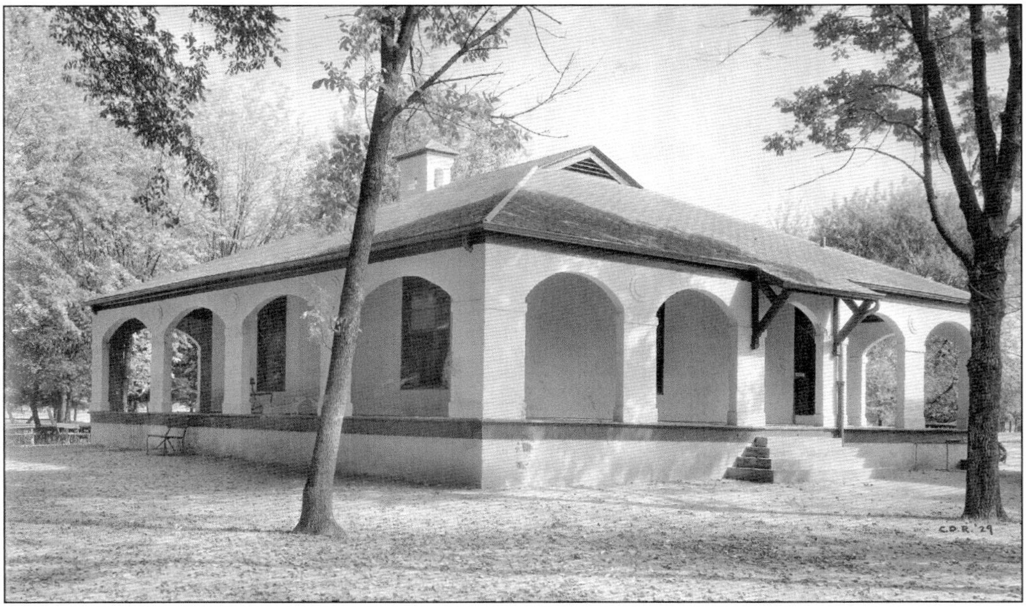

Chickasaw Park, 1929. The only park that was open for African Americans in the early 1900s was Chickasaw Park in the Parkland neighborhood. It was a place where African American families could find togetherness in fun activities, discuss civic issues, eat, and enjoy entertainment freely. The outdoor facility was a place for families to participate in large gatherings, birthday celebrations, outdoor wedding events, and parties.

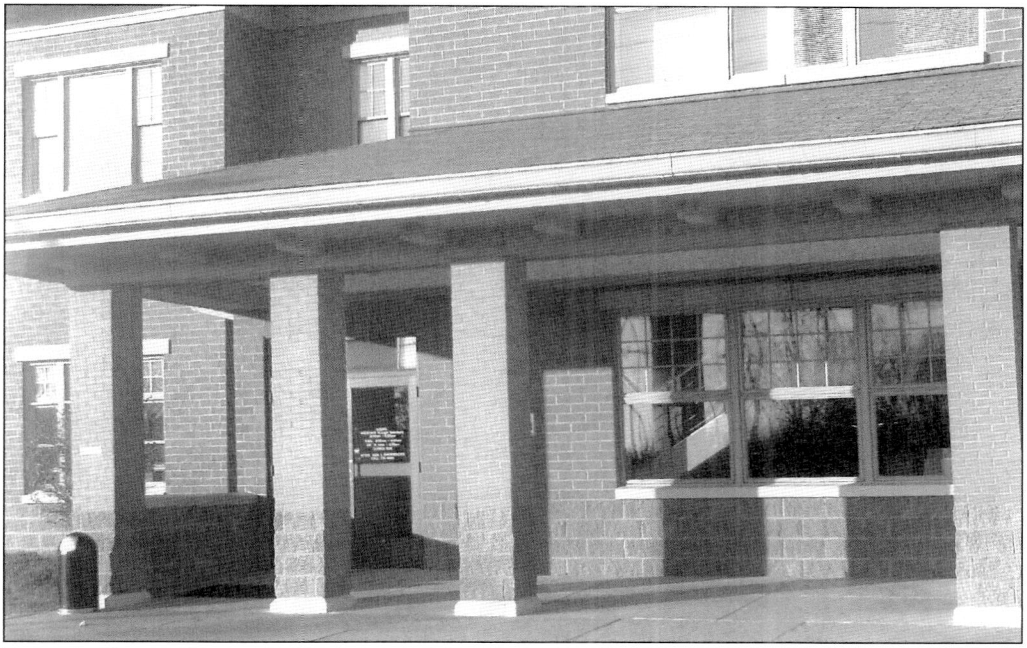

PARK DUVALLE COMMUNITY HEALTH CENTER. Located at 3015 Wilson Avenue, the Parkland neighborhood health clinic has been operating since 1968. Dr. Harvey L. Sloane was the its first director. The center's services include primary care, women's health, family planning, pediatrics, pharmacy, full-service X-rays, WIC program, dermatology, diabetes counseling, nutritional counseling, dental care, a lab, eye clinic, social services, and transportation. (Photograph courtesy of the author.)

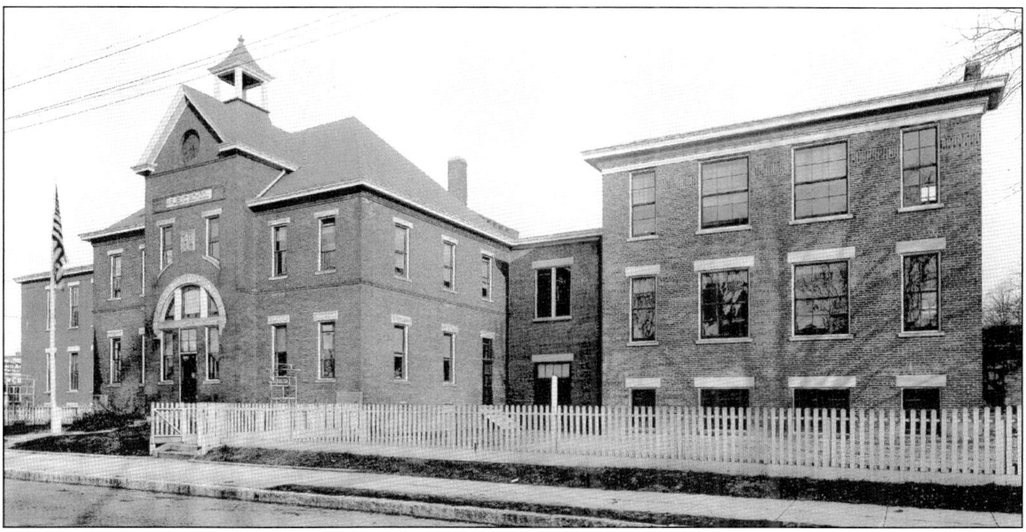

PARKLAND ELEMENTARY SCHOOL, 1923. Parkland Elementary School, located at 1309 Catalpa Street in Louisville, Kentucky, consisted of a brick building in two and three-story sections. The two-story section with the entrance (topped by domed windows) has a peaked roof and turret as well as a high circular window under the roof and, below that, letters that say "Public School." In front of the school are a United States flag and a white picket fence.

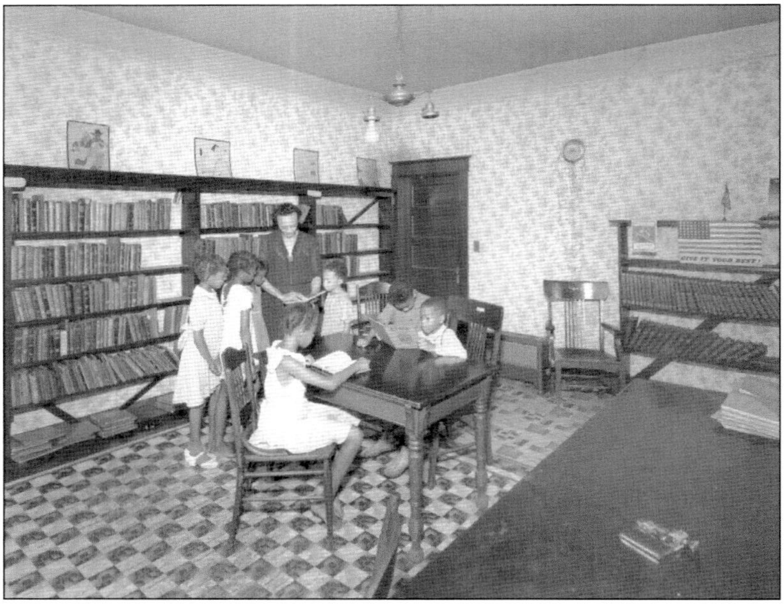

STORY TIME ROOM, 1958. Parkland Branch was located at the corner of Twenty-eighth Street and Virginia Avenue near the Parkland Business District. Its cornerstone was laid on September 20, 1907, and the completion of the building was on October 15, 1908. The branch library opened to blacks in January 1931.

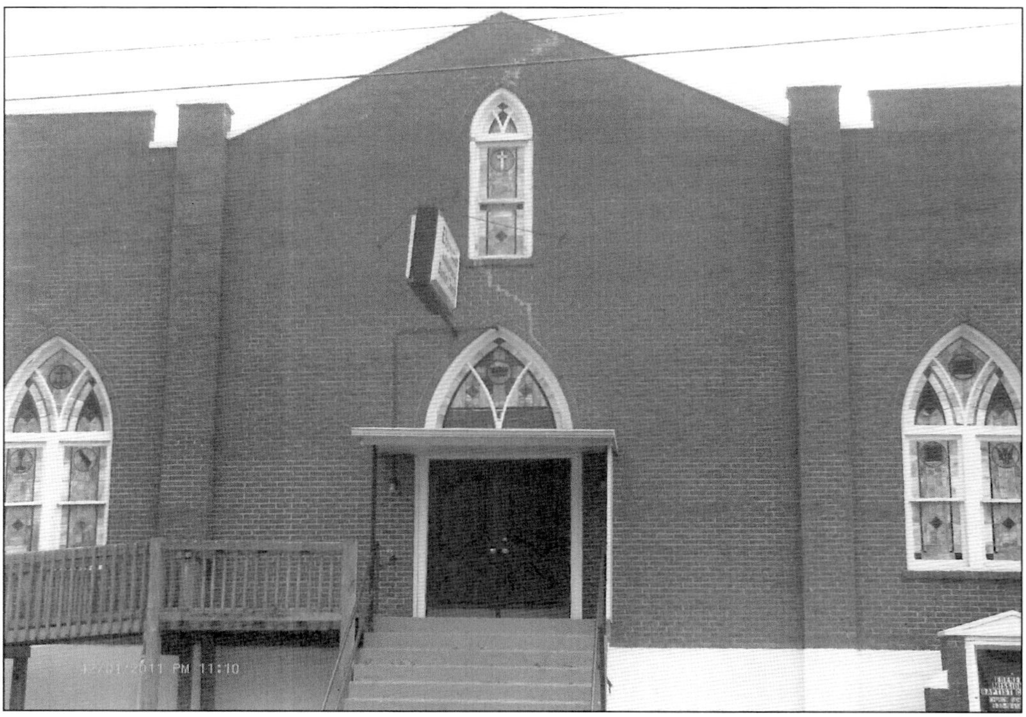

PARKLAND'S HISTORIC AFRICAN AMERICAN CHURCH, 1884. Ebenezer Missionary Baptist Church was organized in October 1884, under its original name, Good Shepherd Baptist Church. Rev. James Mitchell was its first pastor. In 1913, the name was changed to Ebenezer Missionary Baptist Church. The word *ebenezer*, Hebrew in origin, means "stone of help." Rev. Dr. Moses H. Gant led the membership in its purchase of the present location at 1057 South Twenty-eighth Street, and the new building was dedicated on October 26, 1959.

Three

Central Business District

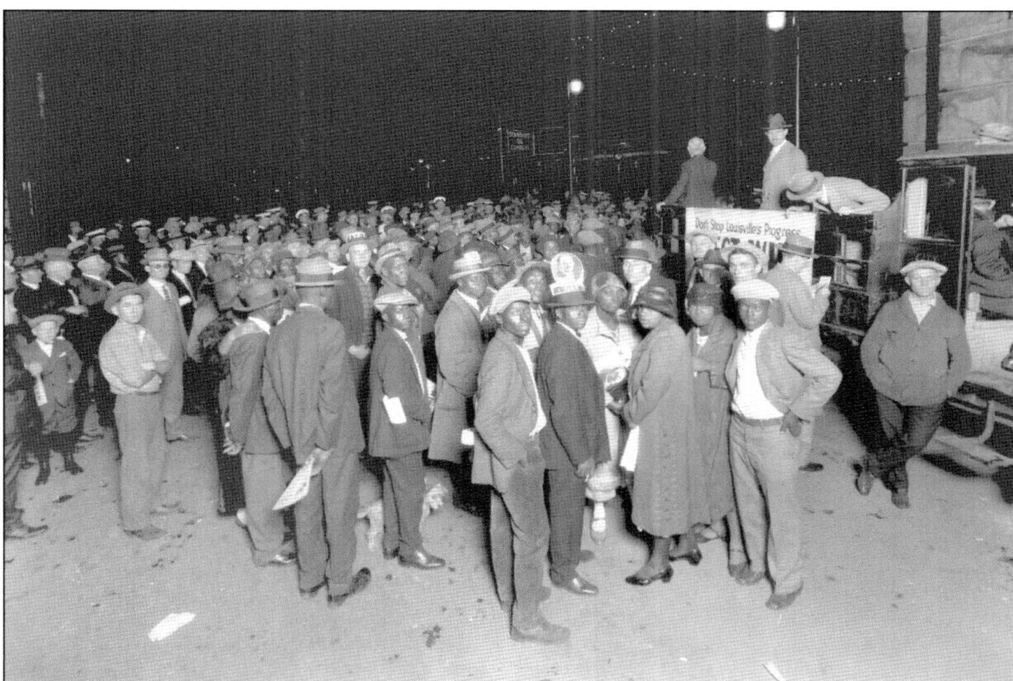

Crowd in Front of Jefferson County Armory, October 9, 1925. A crowd of people gathers for a campaign rally for Republican mayoral candidate Arthur A. Will on October 9, 1925, in front of the armory (now Louisville Gardens) at 514 West Walnut Street (now Muhammad Ali Boulevard). The group is a mix of African Americans and whites, men and women. A banner on a truck reads, "Don't Stop Louisville's Progress."

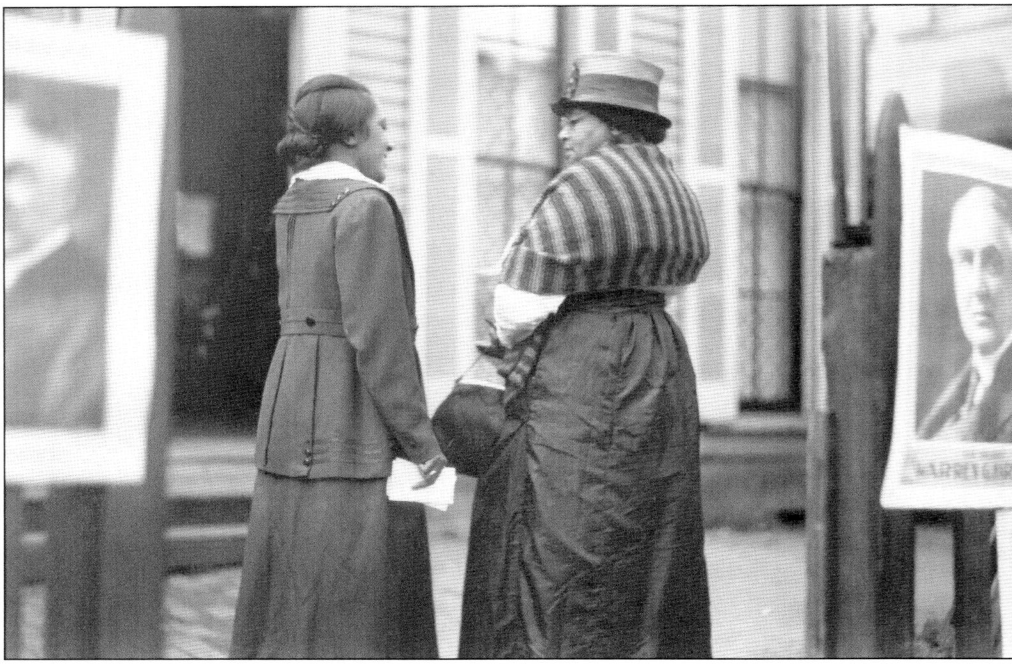

AFRICAN AMERICAN WOMEN IN CAMPAIGN SEASON, 1920. Two distinguished-looking African American women talk outside a building in this photograph taken on October 5, 1920. Political posters, visible on both sides, advertise candidates for upcoming elections, including Warren Gamaliel Harding.

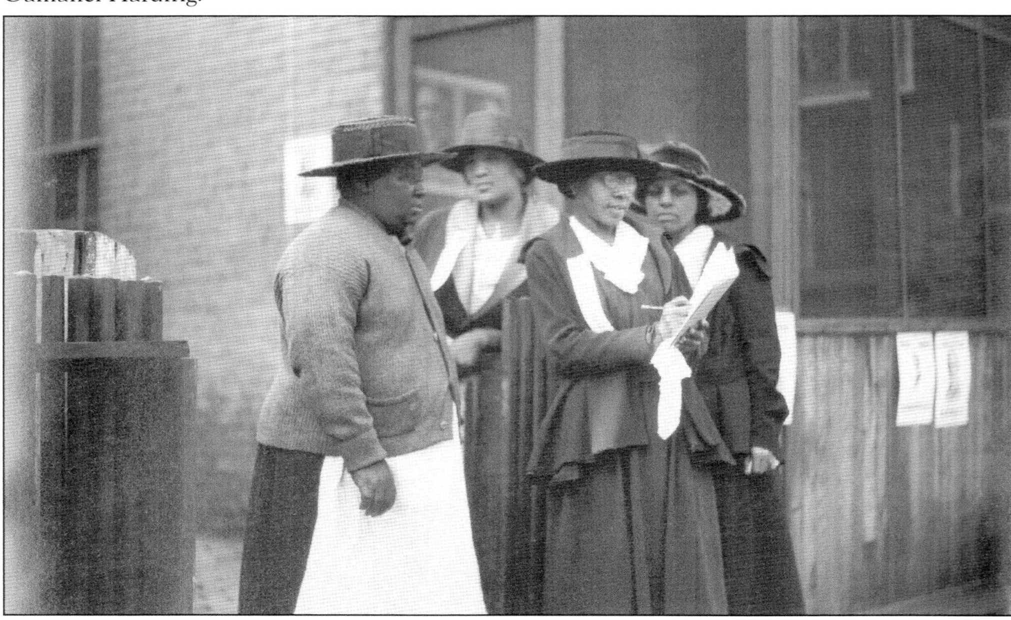

AFRICAN AMERICAN WOMEN AND VOTING REGISTRATION, OCTOBER 5, 1920. Four African Americans stand in the street, possibly registering to vote. One of them is writing on a sheet of paper. All of the women wear hats and jackets. Political advertising is visibly posted on the walls behind the women.

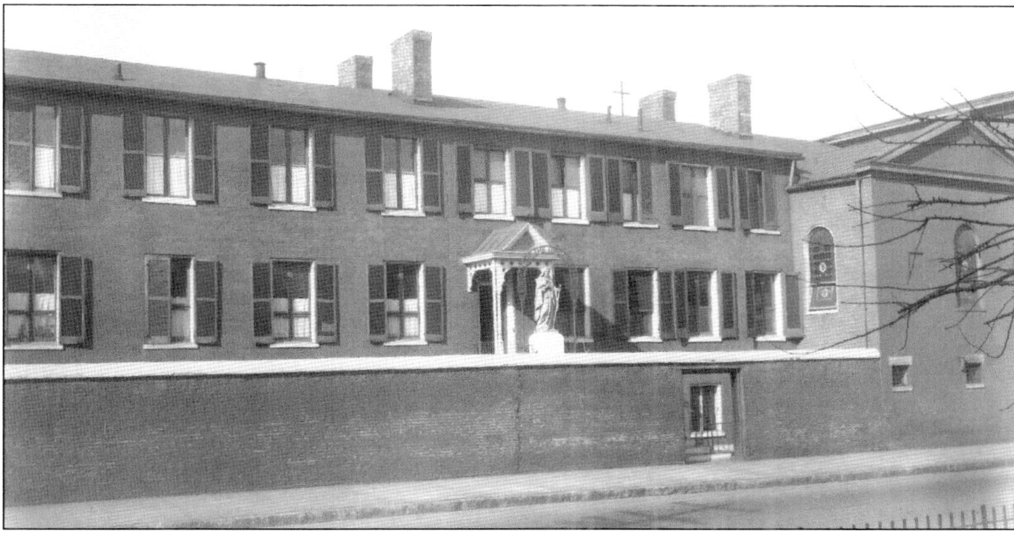

Convent of the Good Shepherd Home for Colored Girls, 1931. Convent of the Good Shepherd Home for Colored Girls had two locations, 800 West Walnut Street (now Muhammad Ali Boulevard) and 518 South Eighth Street. The convent was a long, two-story building with a statue of Jesus holding a lamb and staff in front.

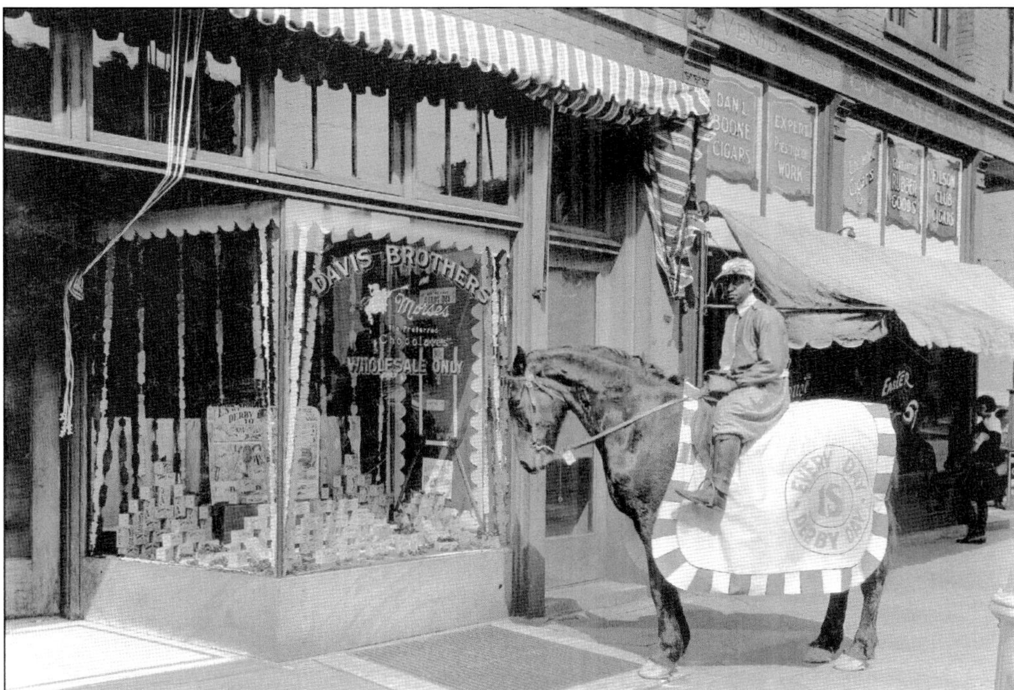

Davis Brothers Storefront, 1924. This storefront was originally located at 103 West Walnut Street (now Muhammad Ali Boulevard), in Louisville. A young African American man sits on a horse wearing a blanket proclaiming, "Every Day is Derby Day." Man and horse are on the sidewalk outside the Davis Brothers Candy Shop, which features a Derby Day display in its window. Next door is Badger Drug Co., which advertises Venida hairnets and cut-rate drugs.

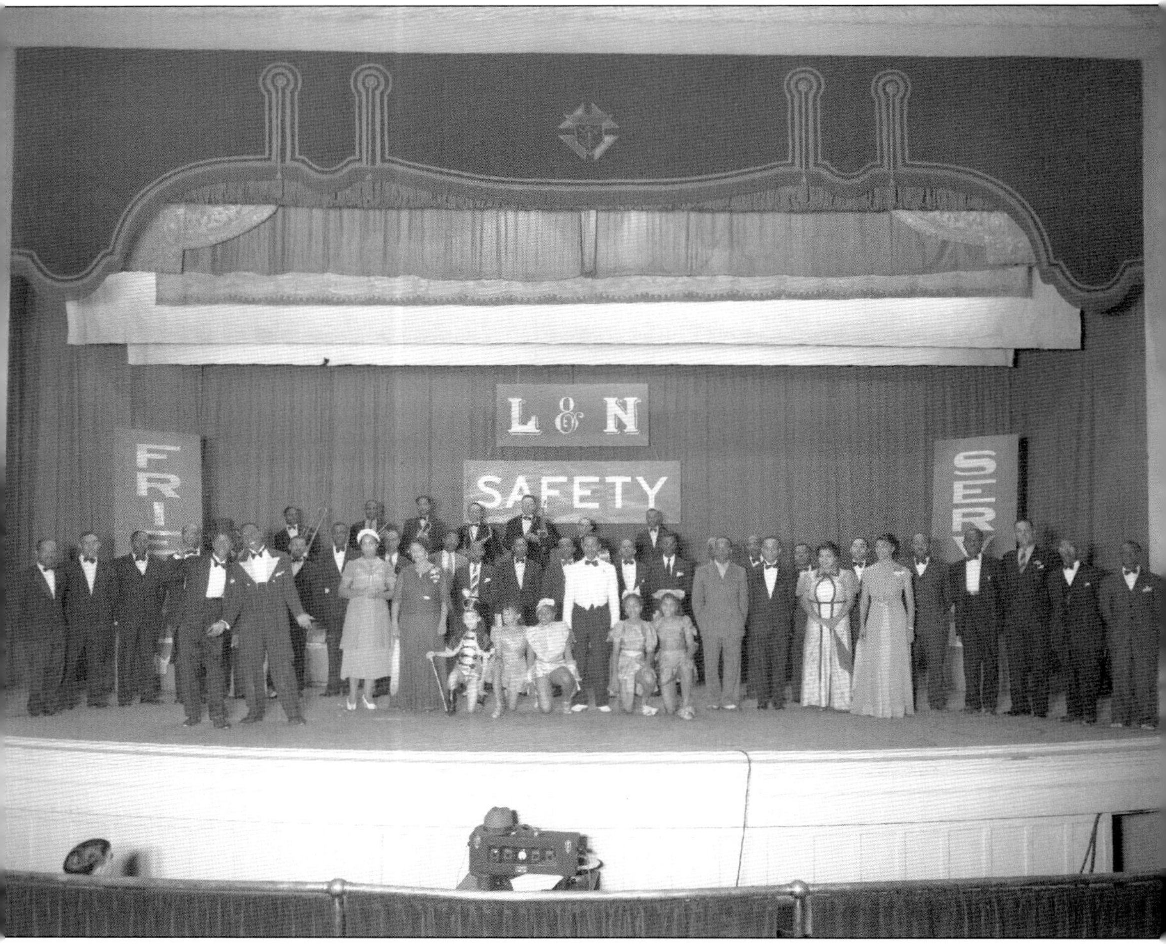

AFRICAN AMERICAN EMPLOYEES OF LOUISVILLE & NASHVILLE RAILROAD SAFETY PARTY. In 1938, a safety party was held in the Columbia Auditorium, located at 830 South Fourth Street. Pictured on the stage, men wear either tuxedos or suits. The women are in dresses, and a couple have corsages pinned to their shoulders. Five young girls are dressed in dance costumes and kneel center stage. A band is present—with a trombone, two saxophones, two trumpets, and a drum among the instruments visible. Hanging above the stage are signs reading "L&N" and "Safety," while two signs frame the stage at left and right reading "Friendly" and "Service." In 1954, Columbia Gym, in the basement of Columbia Auditorium, was where a preteen Cassius Marcellus Clay Jr., age 12, began his boxing career with trainer Joe Martin. Martin continued with the young fighter through his challenging six-year amateur career. ("Life As Muhammad Ali.")

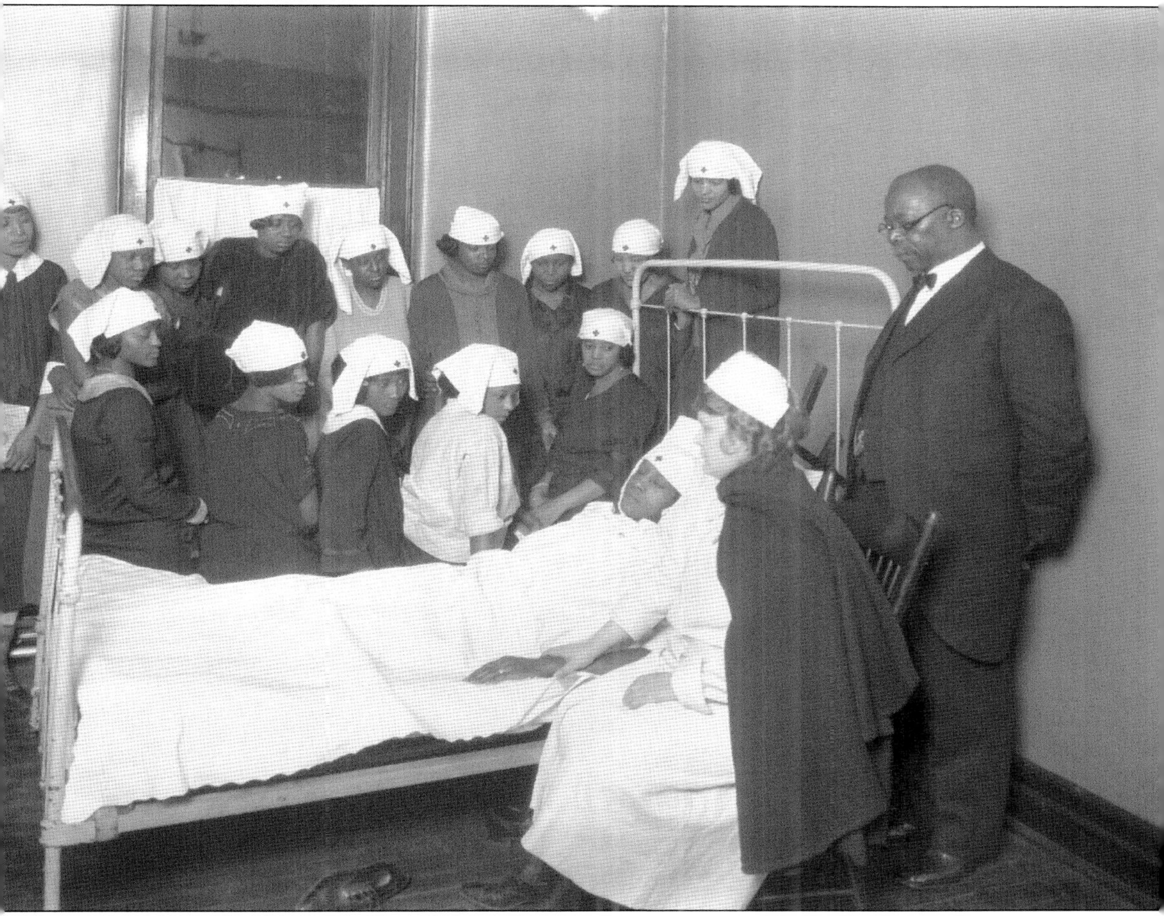

HOME HYGIENE CLASS, FEBRUARY 28, 1925. A number of young African American women surround the bed of a pretend patient as a Red Cross nurse talks to them and a man in a suit observes. The American Red Cross was located at 618 South Fourth Street. According to its website, "Today, in addition to domestic disaster relief, the American Red Cross offers compassionate services in five other areas: community services that help the needy; support and comfort for military members and their families; the collection, processing and distribution of lifesaving blood and blood products; educational programs that promote health and safety; and international relief and development programs."

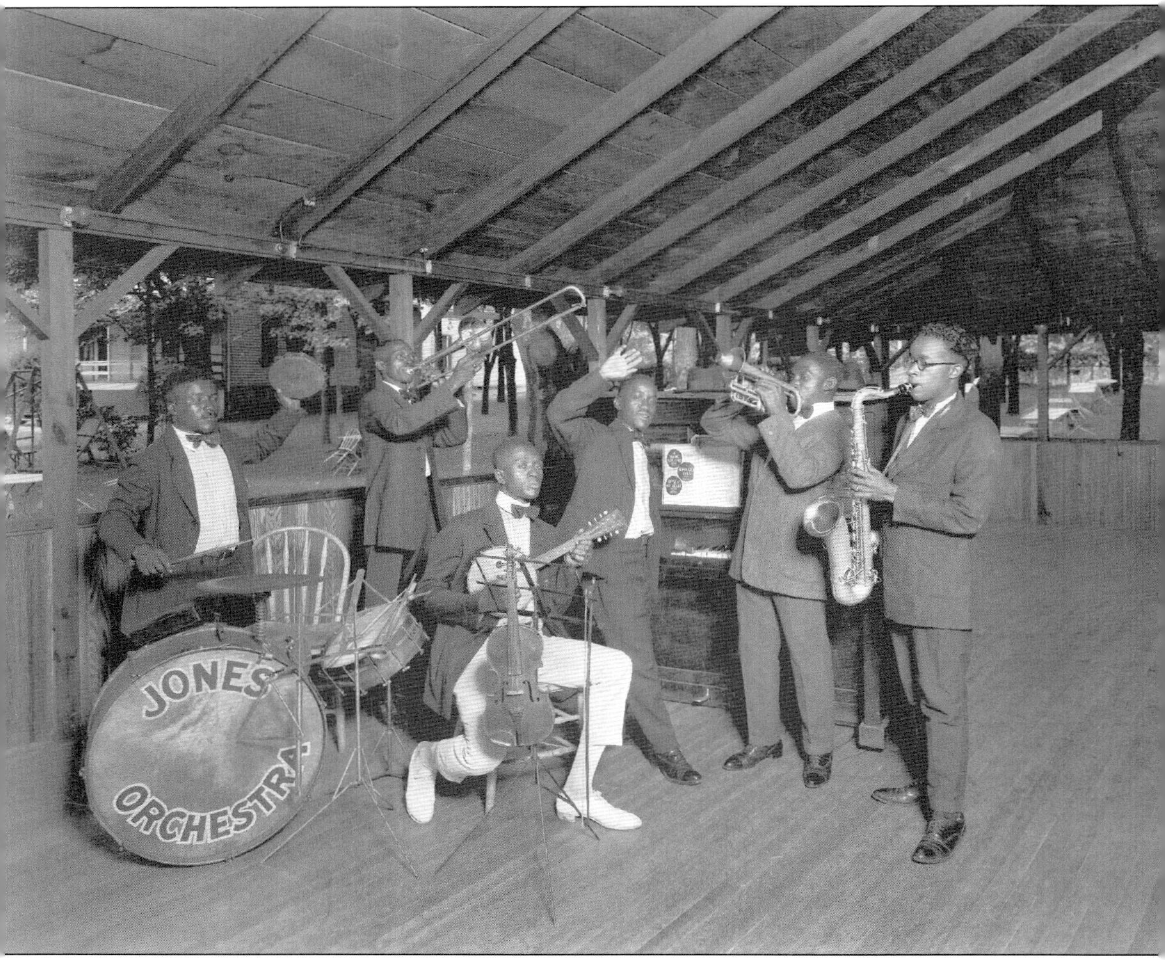

Jones Orchestra at Schneider's Roadhouse, 1921. Six African American teen musicians are seen performing in an open pavilion. The drum reads "Jones Orchestra." Other instruments include the tambourine, trombone, violin, banjo, piano, trumpet, and saxophone. It is not clear whether Jonah Jones, born Robert Elliott Jones, is the trumpeter in this photograph or a descendant, but his magnificent successes as an acclaimed musician deserves recognition. Born on December 31, 1908, Jones was a Louisvillian. He began playing music at approximately age 11. An account on the African American Registry website relates: "He watched the Booker T. Washington Community Center Band march through town as a boy and the flashy trombones impressed him. The band's organizer gave him his chance, but Jones' arms were too short for trombone, so he moved on to the trumpet. Jones started out playing on a Mississippi riverboat in the 1920s." Jones had a long series of popular albums for Capitol before switching to Decca for a few more quartet albums from 1965 to 1967. Jones died on April 30, 2000, in New York, New York, at the age of 91.

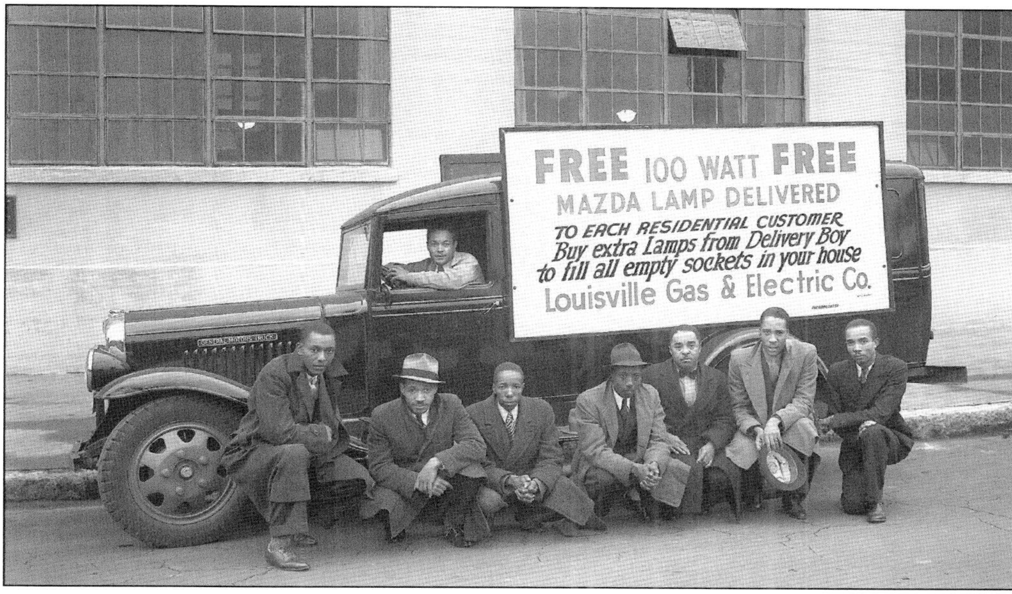

LAMP SALESMEN AND TRUCK, OCTOBER 26, 1936. A group of African American salesmen poses in front of a truck. One man sits behind the wheel. They wear suits, and some of them have on overcoats and/or hats. A sign on the truck reads, "Free 100 Watt Free Mazda lamp delivered to each residential customer. Buy extra lamps from delivery boy to fill all empty sockets in your house. Louisville Gas & Electric Co."

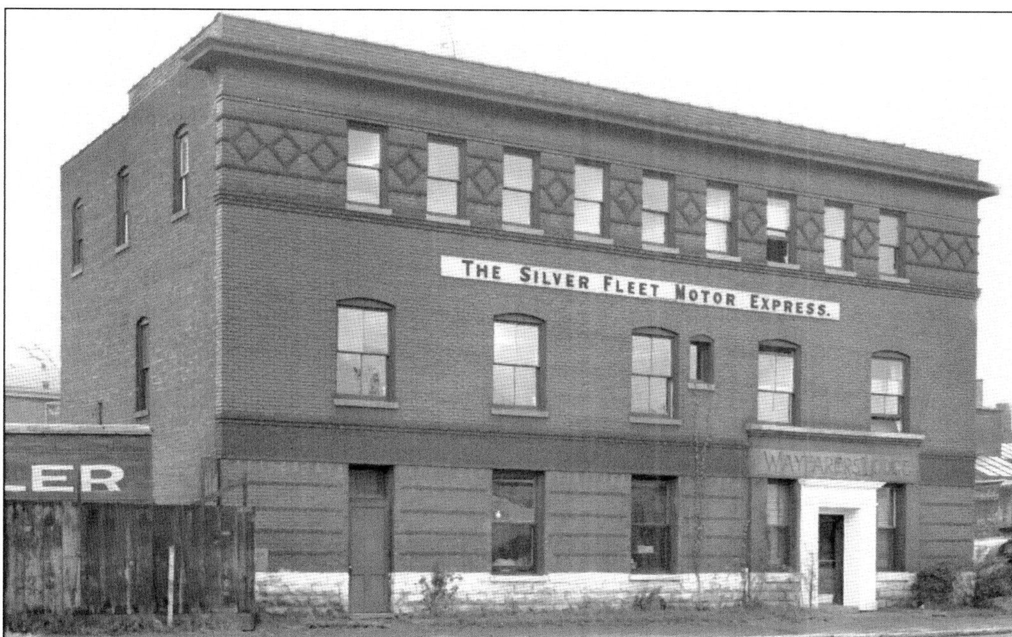

THE SILVER FLEET MOTOR EXPRESS BUILDING, 1940. This building was listed in the 1963 Louisville city directory with an address of 216 East Liberty Street. In the 1964 directory, Mason Dixon Trucking Co. was listed at the same address, and the Silver Fleet Motor Express Co. was not listed.

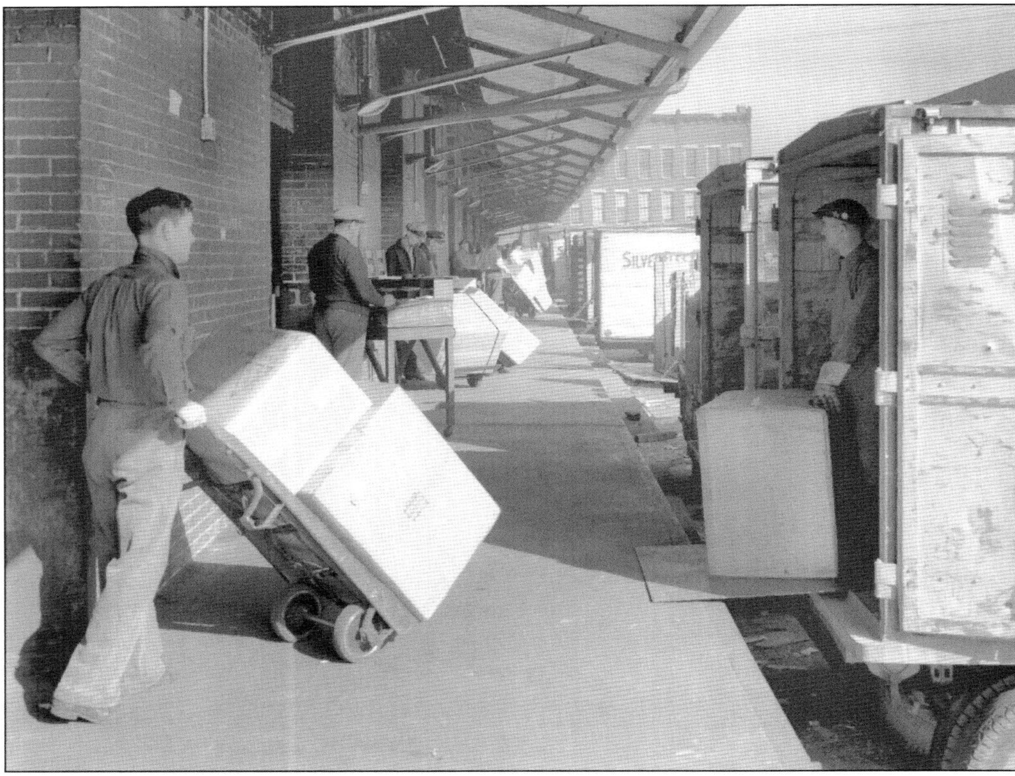

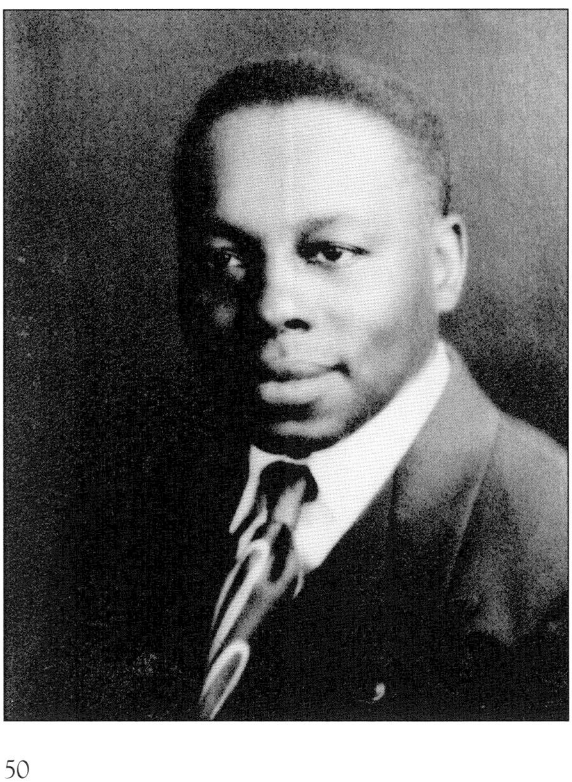

SILVER FLEET LOADING DOCK, 1940. Shown at the loading at the Silver Fleet Building, men push dollies to trucks at the dock. The Silver Fleet Building is a three-story brick structure with the words "The Silver Fleet Motor Express" across the front. Silver Fleet production workers loaded and transported freight and also checked it for damage.

THOMAS JOHNSTON BROWN SR., 1951. Thomas Johnston Brown Sr. was the Silver Fleet Motor Express Company's first African American employee. In 1964, Mason Dixon Trucking Company replaced Silver Fleet Motor Express, and Brown continued with the new company. For over 22 years, he held a position as freight checker, receiving service pin awards and acknowledgments.

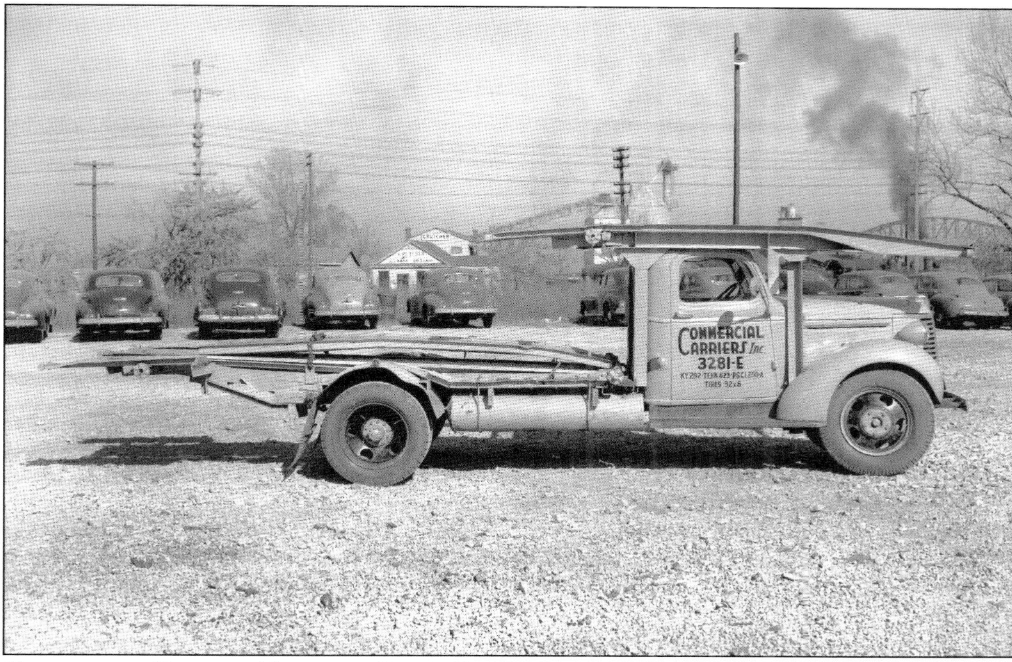

COMMERCIAL CARRIERS TRUCK AT SILVER FLEET, OCTOBER 31, 1940. In this scene, a tow truck sits in a gravel lot with a row of cars parked behind it. Painted on the truck door is "Commercial Carriers Inc. 3281-E."

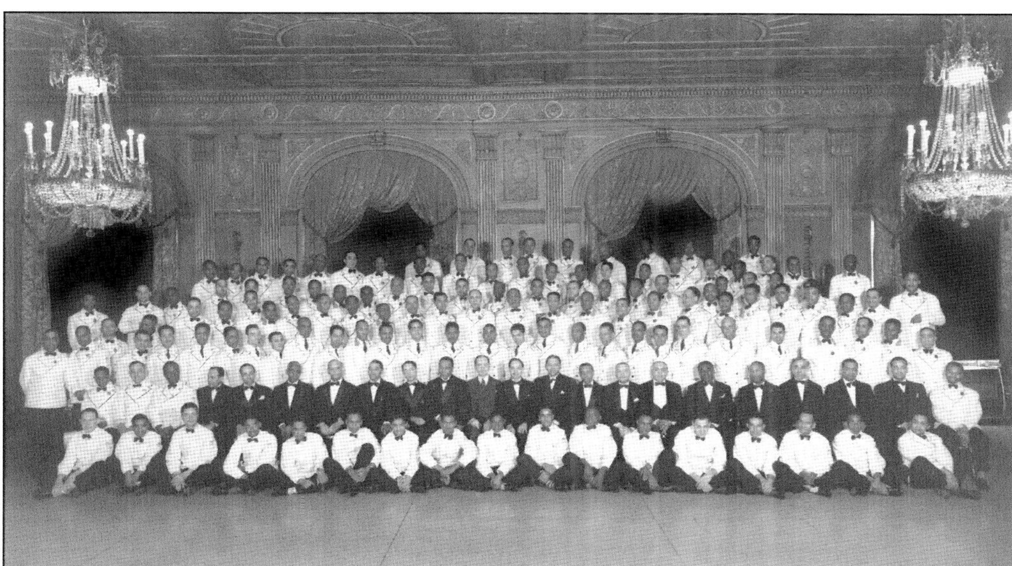

BROWN HOTEL EMPLOYEES, 1936. A group of Brown Hotel employees wearing uniforms poses at the lodging at 335 West Broadway. Some of the men are wearing white jackets, black pants, and black bow or straight ties, while other men wear black jackets, black pants, and black bow ties. Each uniform represents the role the employee performs—bellman, room service, chef, waiter, or front desk agent.

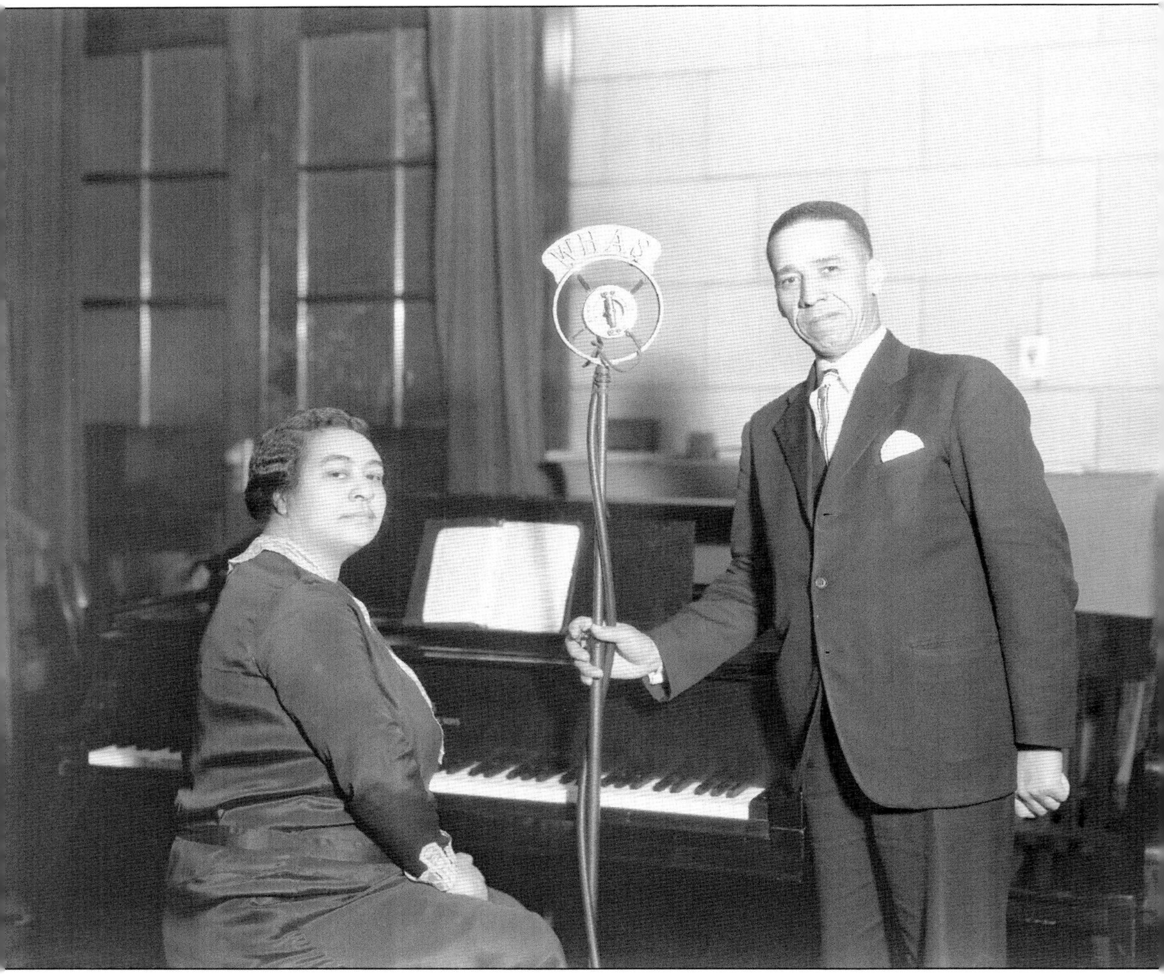

WHAS Broadcast, December 28, 1931. A man in a suit stands holding a WHAS microphone. Next to him is a woman seated at a piano as if ready to play. Sheet music is propped on the piano's stand, and the piano keys are exposed. WHAS-AM signed on July 18, 1922, with 500 watts of power. It was owned by the Bingham family, who also owned the *Courier-Journal* newspaper. Regular programming broadcast on 360 meters and weather and farm programming on 480 meters. Power transmitter and studios were located at Third and Liberty Streets. The first radio broadcast of the Kentucky Derby was on WHAS on May 16, 1925.

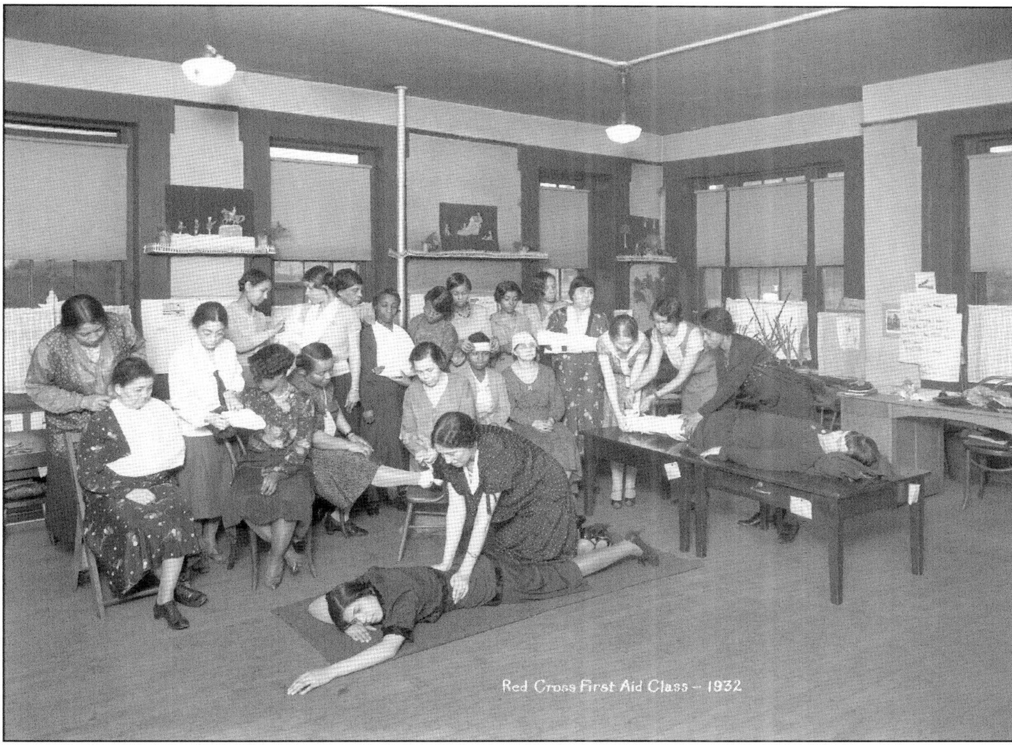

RED CROSS FIRST AID CLASS, 1932. Women practice first aid techniques at the Dunbar School located at 908 Magazine Street. Many women wear bandages on their arms and legs as others practice their bandaging techniques. Since its founding in 1881 by visionary Clara Barton, the American Red Cross has been the nation's leading emergency response organization.

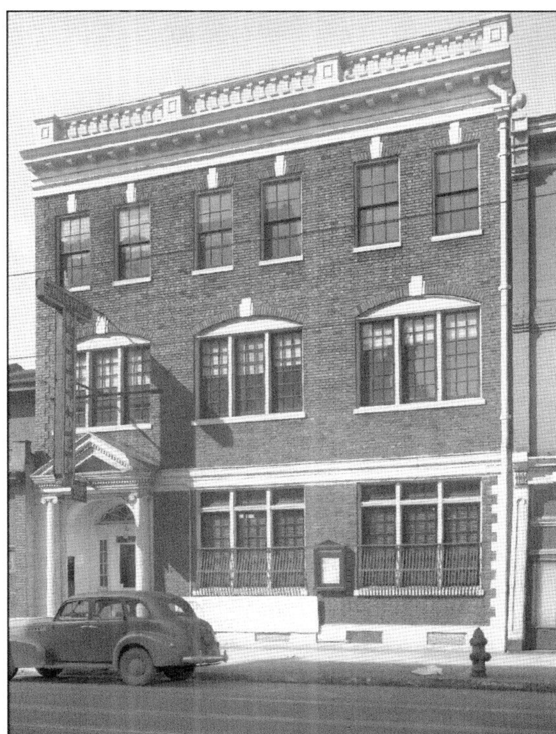

LOUISVILLE DEFENDER BUILDING. This photograph shows an exterior view of the Louisville Defender Building, a three-story brick structure with a sign above the front door. Frank L. Stanley Sr. (1906–1974) served as editor, general manger, and president of the *Louisville Defender* from 1938 through 1974. His papers were donated to University of Louisville by his widow, Vivian Stanley, and his son, Kenneth Stanley, in 1983. Stanley's personal papers and the written material relating to the *Louisville Defender* are held by UARC.

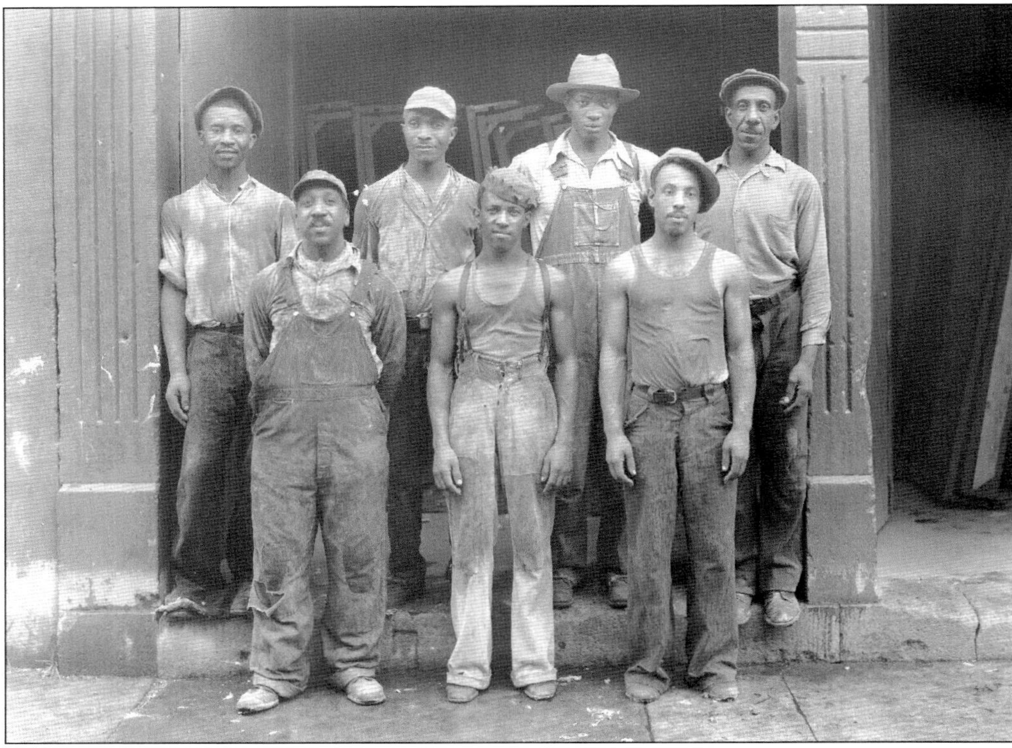

REPUBLICAN ADMINISTRATION ORGANIZATION, JULY 24, 1933. Seven African American men pose for a group portrait. They all wear some type of hat or cap and work clothes, which include overalls, jeans, tank tops, and long-sleeved shirts. Some of the clothes show evidence of dirt and patches. This photograph was taken at 416 West Liberty Street.

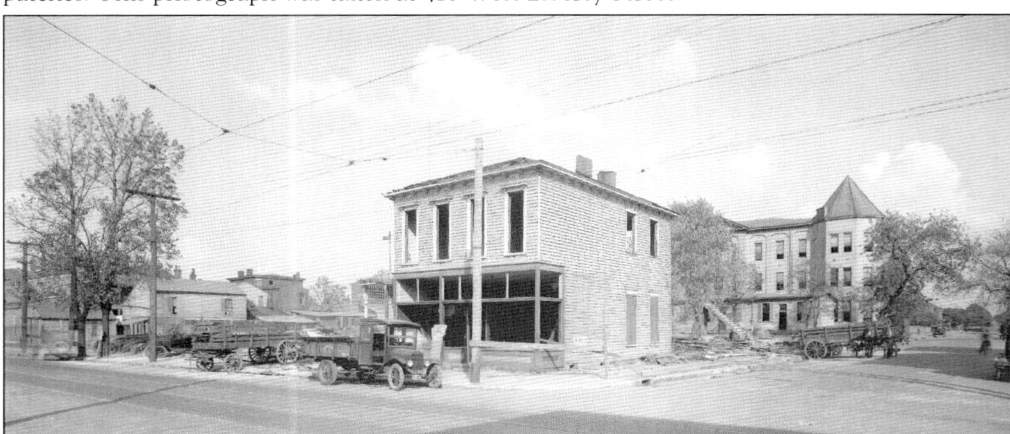

MADISON STREET DEPARTMENTAL COLORED SCHOOL RENOVATION PROGRESS, LOUISVILLE, KENTUCKY, OCTOBER 11, 1928. The school's location is documented as 1713 West Madison Street in Louisville. This photograph, commissioned by the board of education, was shot to keep track of the progress on the renovation of this building into a new high school for African American children. According to the 1928 *Caron's Louisville City Directory*, the property was called the Madison Street Departmental Colored School.

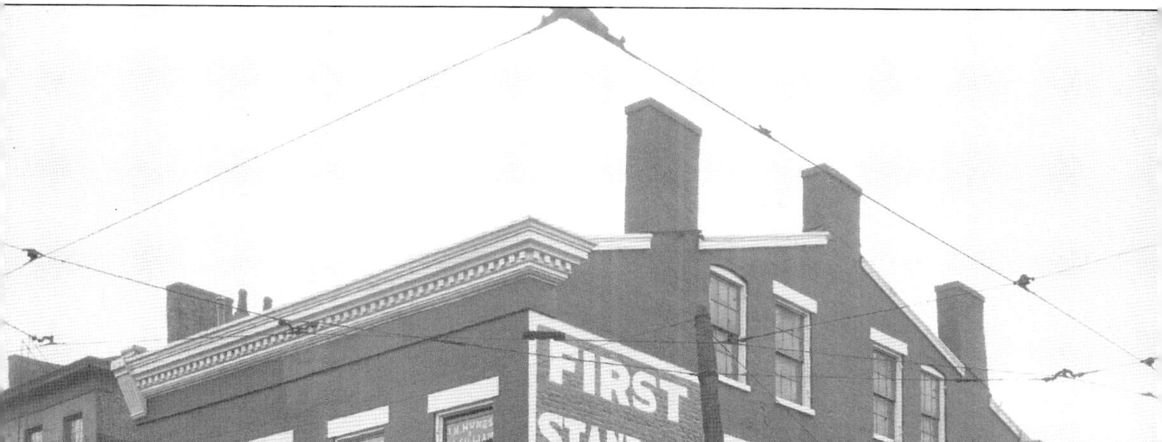

First Standard Bank, February 14, 1921. The First Standard Bank is located at 600 West Walnut Street (now Muhammad Ali Boulevard) in the Central Business District. It was the home of Louisville's first African American bank. The pediment over the door, mock Doric columns, and dentils bring a Greek Revival influence to the building, while white, globed lights frame the entry. Signs on the front window indicate the hours as "Open 9 a.m. – 2 p.m. Saturday Eve. 4 p.m. – 7 p.m." and "Bank Closed / Legal Holiday." Upper windows have advertisements for Humes & Gillian, Real Estate Agents. The building to the left with a fire escape down the front has a shoe-shining stand on its first floor. Around the corner is a poster for a show at the Majestic Theatre.

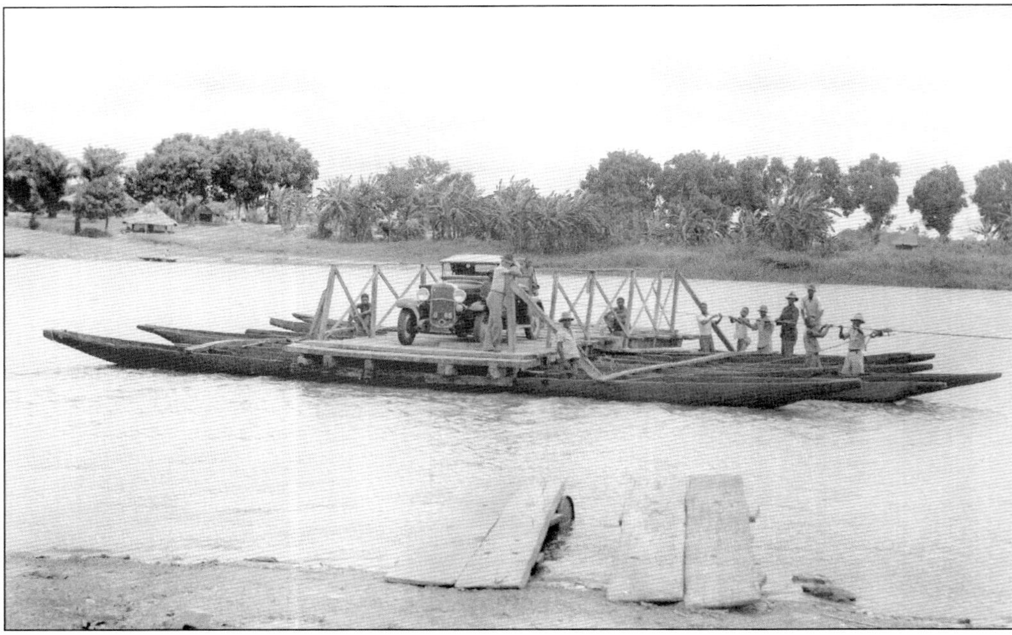

AFRICAN FERRY, APRIL 11, 1935. Made on a trip to the African Congo, this photograph shows a ferry carrying an automobile and several men—mostly African and one white—across a river. Howard Y. Bary submitted the information about this unique and informative image.

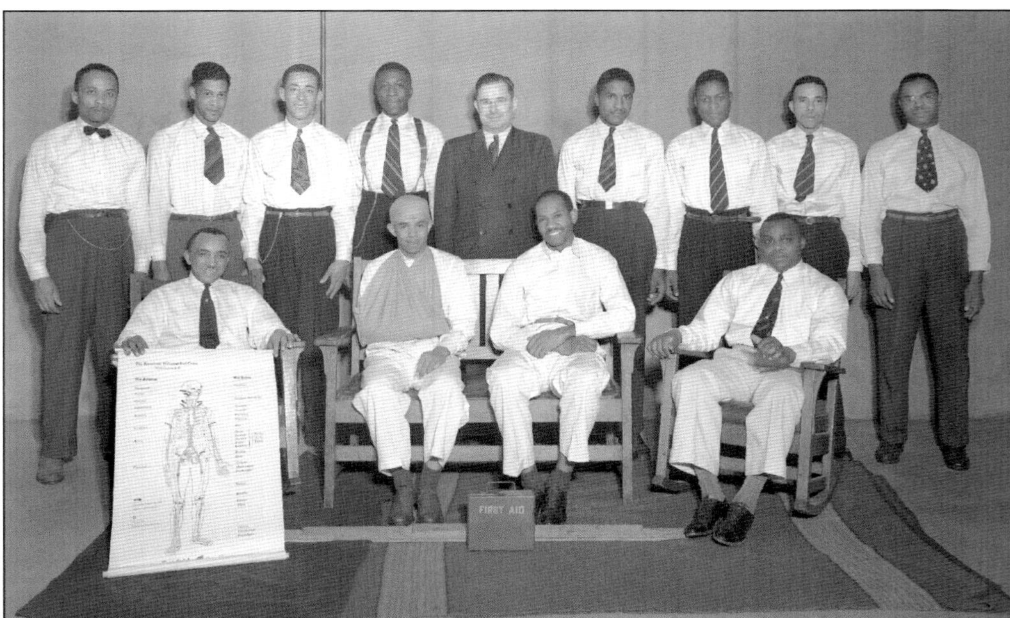

SOUTHERN BELL TELEPHONE CO., FEBRUARY 6, 1942. Shown here is a group of African American men in two rows, with a white man standing in the center of the back row. One is holding a diagram of the human skeletal system, another has his arm in a sling, and a first aid box is on the floor in front of them.

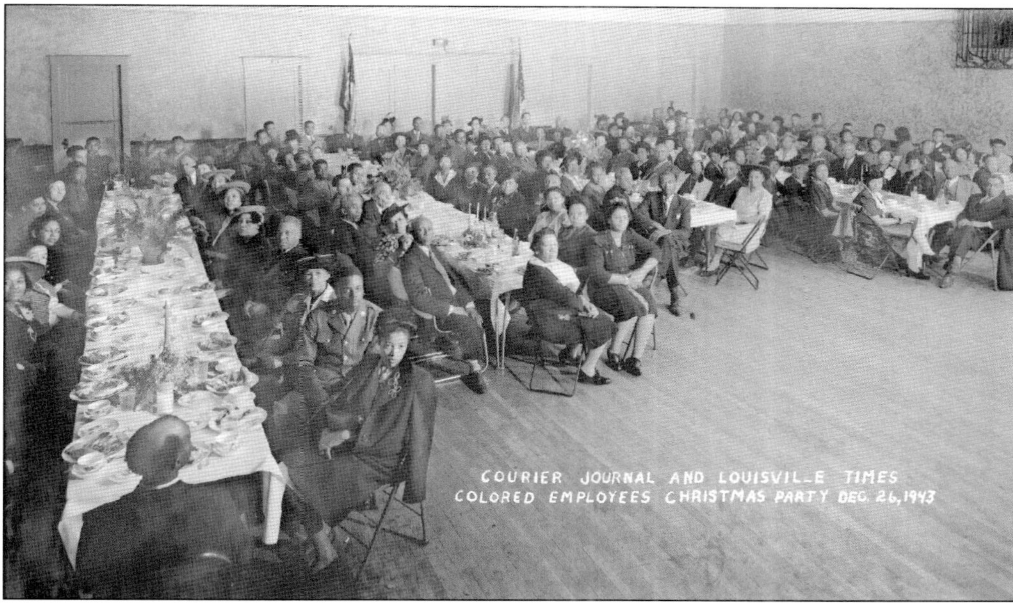

COURIER JOURNAL AND TIMES DINNER PARTY AT THE BROCK BUILDING, DECEMBER 26, 1943. African American men and women sit on either side of dining tables set up in rows during a dinner party at the Brock Building for employees of the *Courier-Journal* and *Louisville Times*. The Brock Building was located at 639 South Ninth Street, in the Central Business District.

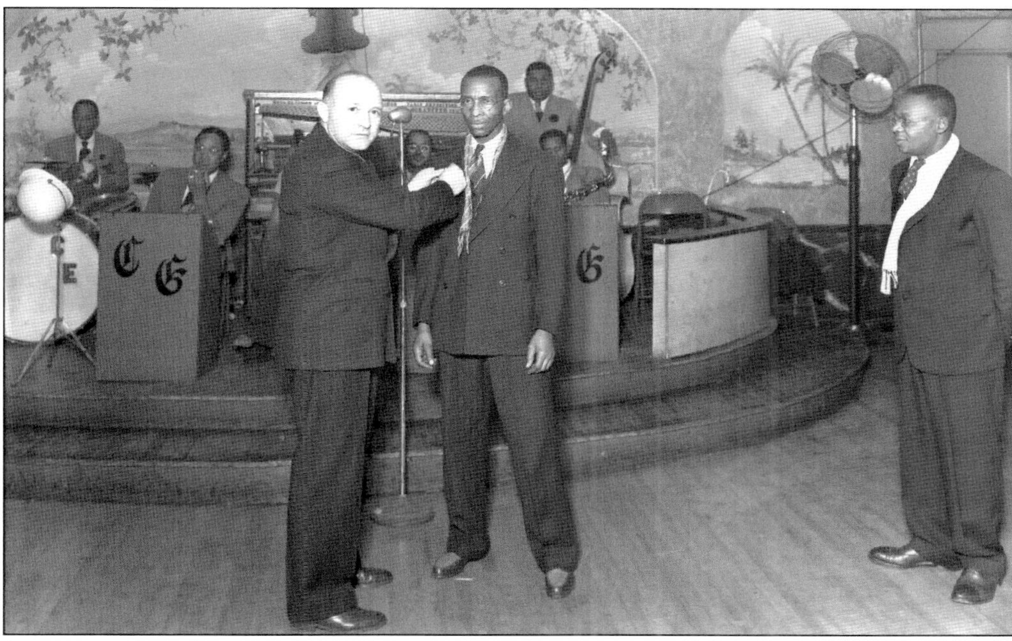

SOUTHERN BELL TELEPHONE CO. PIN AWARD RECOGNITIONS, DECEMBER 15, 1944. At this ceremony, pins are being awarded to African American men for their high work performance at the Southern Bell Telephone Company. All of the men are dressed in dark suits, and a band is playing in the rear. Five musicians are shown, including a string bass player, saxophonist, trumpeter, and a drummer.

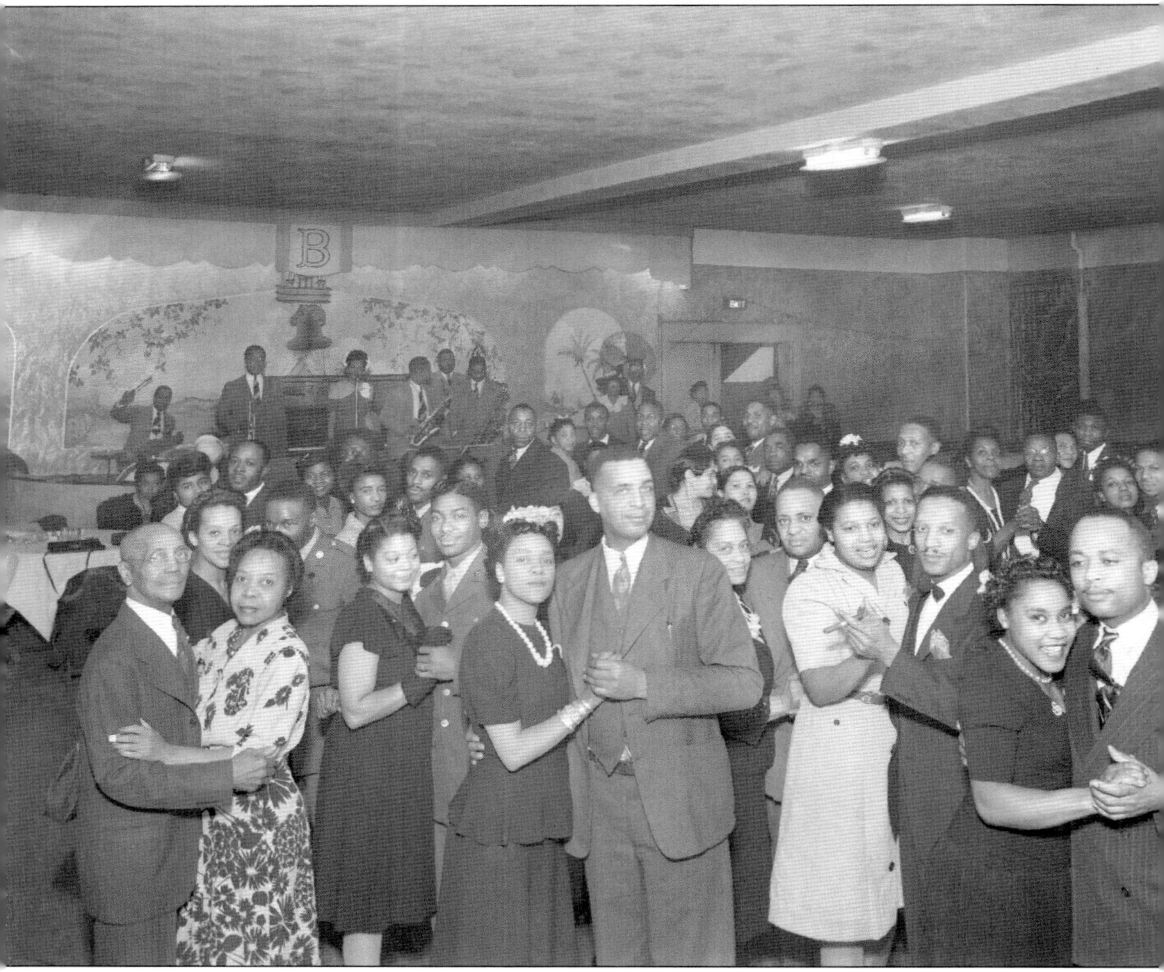

Southern Bell Telephone Co. Dance at Brock Café. December 15, 1944. This dance for Southern Bell employees was held at the Brock Café. A group of African American couples is on a dance floor. Most of the dancers have turned to face the camera and stand cheek to cheek. The men are wearing military dress uniforms or suits. The back wall behind the stage is decorated with a floral or ivy design, and a banner with a *B* hangs at the top. The five-member, all-male band and a female singer are on the stage in the rear. In the left of the image, a man sits playing the drums, next to him is a man holding a trumpet, then a female singer, a man holding an "E-flat" saxophone, a man with a tenor saxophone, and the bass player, in back.

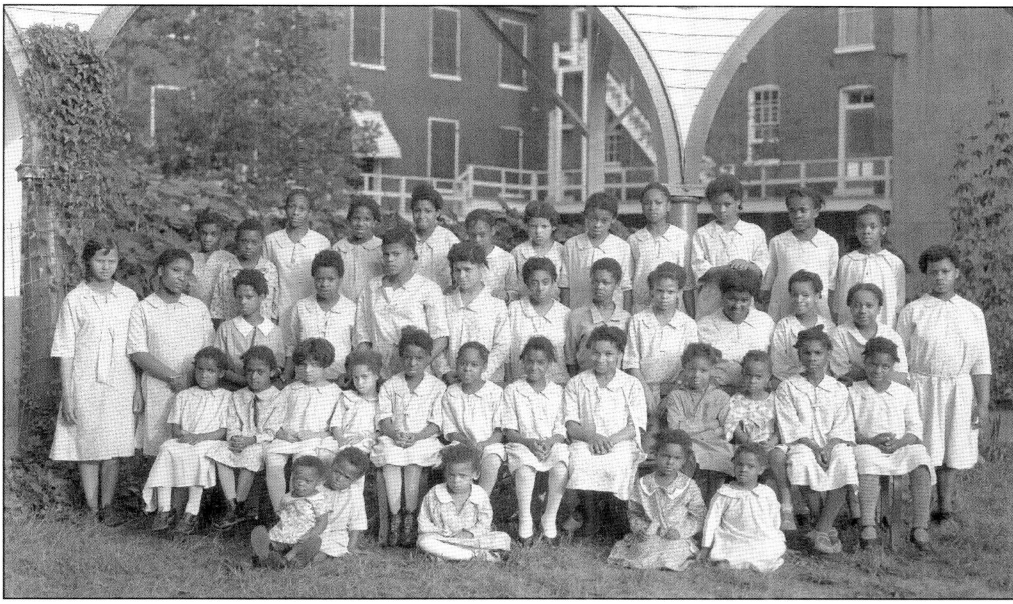

CONVENT HOME FOR COLORED CHILDREN, JULY 1, 1931. This convent stood at 518 South Eighth Street on the corner of Walnut (now Muhammad Ali Boulevard) and Eighth Streets. This photograph shows a group of girls posed under an archway. The children mostly wear plain white dresses, although some have patterns.

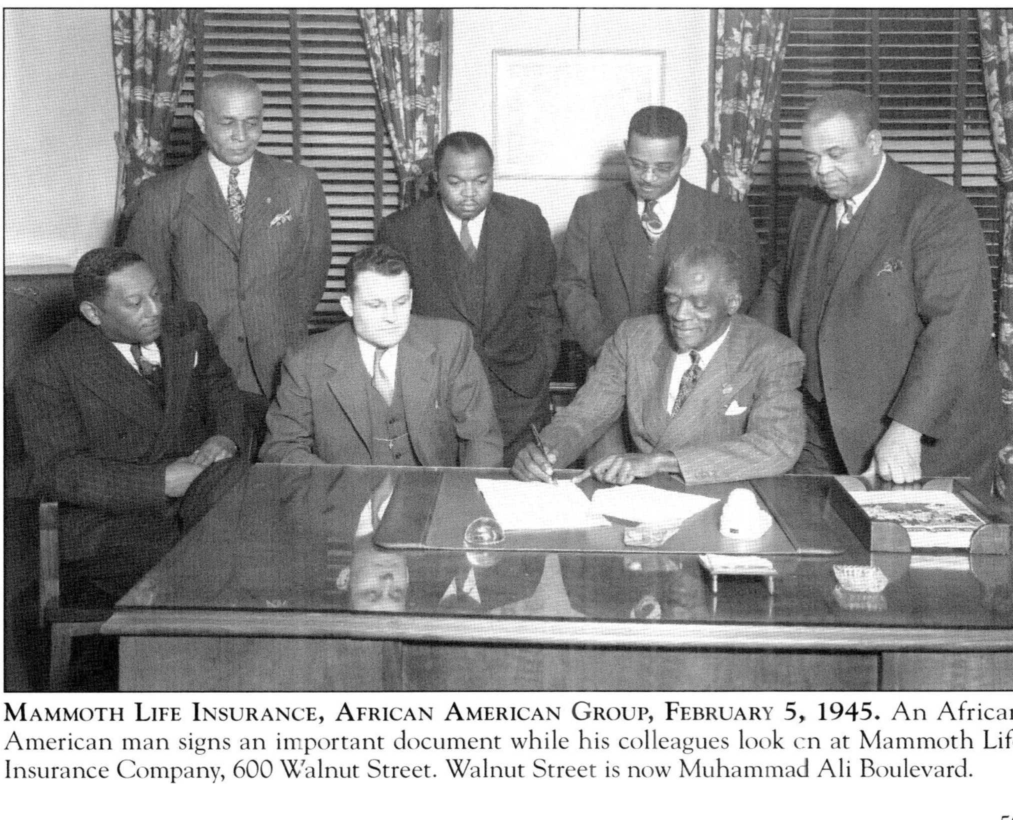

MAMMOTH LIFE INSURANCE, AFRICAN AMERICAN GROUP, FEBRUARY 5, 1945. An African American man signs an important document while his colleagues look on at Mammoth Life Insurance Company, 600 Walnut Street. Walnut Street is now Muhammad Ali Boulevard.

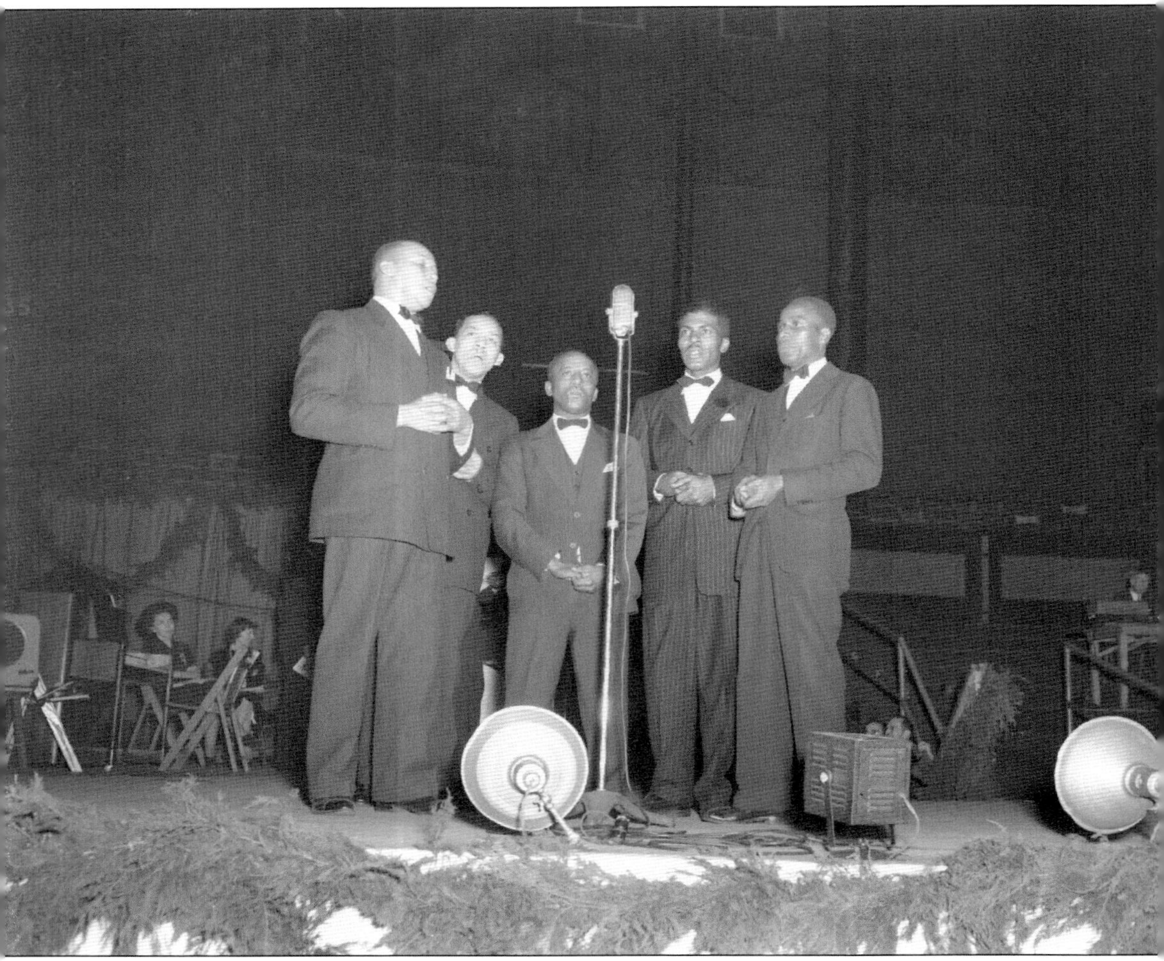

The Mengel Co. Christmas Party at Jefferson County Armory, December 18, 1942. Five African American men are singing around a microphone on a stage at the Jefferson County Armory during a Christmas party. In the background behind the stage, two women and two men are seen viewing the singing group. At the far right, a man sits at a soundboard table. On stage, a small speaker and sound system are visible. The Royal Photo Company documented the event. The Mengel Box Company was founded in 1877 and was originally named Mengel Company. Mengel was one of the leading regional producers of wood products.

Four

Berry-Griffy Towns, Petersburg, Newburg

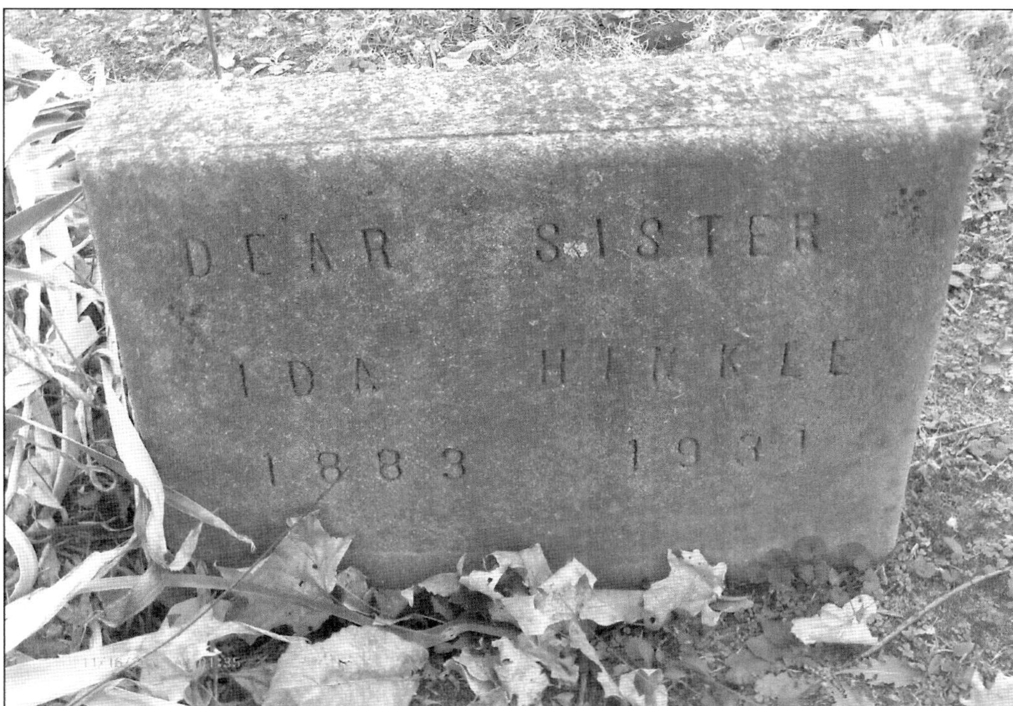

Berrytown Historic Tombstone for "Dear Sister Ida Hinkle 1883–1931." This tombstone is located in the Berrytown Cemetery. Hinkle was a prominent woman in her time, earning the right to rest in one of the oldest African American cemeteries in the country. (Photograph courtesy of the author.)

The Berry Family Tombstone—Mildred (1871–1906), William (1869–1906), and Alfred (1840–1920). Alfred Berry and his family are listed in the 1880 census, which notes that Alfred is 39 years old and Lizzie, his wife, is 29 years old. At the time, they had seven children: Mattie, age 12; William, 11; Mildred, nine; Isaiah, seven; Lewis, six; Henrietta, four; and James, one. The Berry family lived in Anchorage, Kentucky, but their family tombstone can be found at the rear of the Berrytown Cemetery. (Photograph courtesy of the author.)

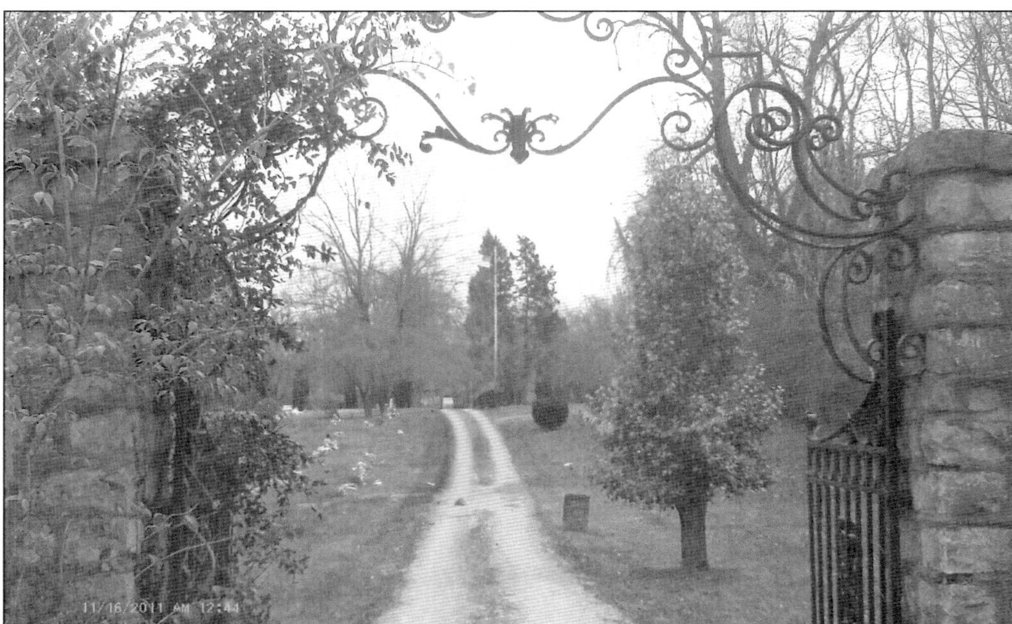

Berrytown Cemetery Gates. This photograph shows the main gate to the Berrytown Cemetery. The opened gate allows access to a dirt road leading into the old cemetery. (Photograph courtesy of the author.)

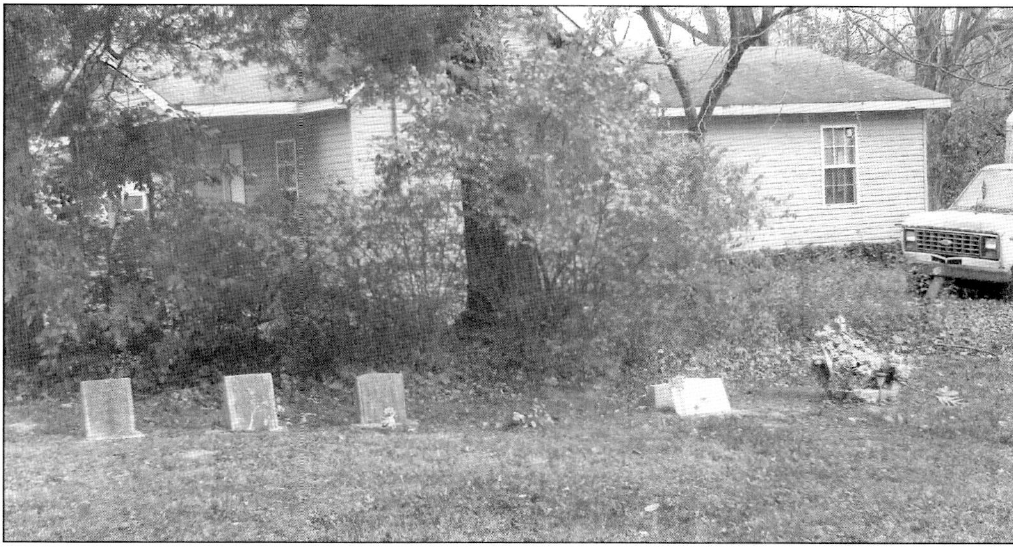

Berrytown Cemetery. Pictured here is Berrytown Cemetery at Old Henry and Berrytown Roads. It is centered in the midst of everyday activities and routines. A vibrant connection to a past that continues into the present is evident in an environment that embraces the cemetery as part of a historic landscape. The well-kept graves are decorated with floral artifacts and small American flags. Despite being associated with the death of loved ones, the cemetery is also a celebration of a unified community that embraces its roots. (Photograph courtesy of the author.)

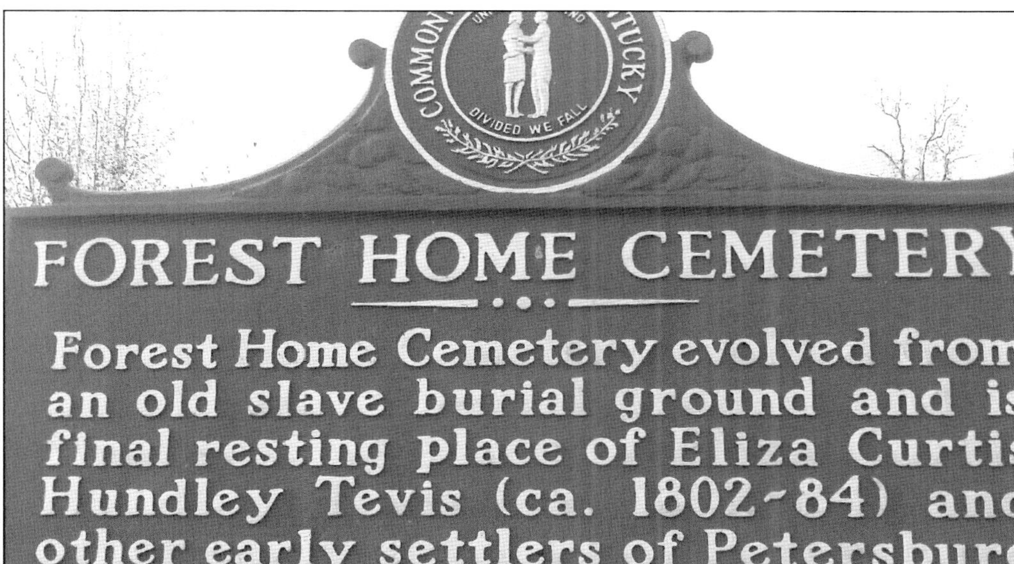

Forest Home Cemetery, Petersburg Neighborhood. This cemetery is one of the oldest dedicated slave burial grounds in Kentucky, dating back to 1851. Forest Home Cemetery evolved from an old slave burial ground and is the final resting place of Eliza Curtis Hundley Tevis (c. 1802–1884) and other early settlers of the Petersburg community. Tevis was born a slave but gained freedom in 1833. She and her husband, Henry, purchased 40 acres in 1851 in Wet Woods. (Photograph courtesy of the author.)

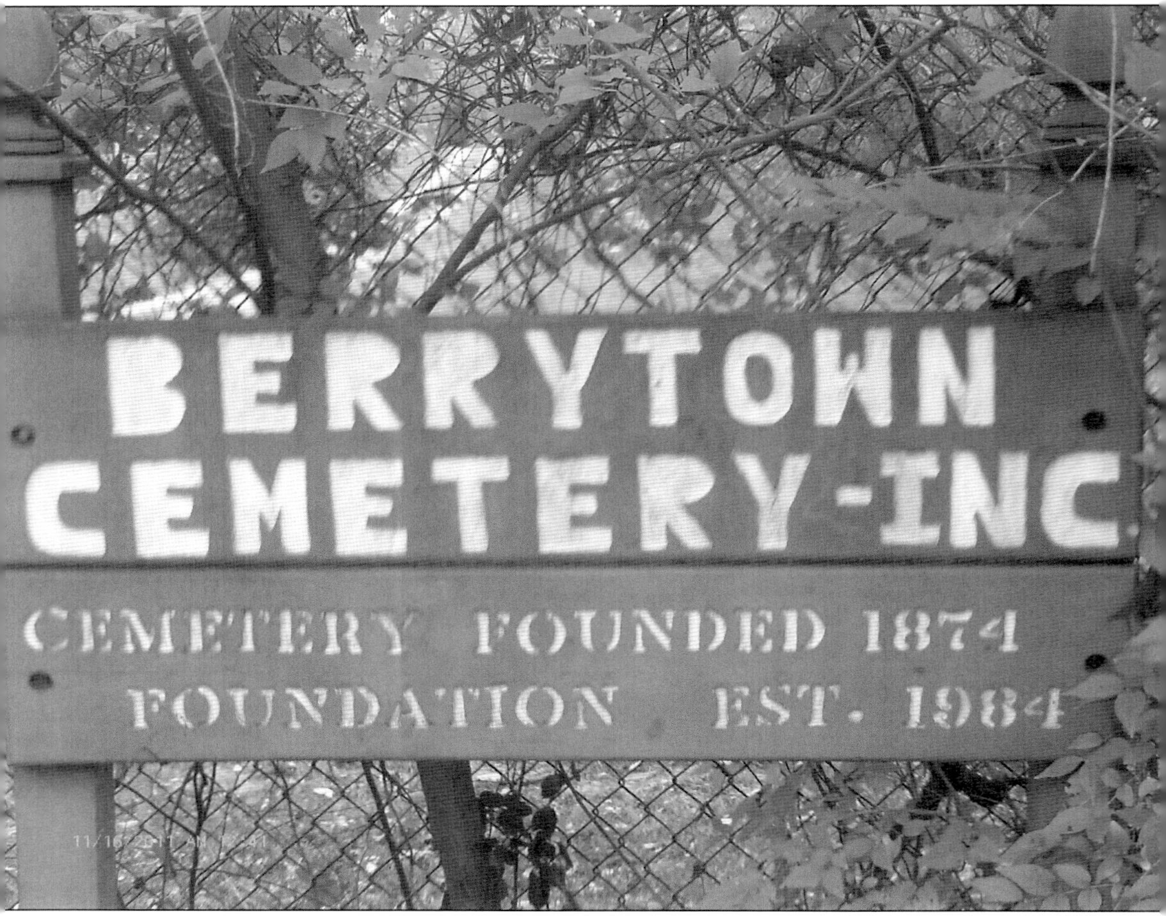

Berrytown Historic Cemetery Incorporated, Founded in 1874. Berrytown is a Louisville neighborhood named after Alfred Berry, a freedman. The historic Berry home built by Alfred also was a vital part of Berrytown's history. Berry purchased this five-acre plot in 1874. The cemetery's current caretaker is Bradley Swearingen, and he is assisted by other concerned community citizens. Griffytown is a nearby neighborhood and is located along Old Harrods Creek Road. In 1879, Dan Griffy, also a freed slave, purchased the land he had been living on in the area. Griffytown was named after this prominent man who, against the odds, bought the property he once lived on as a slave. Citizens of both communities survived by supplying their services as cooks, butlers, maids, drivers, and gardeners to affluent Anchorage families. People in both Berrytown and Griffytown have pride in their rich historic heritage.

PETERSBURG ESTATES "WHERE PRIDE RESIDES" BANNER. These banners can be seen today along Petersburg and Indian Trail Roads. They commemorate a sense of pride and reverence for the community and its history. (Photograph courtesy of the author.)

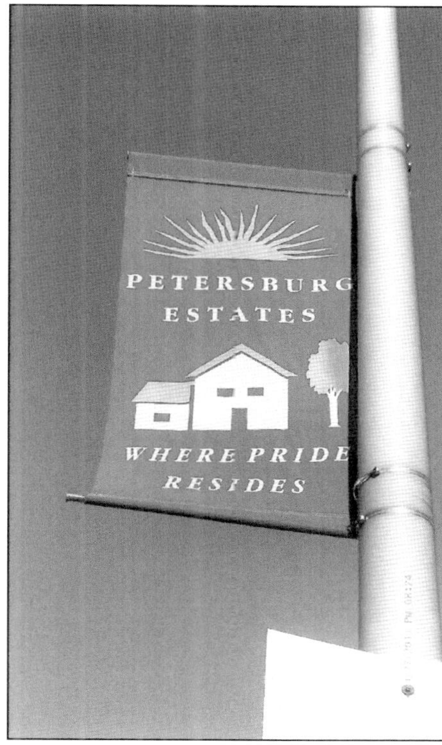

NEWBURG HEALTH CENTER. Newburg Health Center's primary focus is servicing the Newburg and Petersburg residents, but it also receives clients from other neighborhoods. In the 2000 census, Newburg's population was 20,636. The area was annexed by the City of Louisville due to a merger between the city and Jefferson County. Newburg is now a neighborhood within the Louisville city limits. It was settled in the 1820s by four German families and was a small village called Newburgh. The *H* was dropped and the modern spelling emerged by the end of the 19th century. Newburg has historically had a black population, once centered around the nearby Petersburg area. After the Civil War, freed blacks bought land in the area and started farms. (Photograph courtesy of the author.)

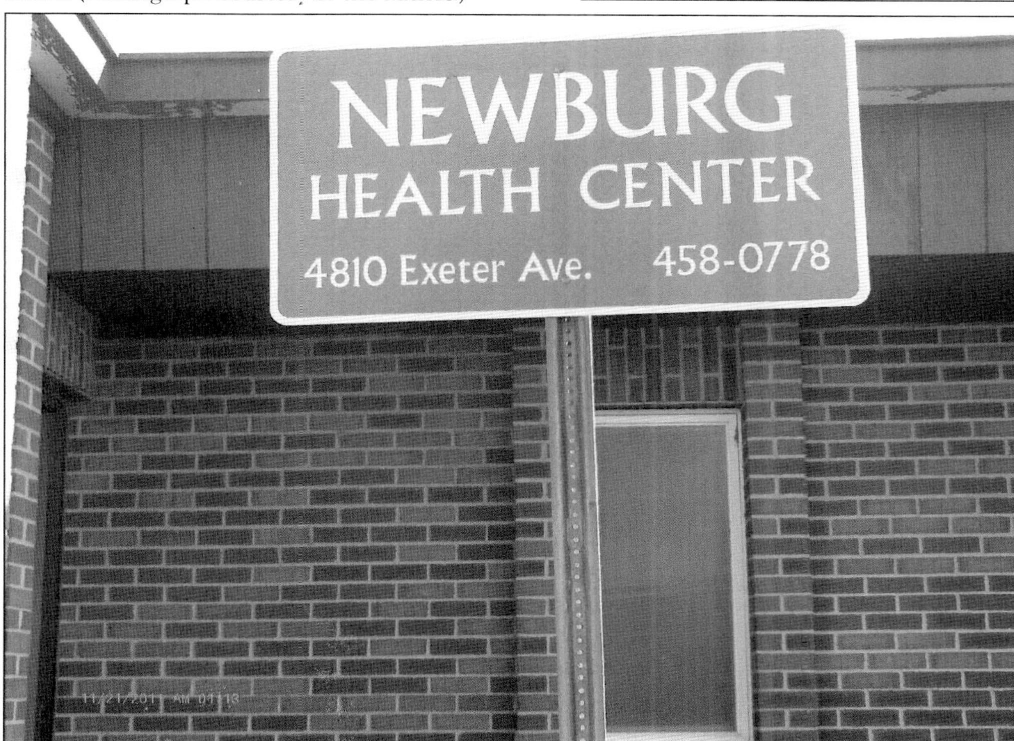

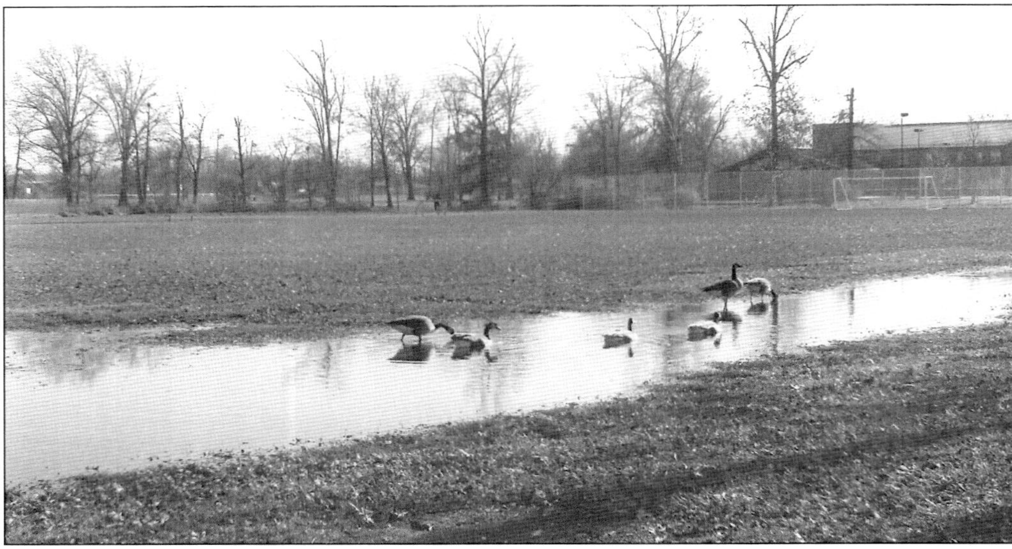

Louisville's Newburg Free Public Library Shallow Pond with Canada Geese. The pond can be found at Exeter Avenue and Indian Trail Road in the Newburg neighborhood. The pond is in a less dense lawn area and provides a very scenic atmosphere. It can be seen when one is entering the newly constructed Louisville Free Public Library Newburg Branch. (Photograph courtesy of the author.)

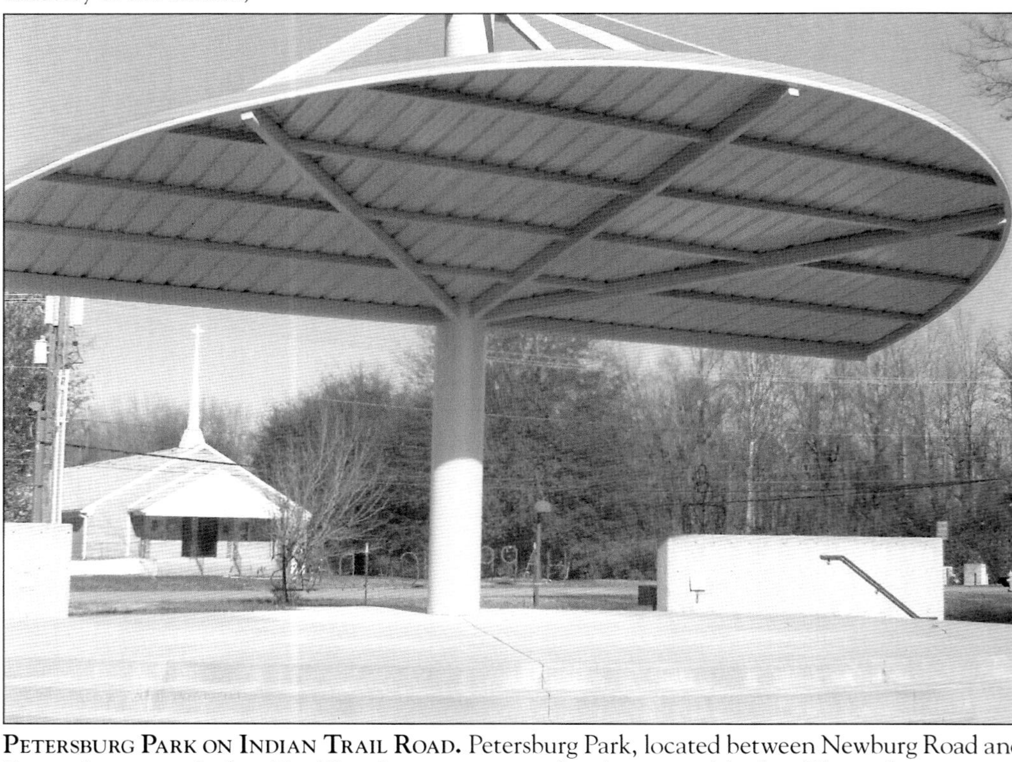

Petersburg Park on Indian Trail Road. Petersburg Park, located between Newburg Road and Exeter Avenue on Indian Trail Road, is a very active family-oriented facility. The park is spacious, with various designated-activity areas. (Photograph courtesy of the author.)

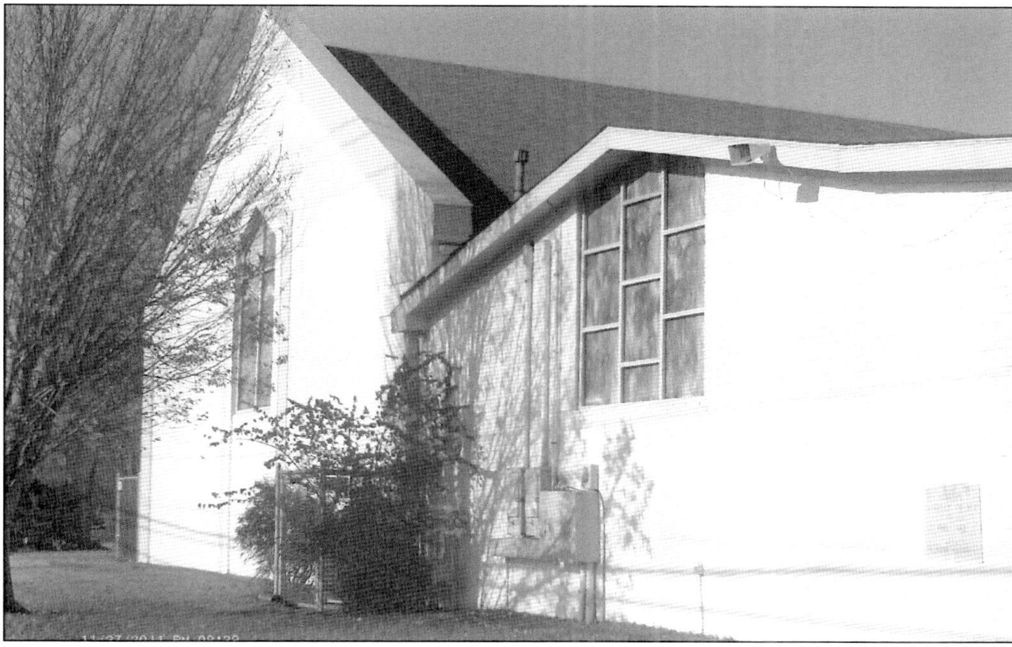

Newburg Apostolic Church. This was the first church in the Newburg area. Newburg Apostolic Church was established by evangelist pastor Mattie Holland in March 1948. Since Pastor Holland's death, her son, elder Waverly Holland, continues to carry the torch of pastorship. (Photograph courtesy of the author.)

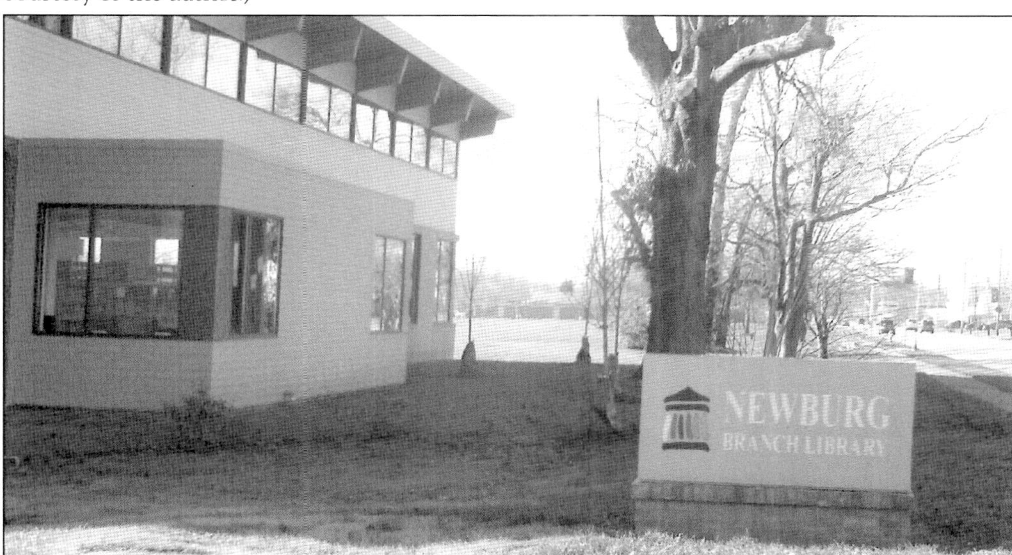

Newburg Branch Free Public Library. Newburg Branch of the Louisville Free Public Library was the first library built in Newburg. Located at 4800 Exeter Avenue, it is education-driven for youth. The focus is on study and tutoring space, computer access, and books to assist students' educational needs. The library, a new addition to the area, accommodates children from all over the Newburg and Petersburg areas, as well as nearby neighborhoods, daily. (Photograph courtesy of the author.)

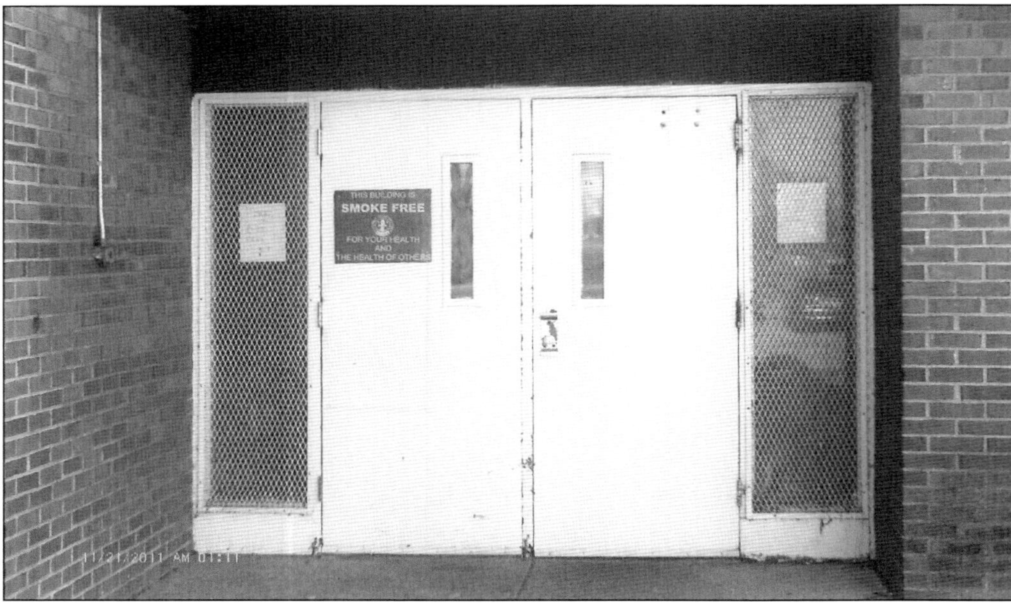

Newburg Community Center. The NCC is equipped with spacious areas for art, music, and cultural activities. It is located at 4810 Exeter Avenue and offers a variety of programs such as tap dancing, senior programming, a teen girls' club, aerobics, noon basketball (18 years and older), a boys' basketball league, and a girls' basketball league. A performing arts hall is also available at the center. (Photograph courtesy of the author.)

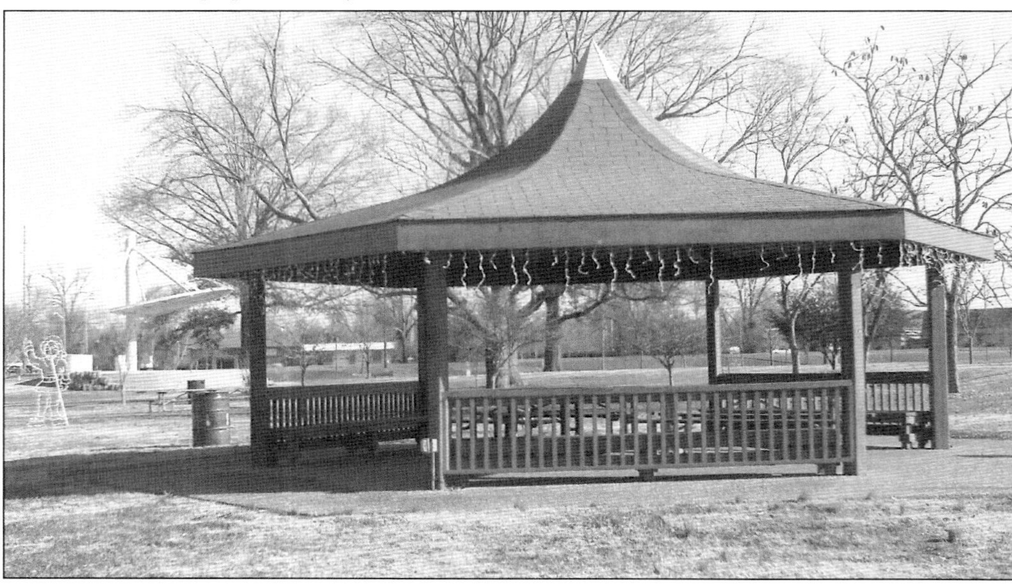

Petersburg Park Pavilion. Petersburg Park Pavilion's walking trail area is very accessible, inviting, and convenient. Families, including residents from areas other than Petersburg-Newburg, are often seen enjoying its spacious campus. Every year, the park holds "Newburg Day," bringing Ferris wheels and many other recreational features, food, games, and entertainment to the park. Crowds of families come to enjoy this vibrant community fellowship. (Photograph courtesy of the author.)

Five

South Louisville and Black Horsemen in the Kentucky Derby

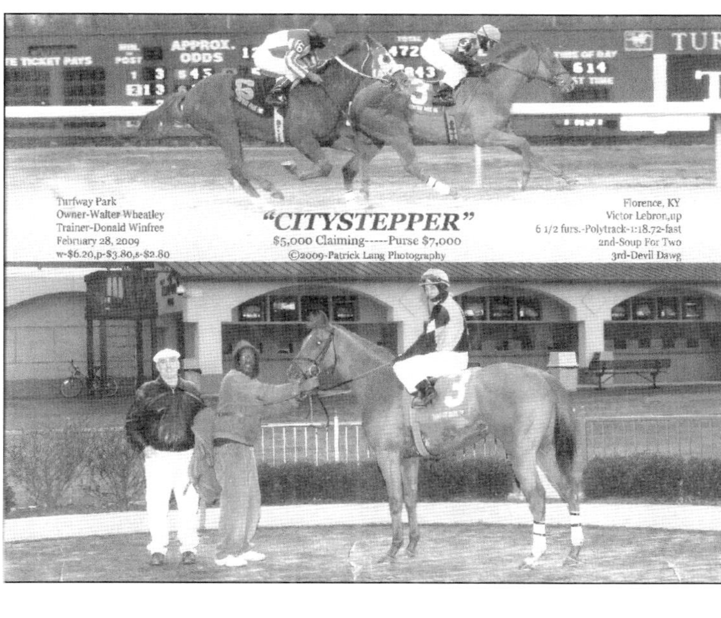

Ray "Dittle" Smith, Black Horseman-Groomer, Churchill Downs. Called "Dittle" at the tracks, Ray is Louisville born and has been a horseman over 35 years. He was the groomer for the Turfway Park winner City Stepper in February 28, 2009. Ray continues the great legacy of black horsemen, including the early black jockeys, such as Oliver Lewis, rider of the first Kentucky Derby winner, Aristides.

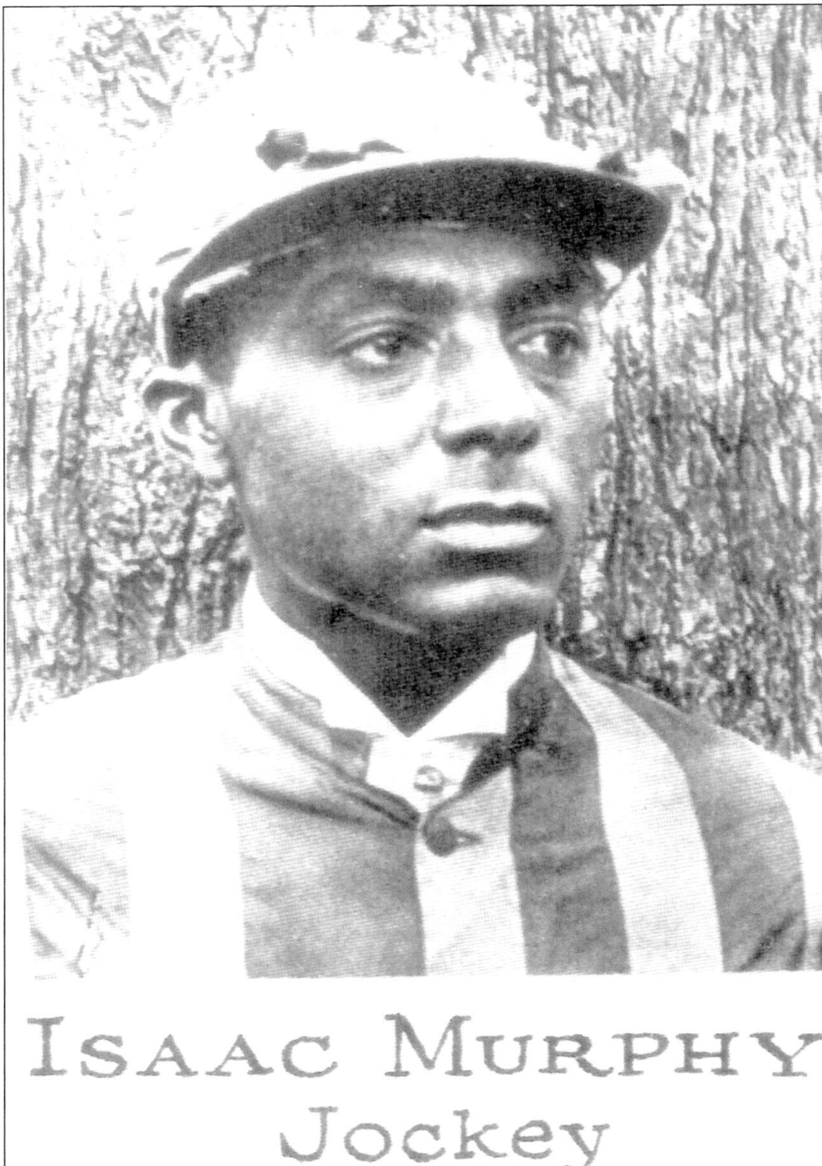

ISAAC MURPHY, AFRICAN AMERICAN HALL OF FAME JOCKEY (APRIL 16, 1861–FEBRUARY 12, 1896.) Isaac Murphy is considered one of the greatest race riders in American history. He was the first jockey to win the Derby on three occasions and consecutive runnings—Buchanan, 1884; Riley, 1890; and Kingman, 1891. He remains the only jockey to win the Kentucky Derby, the Kentucky Oaks, and the Clark Handicap all in the same year, in 1884. His record has not been approached by any other jockey since. He was the first jockey to be inducted into the Jockey Hall of Fame at the National Museum of Racing. Ike, or the "Colored Archer" as he was dubbed in reference to the prominent English jockey of the time, Fred Archer, won 44 percent of all races he rode. Isaac Burns (Murphy) was born in 1861 on David Tanner's Pleasant Green Hill Farm in Fayette County, Kentucky. His father enlisted in the Union army during the Civil War and died as a prisoner of war at Camp Nelson along the Kentucky River.

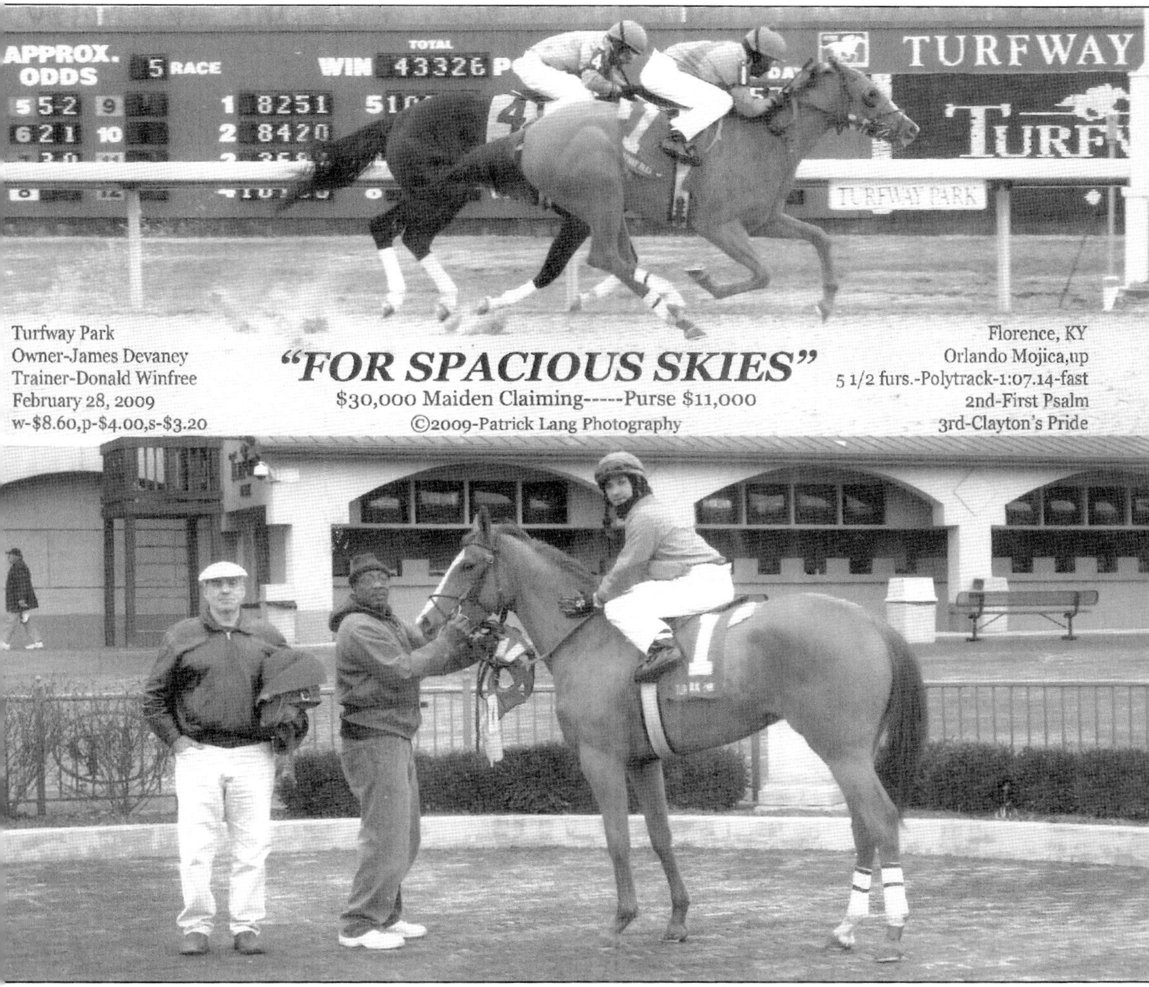

Ray "Dittle" Smith, Churchill Downs. Horseman groomer stands with For Spacious Skies at Turfway Park on February 28, 2009. Dittle continues the legacy of black horsemen following after the great pioneers who paved the way for present and future horsemen and horsewomen. Tribute also goes to the Midwest Black Horsemen Association, Ebony Horsewomen Inc., Michigan Black Horsemen Association, and the Cincinnati Black Cowboys. Willie Simms was the winner of the Derby twice and the other Triple Crown races at least once; Jimmy Winkfield was the 1901 and 1902 Derby winner; Alonzo Clayton won the Kentucky Derby at only 15 years of age; James Perkins also won the Derby at only 15 years of age; and Ed Brown was the trainer for the 1877 Kentucky Derby winner, Baden-Baden.

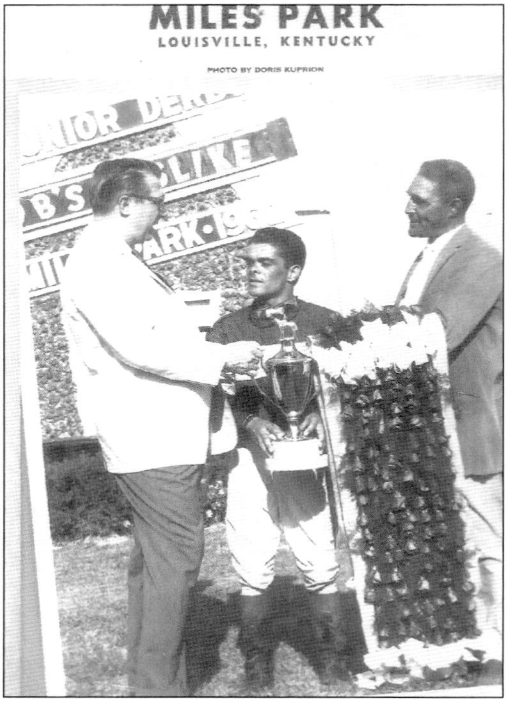

MILES PARK TRACK, LOUISVILLE, KENTUCKY. On July 14, 1962, Carl Sitgraves (born January 27, 1913; died April 20, 2000) receives the winner prize as he stands next to jockey Charles Corolla after the 1:13:1 Junior Derby race. He was one of Louisville's most successful African American thoroughbred trainers, winning the Junior Derby, Miles Park's top stakes event, with a two-year-old colt named Bob's Dislike in 1962.

ENGLISH NEWS AT MILES PARK. Identified here are owner W.C. Hines (far left), trainer Carl H. Sitgraves (fourth from left), and jockey David Niblick, after six and a half furlongs with a time of 1:19 on March 27, 1971. Sitgraves grew up in the "Hill," north of Churchill Downs, near Heywood Avenue and Sixth Street. African American horsemen (walkers, groomers, jockeys, trainers, and owners) lived and worked in this neighborhood. It was the place where deep discussions of racing ethics, track racing, and potential winners occurred.

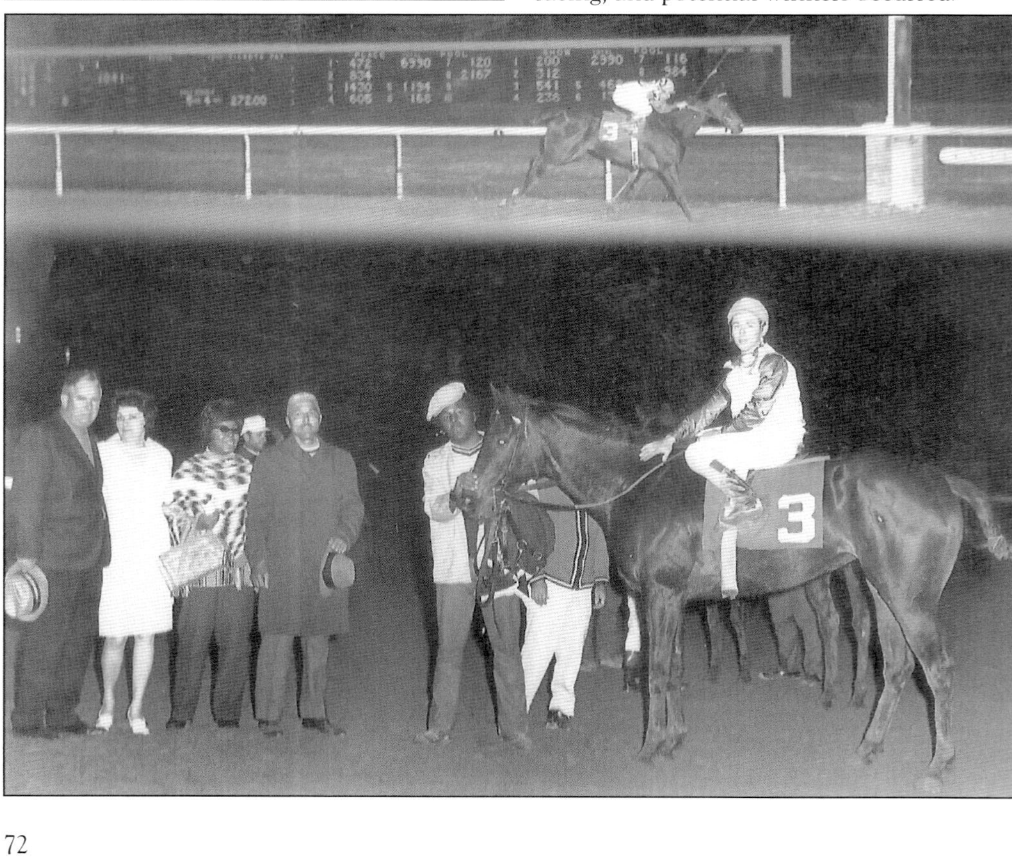

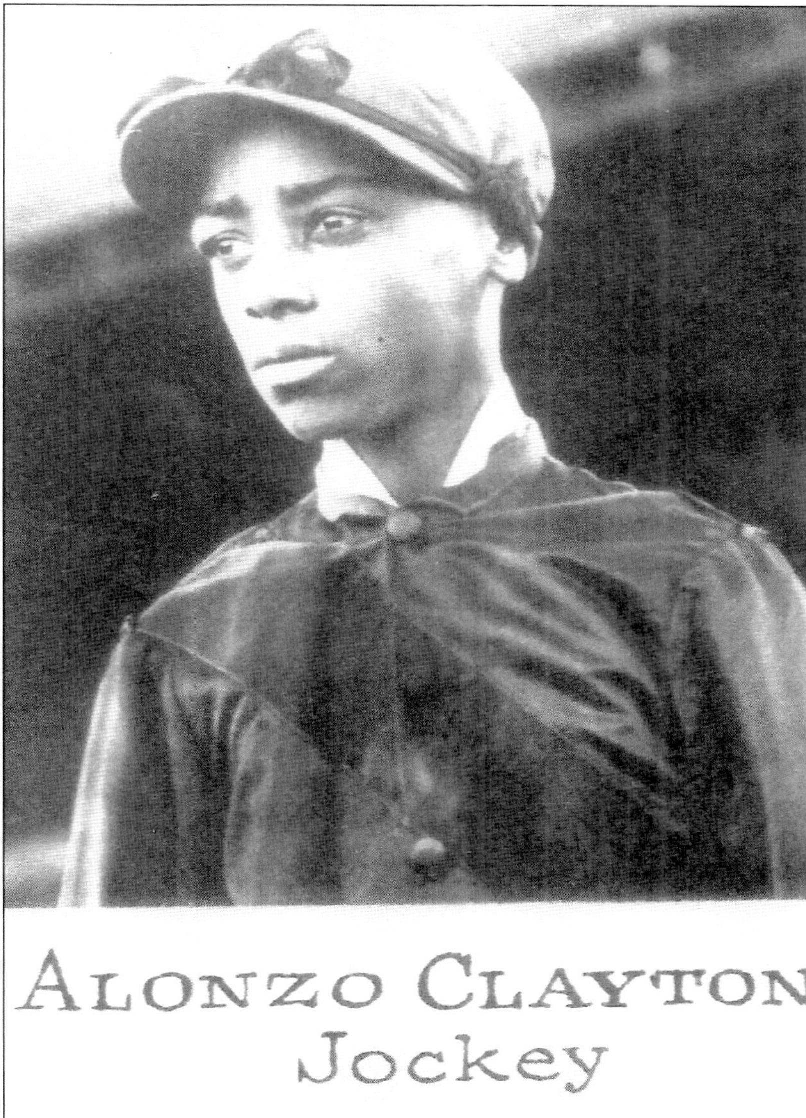

ALONZO "LONNIE" CLAYTON. In 1892, Clayton achieved an impressive victory riding Azra in a three-horse field and became, at age 15, the youngest jockey to win the Kentucky Derby up to that time. Born in Kansas City, Missouri, in 1876, Clayton succeeded his brother in the jockey profession. His career began as an exercise rider for E.J. "Lucky" Baldwin during the summer of 1888 in Chicago, Illinois. Clayton continued his new profession working for D.A. Honig in Clifton, New Jersey. In 1890, Clayton rode Redstone in his first race at the Clifton track and later won his first victory. His Derby career included four mounts—with one victory, two second places, and one third place. Clayton again rode Azra to victories in the Champagne Stakes, Travers and Clark Handicap. Clayton participated in the Kentucky Oaks, riding Selika in 1894 and Voladora in 1895. He also participated at Churchill Downs in 1893 and obtained the jockey crown during a fall meet. Clayton is one of only three African American jockeys to finish third in the Preakness, which he did in 1896.

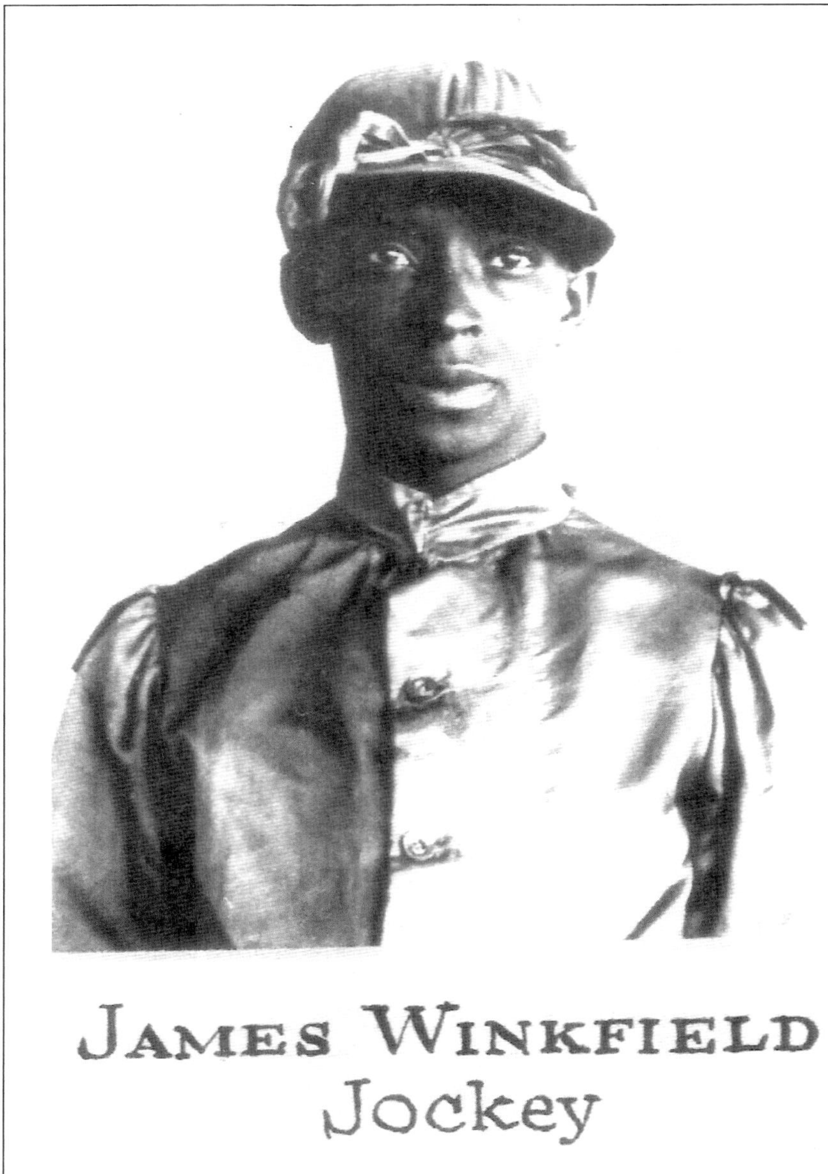

JAMES WINKFIELD. A 1901 and 1902 Kentucky Derby winner, James "Jimmy" Winkfield was the first jockey inducted into the Hall of Fame at the National Museum of Racing. African American Oliver Lewis had ridden Aristides to victory in the inaugural Run for the Roses, on May 17, 1875. His two-length victory time of 2:37 3/4, established a then American record for the 1.5 miles (the distance was changed to 1.25 miles in 1896). In 2000, Marlon St. Julien became the first African American jockey to ride in the Kentucky Derby since Henry King in 1921. St. Julien rode Curule to a seventh-place finish.

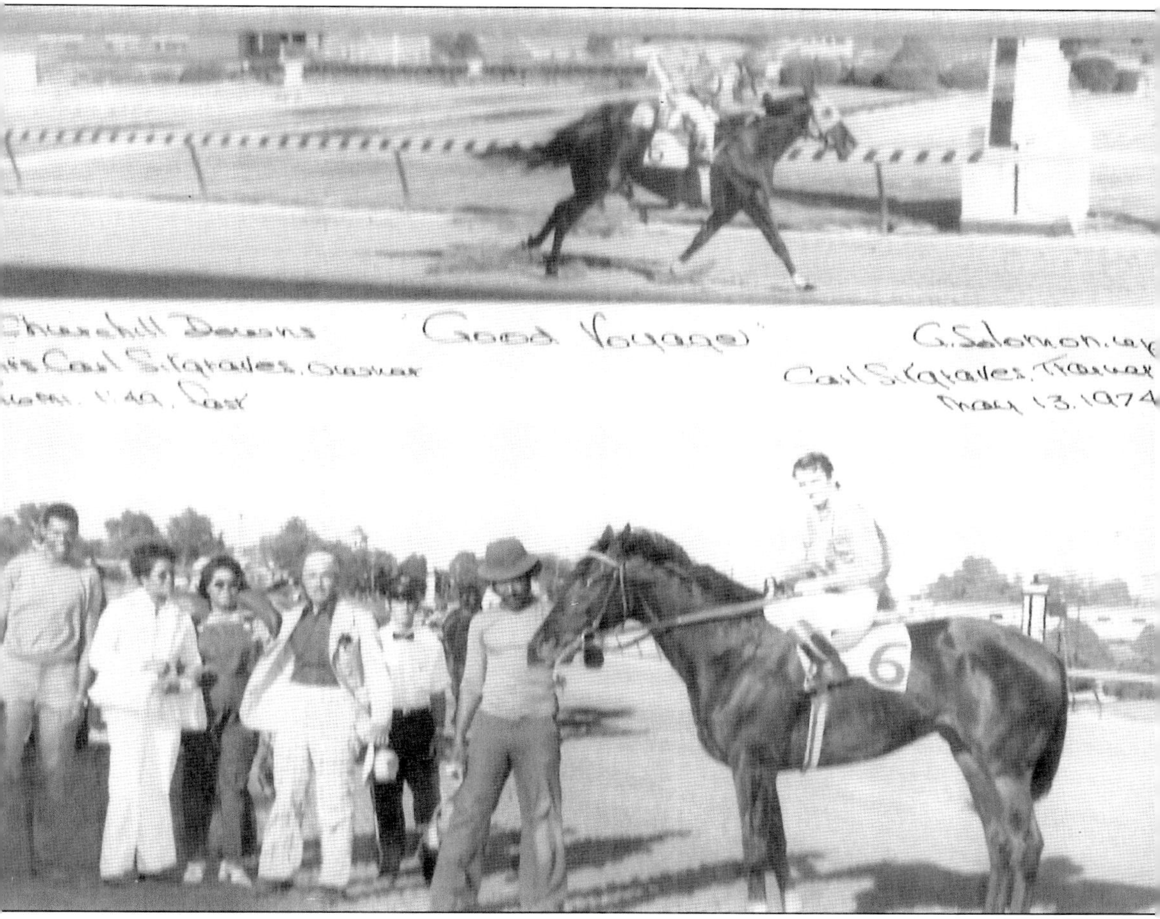

Good Voyage, Churchill Downs. Gene Solomon, jockey of Good Voyage, is pictured here with owner Essie Sitgraves (third from left) and trainer Carl Sitgraves (fourth from left). The horse-and-jockey team recorded a time of 1:49 over a one-and-one-sixteenth-mile course on May 13, 1974. Carl started off walking horses as a teenager and trained and owned them until 1979, at a time when minority trainers were rare. Essie helped her husband train and walk horses and muck stalls. She also made sure he looked good, setting out the outfit she wanted him to wear on race days. Essie was also an owner of several horses her husband trained.

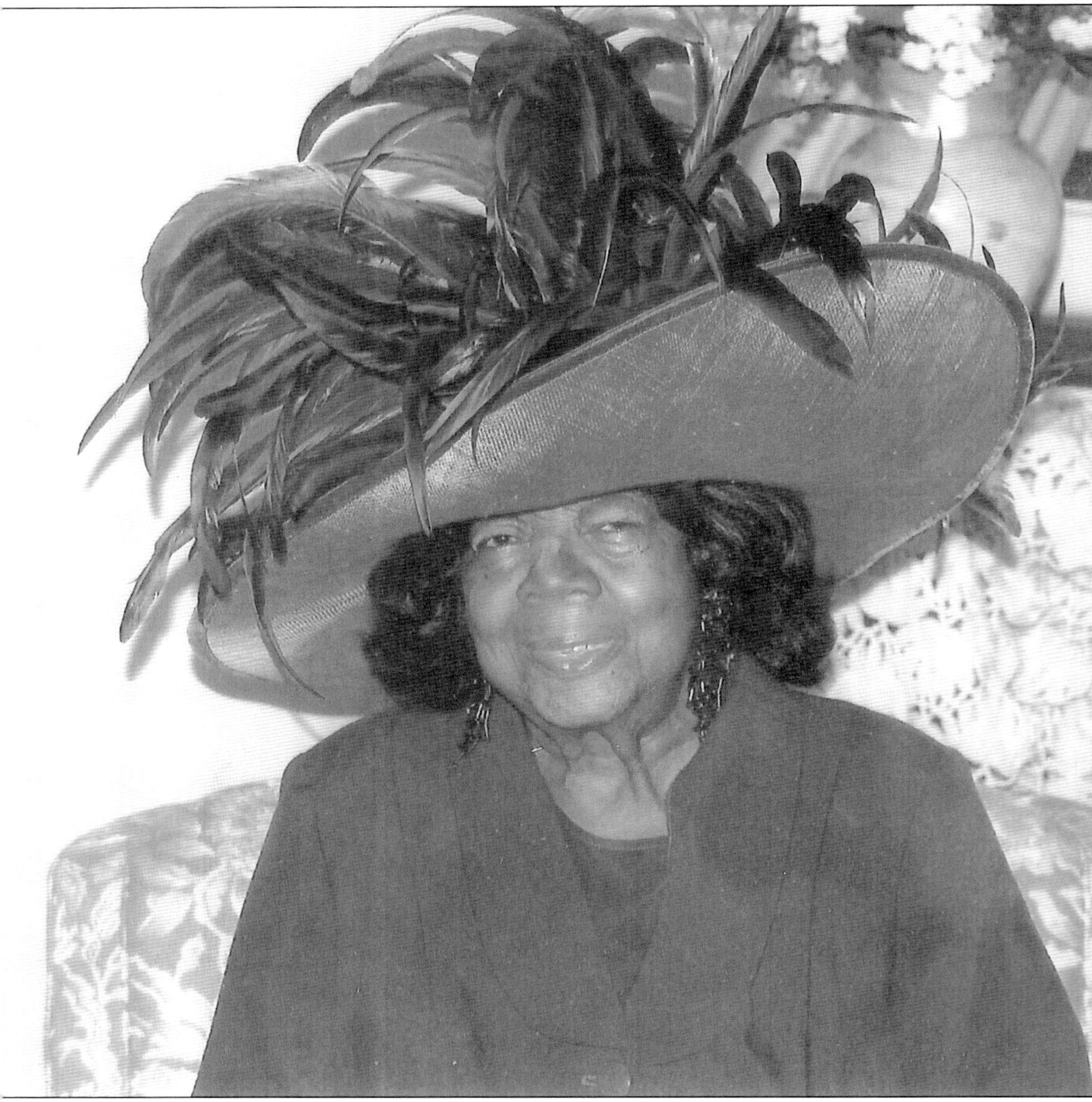

Essie Sitgraves, Dressed for the Kentucky Oaks, 2009. A fashionable headdress, with an elegant fuchsia brim and trimmed in rich purple feathers and border, Essie's headdress was a piece of art. "I love wearing hats. I have many styles to choose from. Hats are my thing," she remarked, adding "I love my hats." Essie continued by explaining a story related to the horse named Bob's Dislike. Several trainers told Carl Sitgraves that Bob's Dislike was not going to bring any wins. Carl, knowing the potential of the horse, disagreed. After Bob's Dislike won the race on July 14, 1962, Carl bought a mare and named it Did Do It. That horse won also on May 5, 1964, at Churchill Downs.

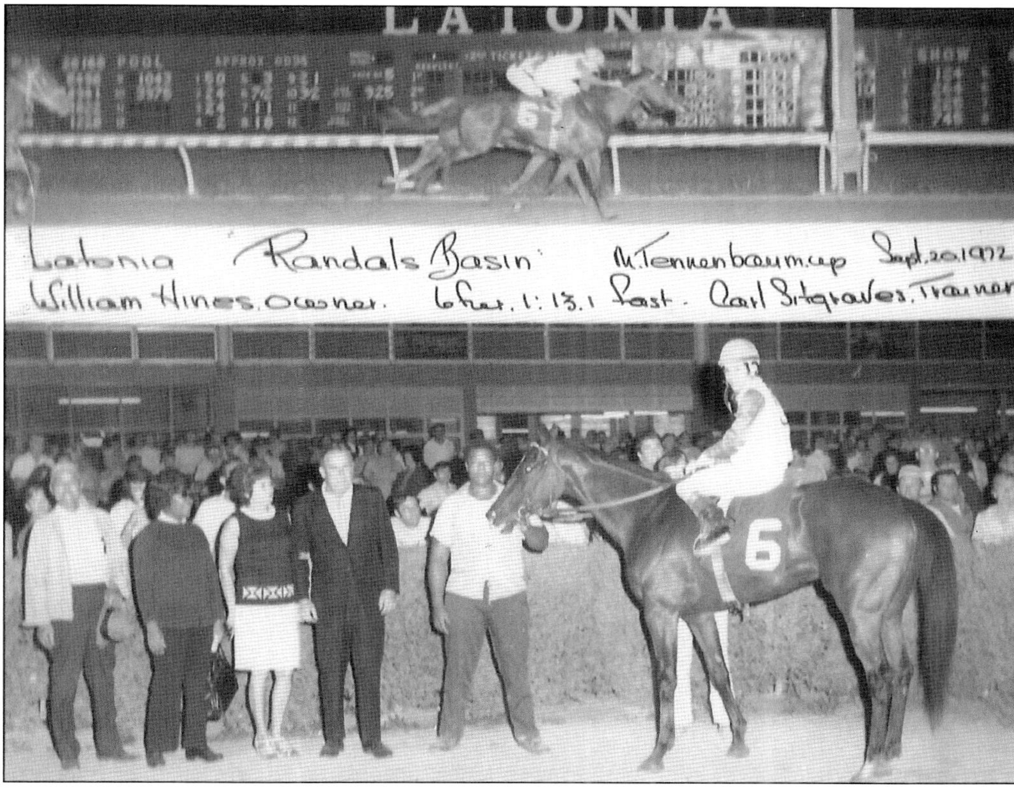

RANDALS BASIN WINS FIRST PLACE, FLORENCE, KENTUCKY. N. Tennenbaum rode Randals Basin, owned by William Hines, to victory with trainer Carl Sitgraves at Latonia Track. The horse-and-jockey team completed the six-furlong race in 1:13.

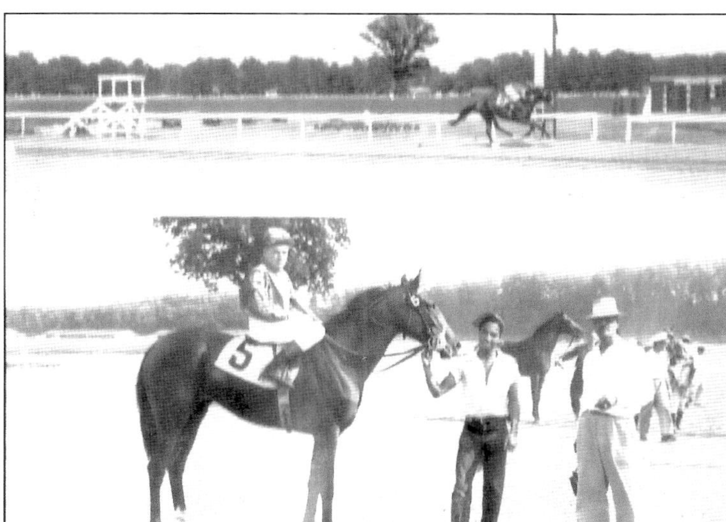

DADDY'S PUNKIN', ELLIS PARK, HENDERSON, KENTUCKY. Pictured here is jockey S. Bielen aboard Daddy's Punkin', with owner Alton More and trainer Carl Sitgraves. The horse and jockey completed five furlongs in 59:3/5.

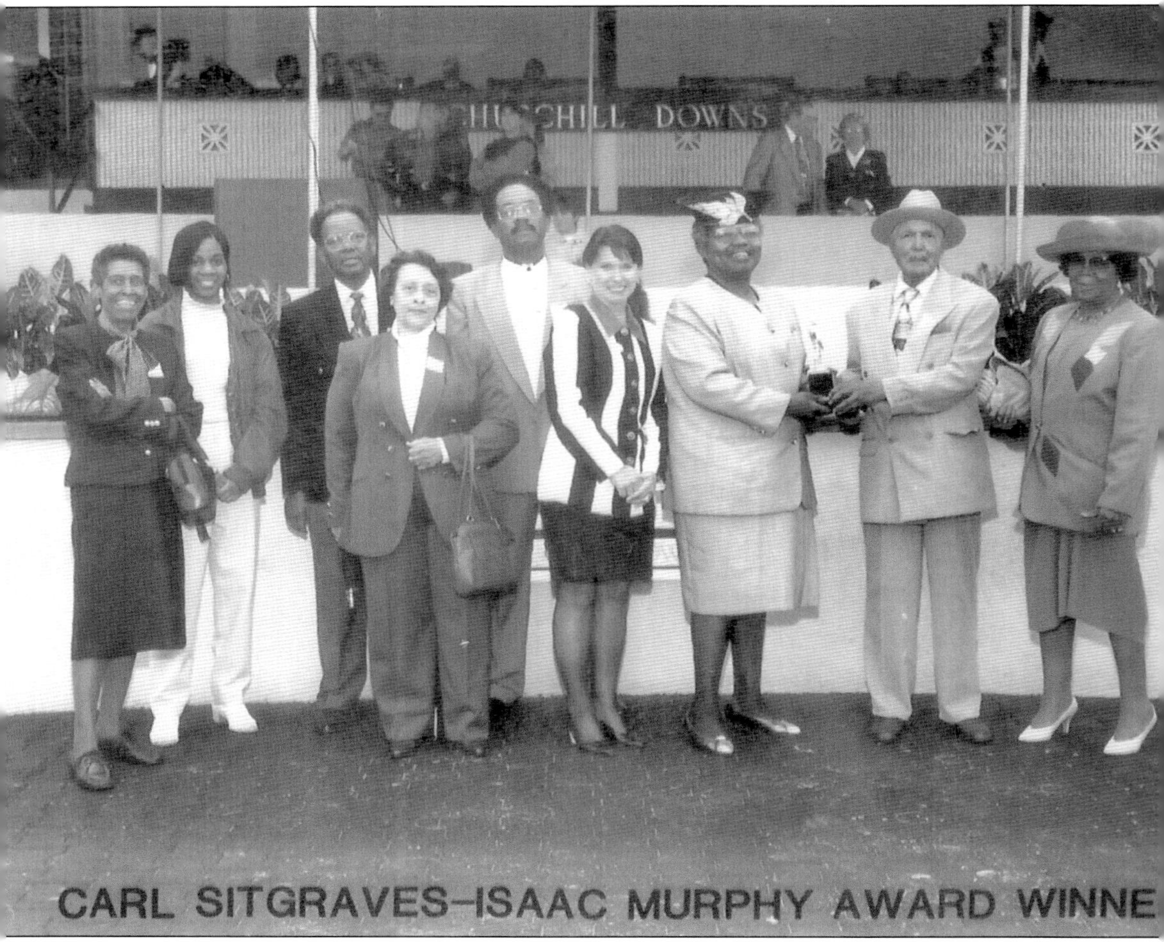

CARL SITGRAVES–ISAAC MURPHY AWARD WINNER, TUESDAY, APRIL 29, 1997. In recognition of his outstanding achievement in the thoroughbred industry, Carl Sitgraves was awarded the Isaac Murphy Award presented by Salute to Black Jockeys Inc. and Churchill Downs Incorporated. Murphy is considered one of the greatest race riders in American history. After the death of his father as a soldier in the Civil War, Isaac's mother moved to Lexington, where the family lived with her father, Green Murphy. Upon becoming a jockey at age 14, Isaac changed his last name to Murphy in honor of his grandfather. Isaac, 35, died of pneumonia on February 12, 1896. He is buried next to Man o' War at the Kentucky Horse Park's entrance.

Willie Simms, African American Hall of Fame Jockey. Born on January 16, 1870, in Augusta, Georgia, Willie Simms was inducted into the National Museum of Racing Hall of Fame in 1977. His riding career spanned from 1887 to 1901. Throughout his career, he boasted 4,532 mounts, 1,125 wins, and an overall winning percentage of 24.8.

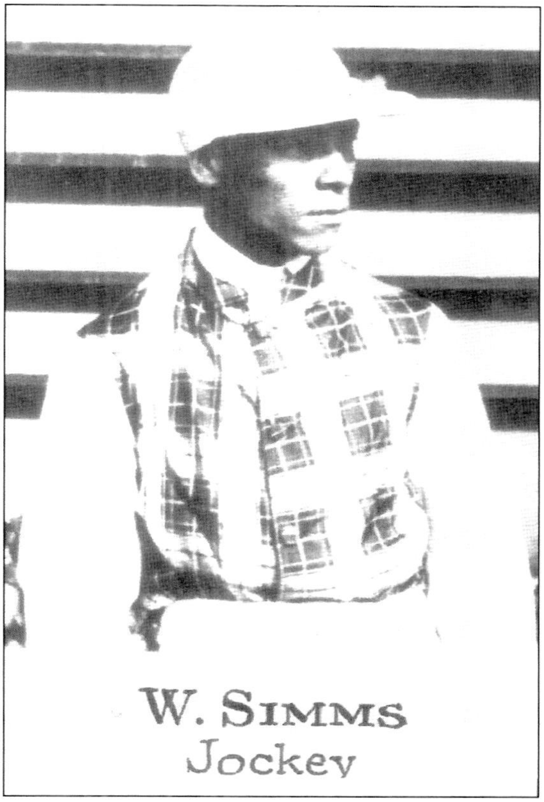

Regards at Beulah Park, October 3, 1936. This image commemorates Carl Sitgraves's legendary first win. He poses on the left as the owner and trainer of Regards.

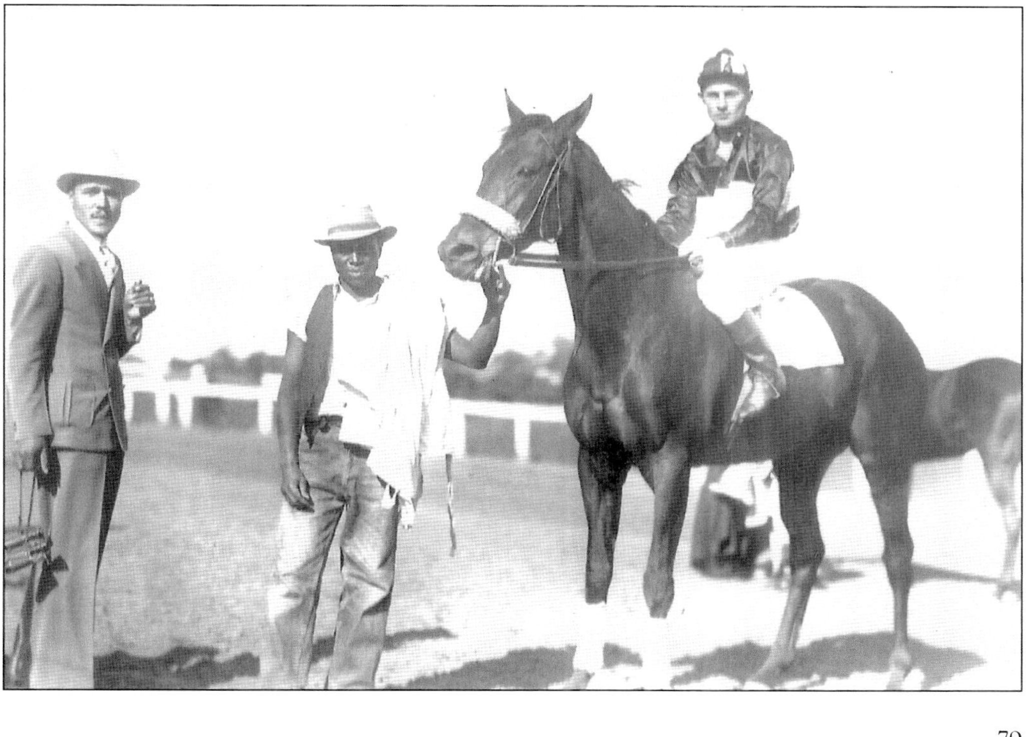

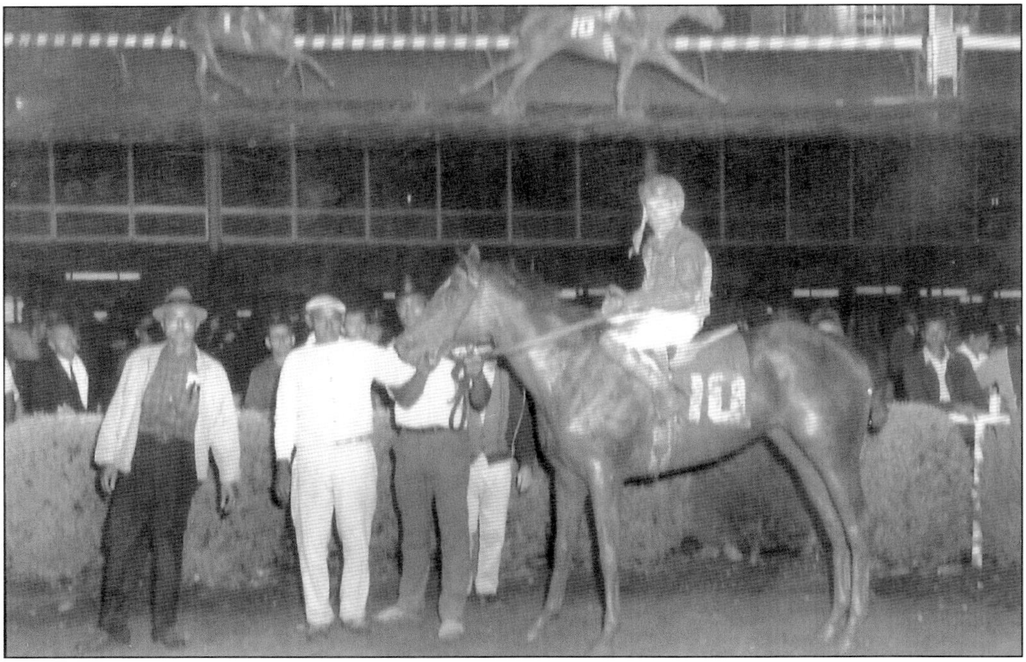

My Tressie at Latonia Track in Florence, Kentucky. On October 2, 1969, My Tressie was the winning horse at the Latonia Track in Florence. Trainer Carl Sitgraves (far left) and owner Alto Moore (second from left) are seen standing, with jockey J. Piaxxa astride the horse.

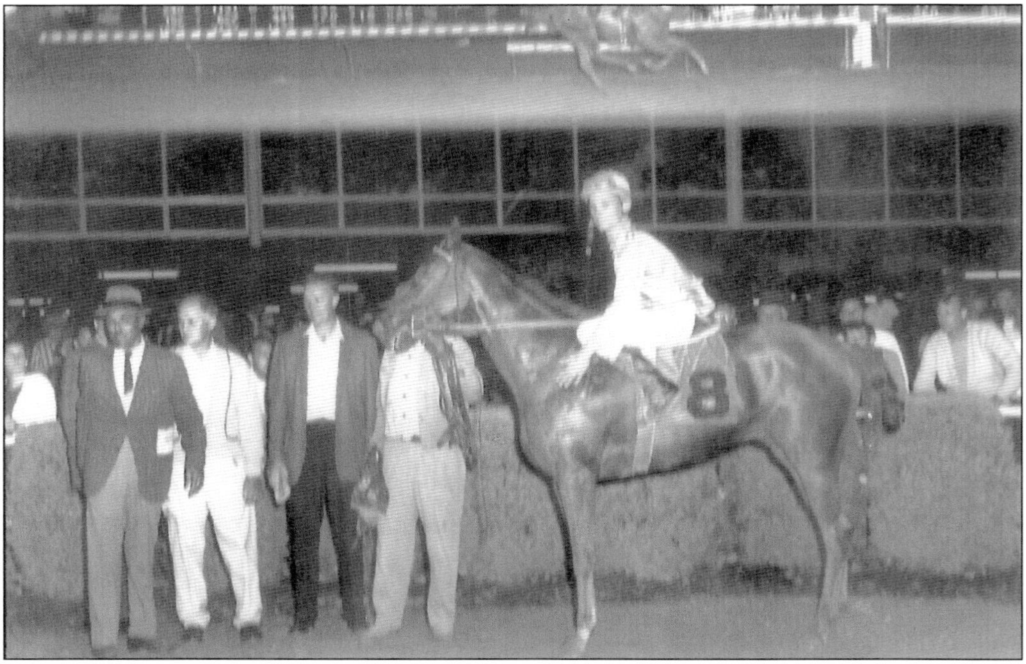

Peper Wan at Latonia Track in Florence, Kentucky. On September 17, 1968, Peper Wan took first place in the six-furlong race with a time of 1:14. Pictured here are, from left to right, trainer Carl Sitgraves, owners L.J. and N.A. Wanstrath, and jockey M.W. Cook.

WILLIE SIMMS, JOCKEY. Willie Simms won the Kentucky Derby in both 1896 and 1898. In 1896, Simms rode Ben Brush; in 1898, he rode Plaudit. Born on January 16, 1870, in Augusta, Georgia, Simms was the only African American jockey to win all three Triple Crown events. In 1898, he rode Sly Fox in the Preakness, and he won consecutive runs at the Belmont track with Comanche in 1893 and Henry of Navarre in 1894. Simms was the nation's leading jockey in 1893 and again in 1894. He was the first American jockey ever to win a race with an American horse at an English track and was credited in the 1890s for bringing the short-stirrup riding style to England. Later in his career, Simms became a horse trainer and continued until February 26, 1927, when he died at age 47 in Asbury, New Jersey.

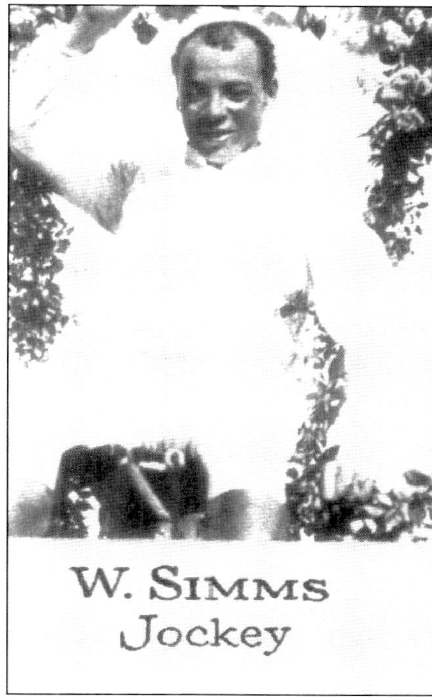

SYNDICATE, THE ARLINGTON STAKE RACE. On October 11, 1944, Syndicate was the winning horse at Keeneland Race Track in Lexington, Kentucky. The horse-and-jockey team recorded a seven-furlong time of 1:24.8. Pictured are trainer Carl Sitgraves (left) and jockey K. Church.

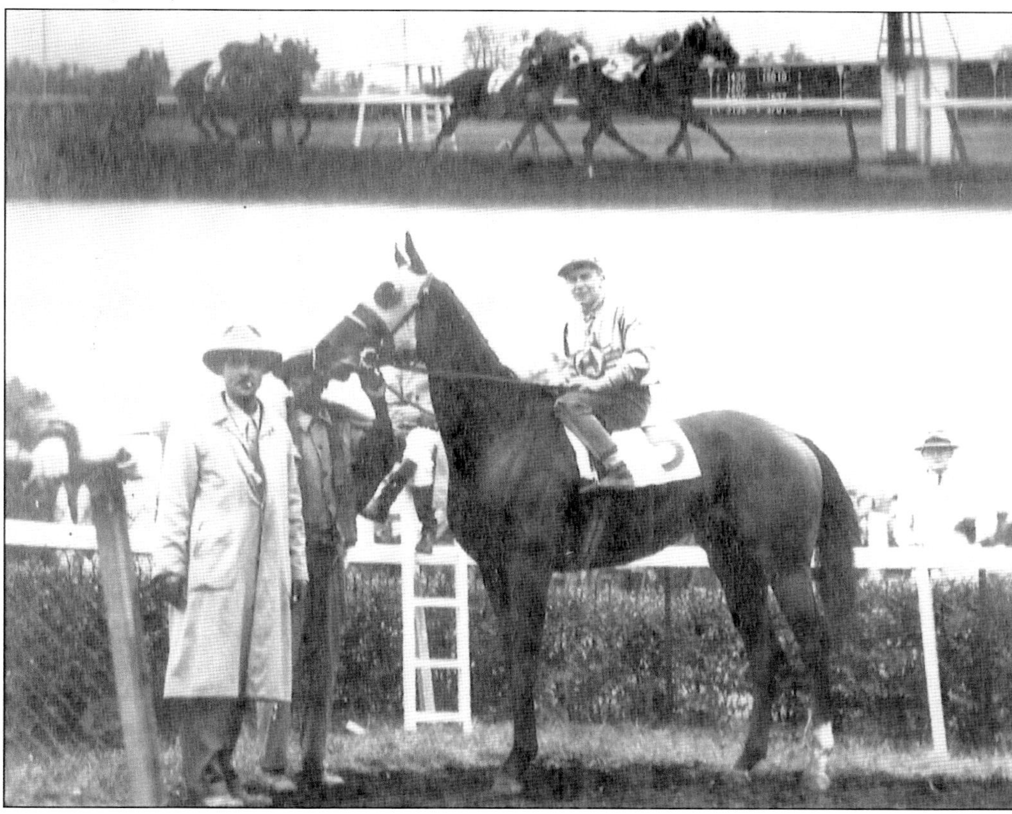

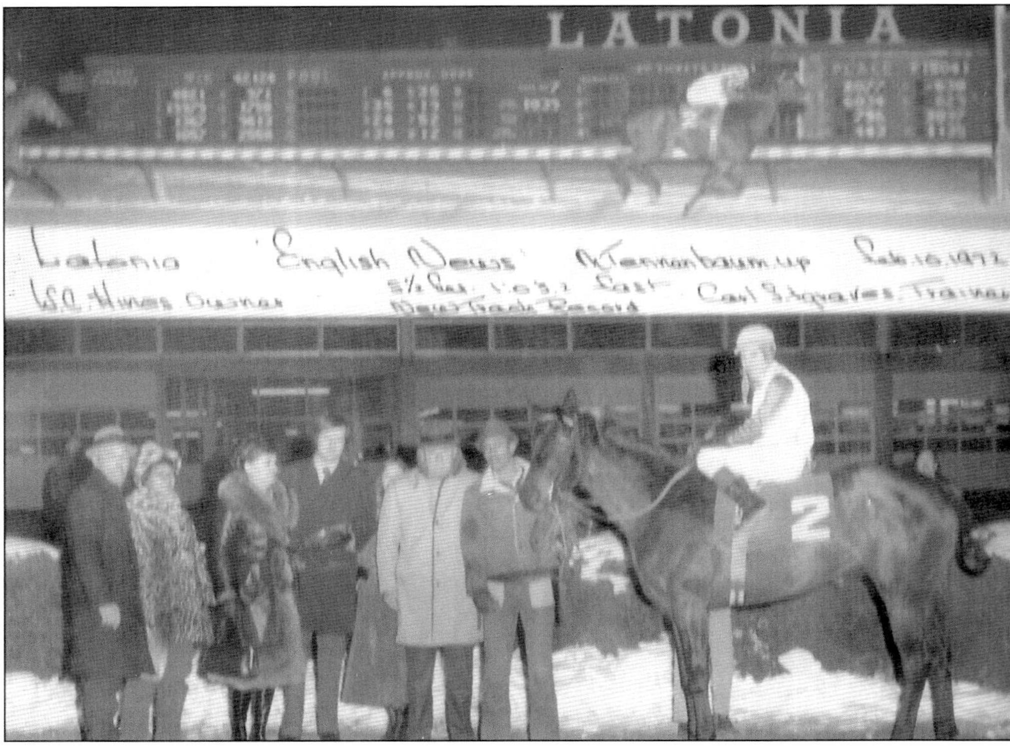

English News, Latonia, Florence, Kentucky. On February 10, 1972, English News was the winning horse at the Latonia Track, setting a new track record of five and a half furlongs in 1:03.2. Identified here celebrating their victory are trainer Carl Sitgraves (far left), owner W.C. Hines (fifth from left), and jockey N. Tennanbaum.

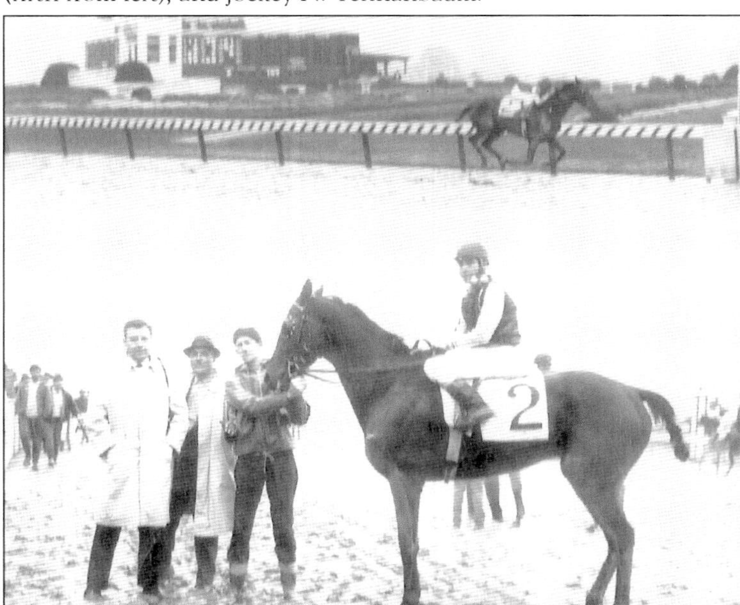

Bodoni, Churchill Downs, November 6, 1968. In sloppy track conditions, Bodoni ran the 1.0625 miles to the winner's circle in 1:48. Jockey L.G. Rivera holds the reigns for owner George Grassle (far left) and trainer Carl Sitgraves (second from left).

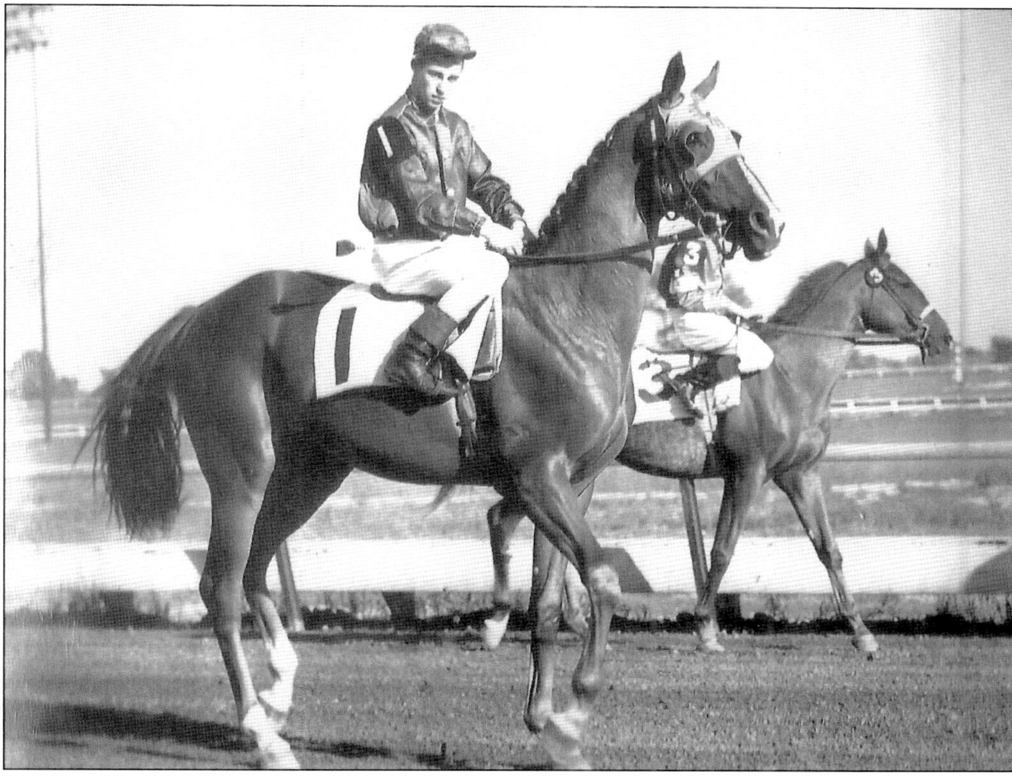

Abe's Choice, Detroit, 1950. Abe's Choice took the blue ribbon for the six furlongs in Detroit with a time of 1:13. Jockey W.M. Cook is shown here on the winning horse.

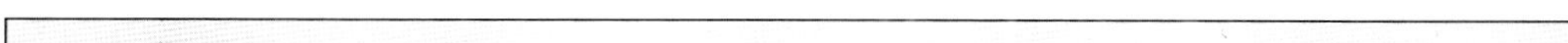

Minnie Hacha, Churchill Downs, October 24, 1945. After six and a half furlongs in 1:23.4, Minnie Hacha was the victor. Trainer Carl Sitgraves (left) is pictured here with owners M.J. (second from left) and C.E. Herbold (in the rear).

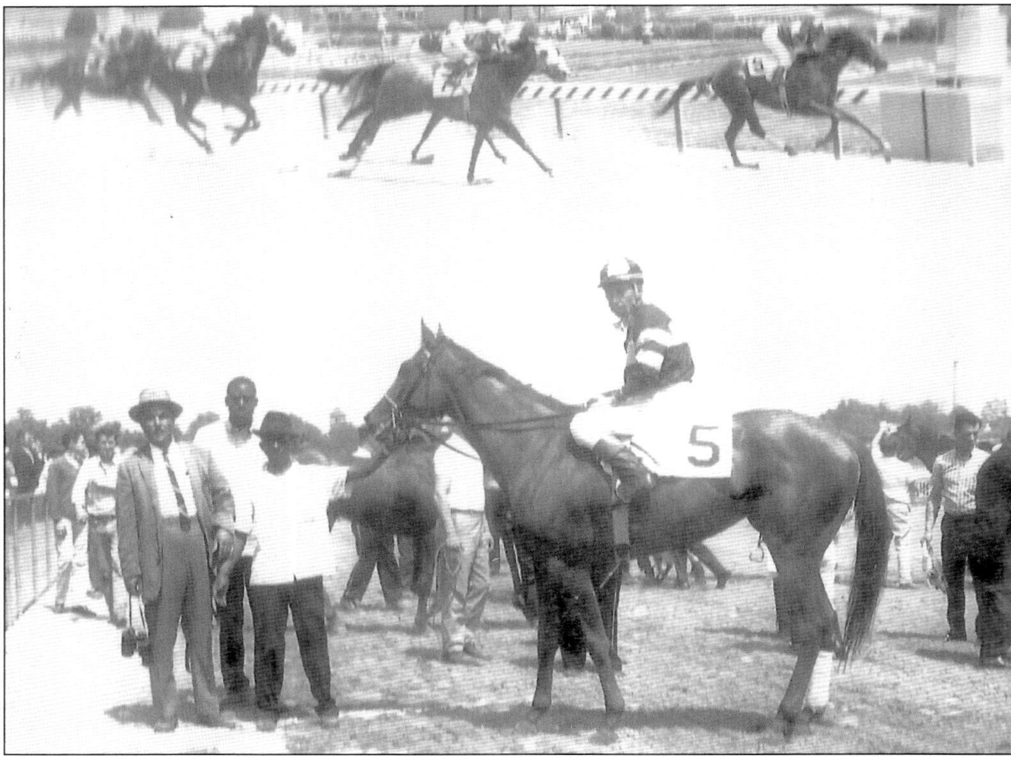

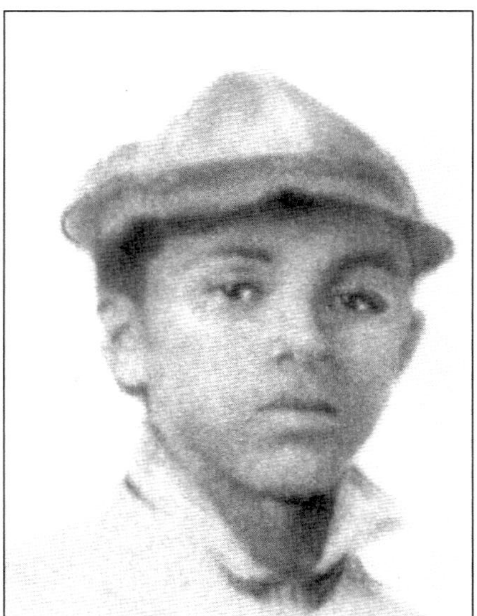

DID DO IT, CHURCHILL DOWNS, MAY 5, 1964. Carl Sitgraves, owner and trainer, bought this mare after his win with Bob's Dislike and named her Did Do It. Several trainers did not think Bob's Dislike could win but he did, coming in first in the Junior Derby on July 14, 1962, with a time of 1:13.1.

WILLIAM WALKER, JOCKEY. Walker won the 1877 Kentucky Derby mounted on Baden-Baden for Ed Brown, an African American trainer. Walker, a native of Woodford County, was born into slavery in 1860 at Gen. Abe Buford's Bosque Bonita Farm near Versailles, Kentucky. In 1871, at only 11 years old, Walker began his riding career with his first win in Lexington at Jerome Park. At age 13, he had obtained his first stakes victory. Walker participated in four Derby races (winning the 1877 Derby) and witnessed 59 consecutive Kentucky Derby races until his death on September 20, 1933, at his home. He is buried in the Louisville Cemetery. In 1996, during Derby Week, Churchill Downs placed a headstone in Walker's honor that commemorates his achievements and triumphs.

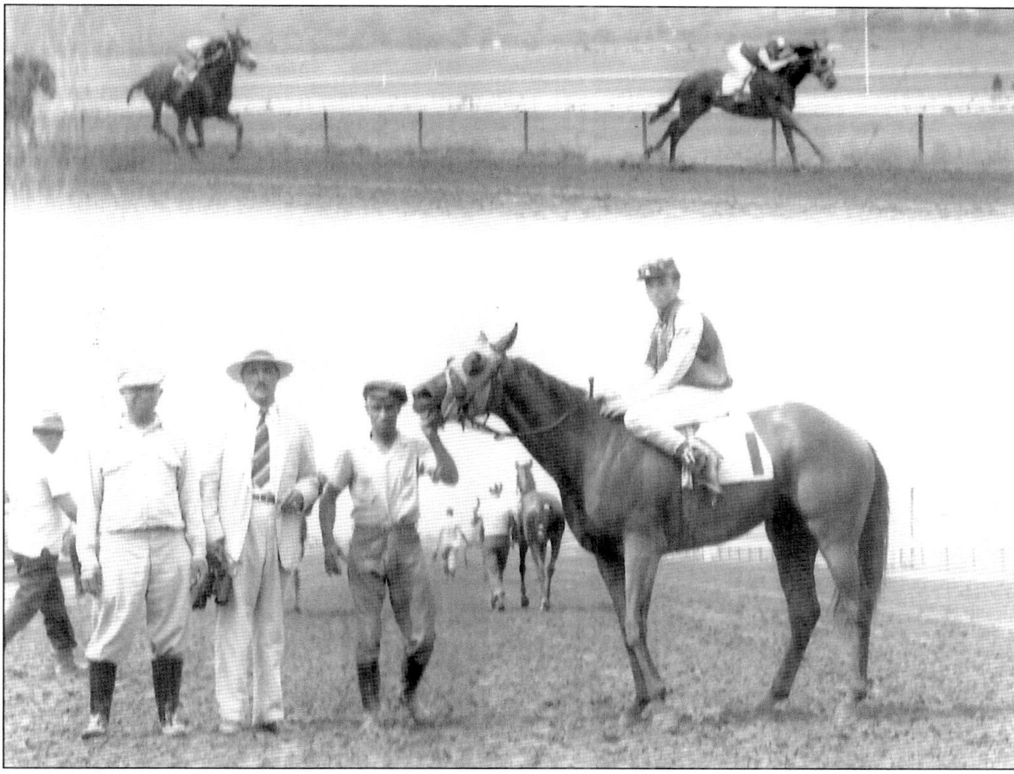

Real Treat, Waterford Park, Ohio. On June 30, 1952, Real Treat ran the five furlongs to victory at Waterford Park with a time of 1:2.2. H. Amos jockeyed for owner B. Hisner and trainer Carl Sitgraves in muddy conditions.

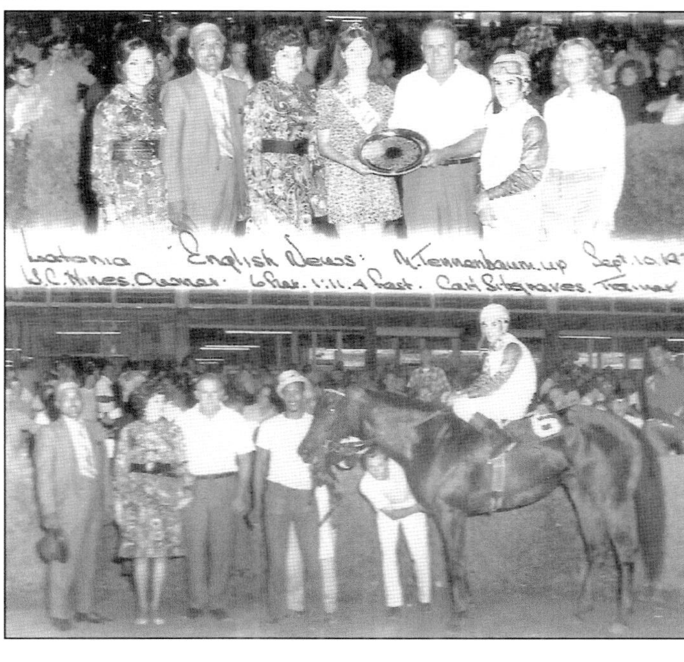

English News, Latonia Track, Florence, Kentucky. On September 10, 1971, English News recorded another victory, completing the six furlongs in 1:14.4. Identified in this image are trainer Carl Sitgraves (far left), owner W.C. Hines (third from left), and jockey N. Tennenbaum.

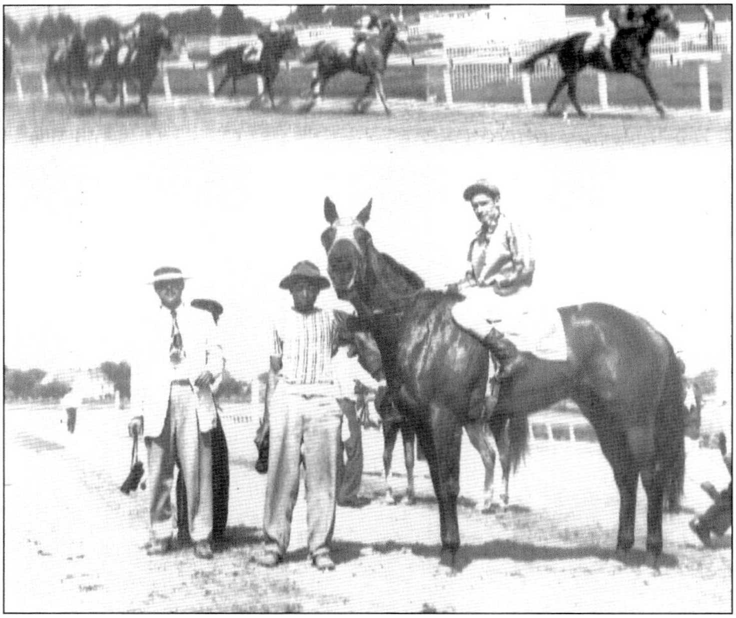

Jessica B, Keeneland Track, Lexington, Kentucky. On October 18, 1950, Jessica B completed the seven furlongs in 1:26 4/5 with jockey R.H. Baird. Pictured with the horse and rider are trainer Carl Sitgraves (left) and owner J.H. Wallace.

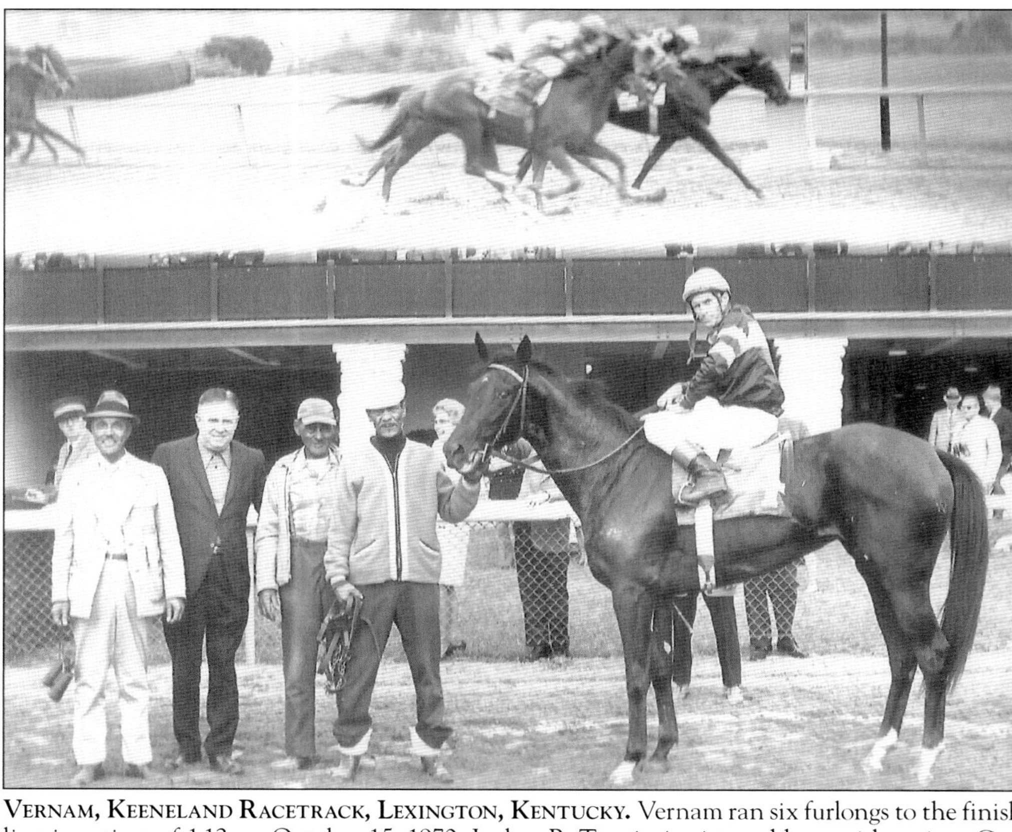

Vernam, Keeneland Racetrack, Lexington, Kentucky. Vernam ran six furlongs to the finish line in a time of 1:12 on October 15, 1970. Jockey B. Tauxin is pictured here with trainer Carl Sitgraves (left) and owner William Hines (second from left).

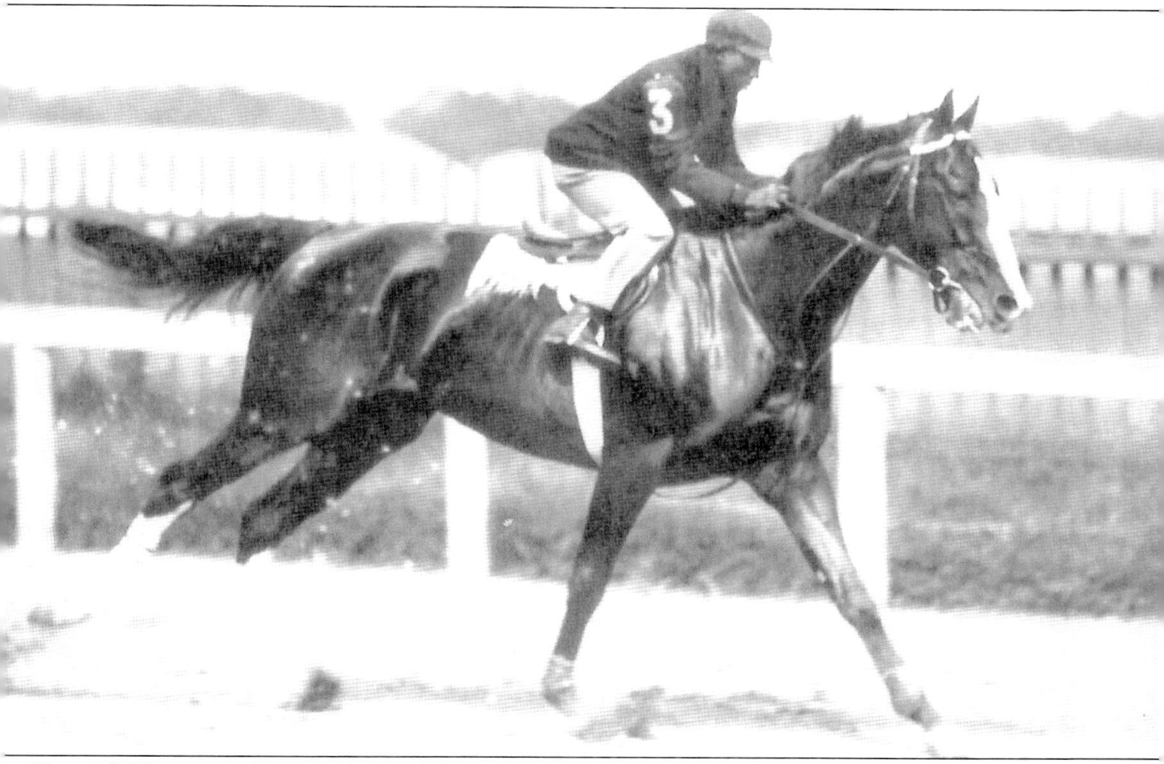

"Jimmy" Winkfield Riding Alan-A-Dale, Churchill Downs Track. Churchill Downs, on Central Avenue in Louisville, began its legacy in 1875 with the first Kentucky Derby and also hosted the Kentucky Oaks in the same year. The winning horse in the inaugural "Run for the Roses" on May 17, 1875, was Aristides, ridden by Oliver Lewis, an African American. African American jockeys dominated the track in early racing, and in the first Kentucky Derby, 13 out of 15 jockeys were African Americans. By 1921, African American jockeys were no longer racing at Churchill Downs and would not surface again until 2000 when Marlon St. Julien rode Curule to seventh place.

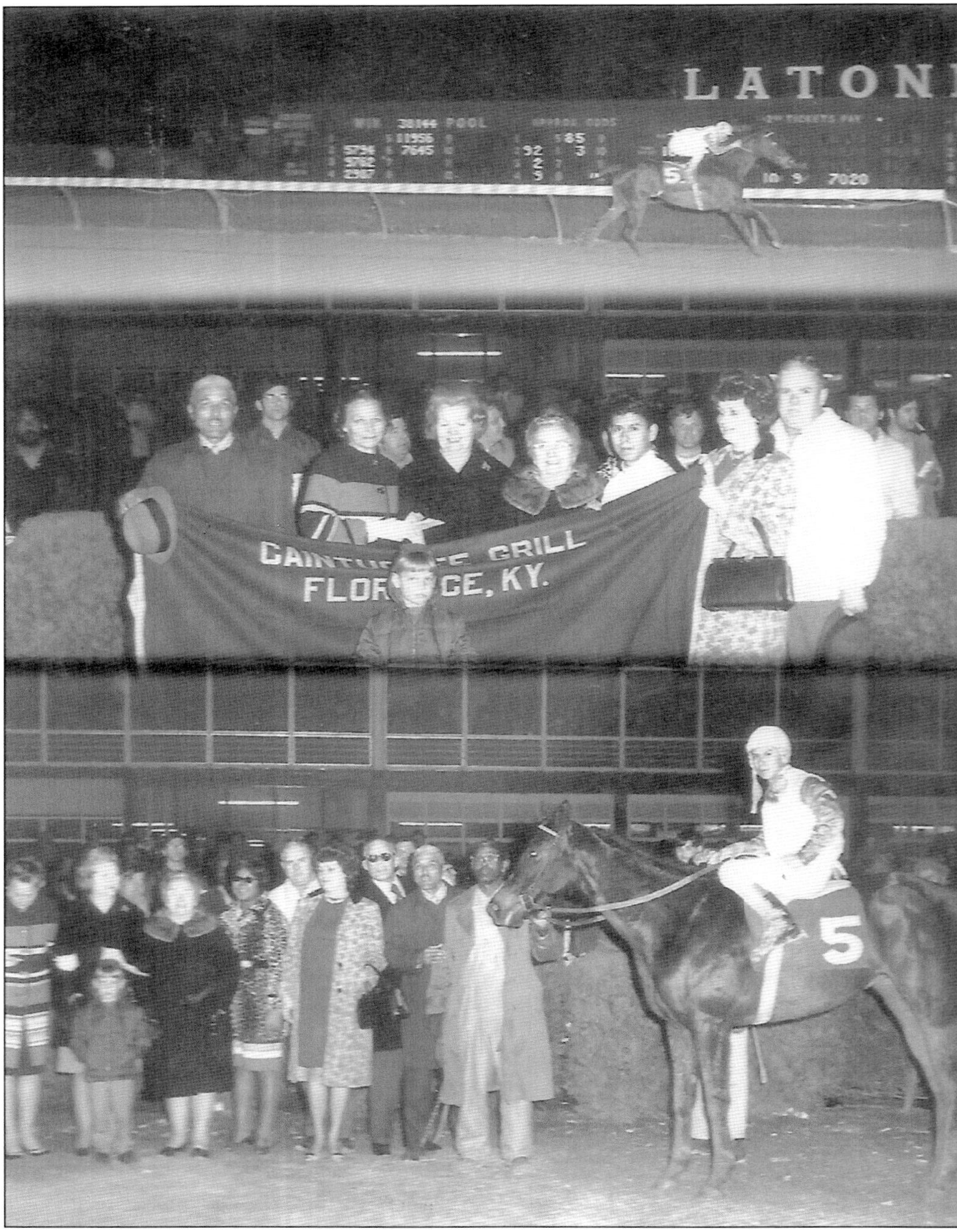

ENGLISH NEWS, LATONIA TRACK, FLORENCE, KENTUCKY. On March 15, 1971, English News was photographed beneath a banner reading "Caintuckee Grill, Florence, Ky." after winning six furlongs in 1:13:3. H. Hidalgo is the jockey pictured here with owner W.C. Hines (fifth from left) and trainer Carl Sitgraves (eighth from left).

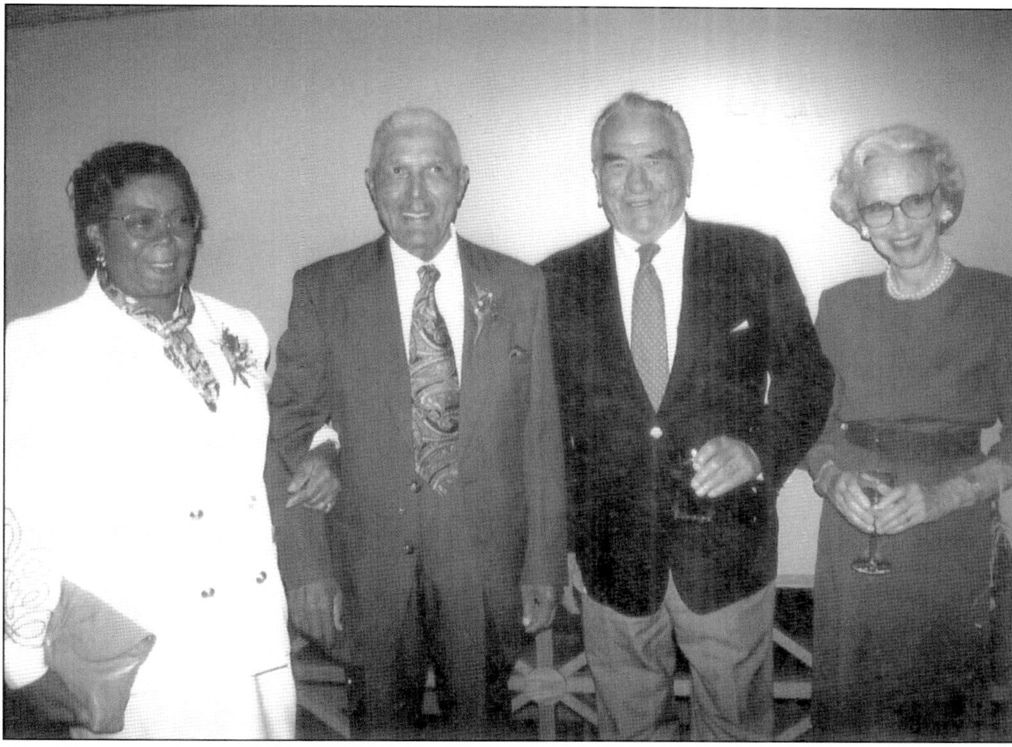

The Kentucky Derby Museum, African American Horsemen, 1997. Pictured here, from left to right, are Essie Sitgraves, Carl Sitgraves, Warner Jones, and Harriet Seelbach Jones. The Kentucky Derby Museum opened to the public in April 1985. The museum sits on land that Churchill Downs donated to the nonprofit corporation. The construction of the facility and seed money for the endowment was provided by the J. Graham Brown Foundation and five banks in the community.

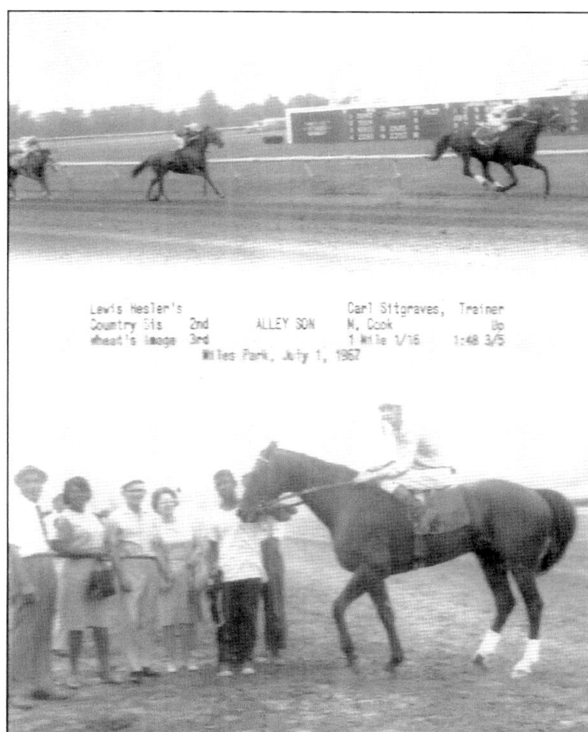

Alley Son, Miles Park, July 1, 1967. Alley Son ran the 1.0625-mile track in 1:48.6 with jockey M. Cook. Trainer Carl Sitgraves (far left) and owner Lewis Hesler (third from left) and are pictured here in the winner's circle.

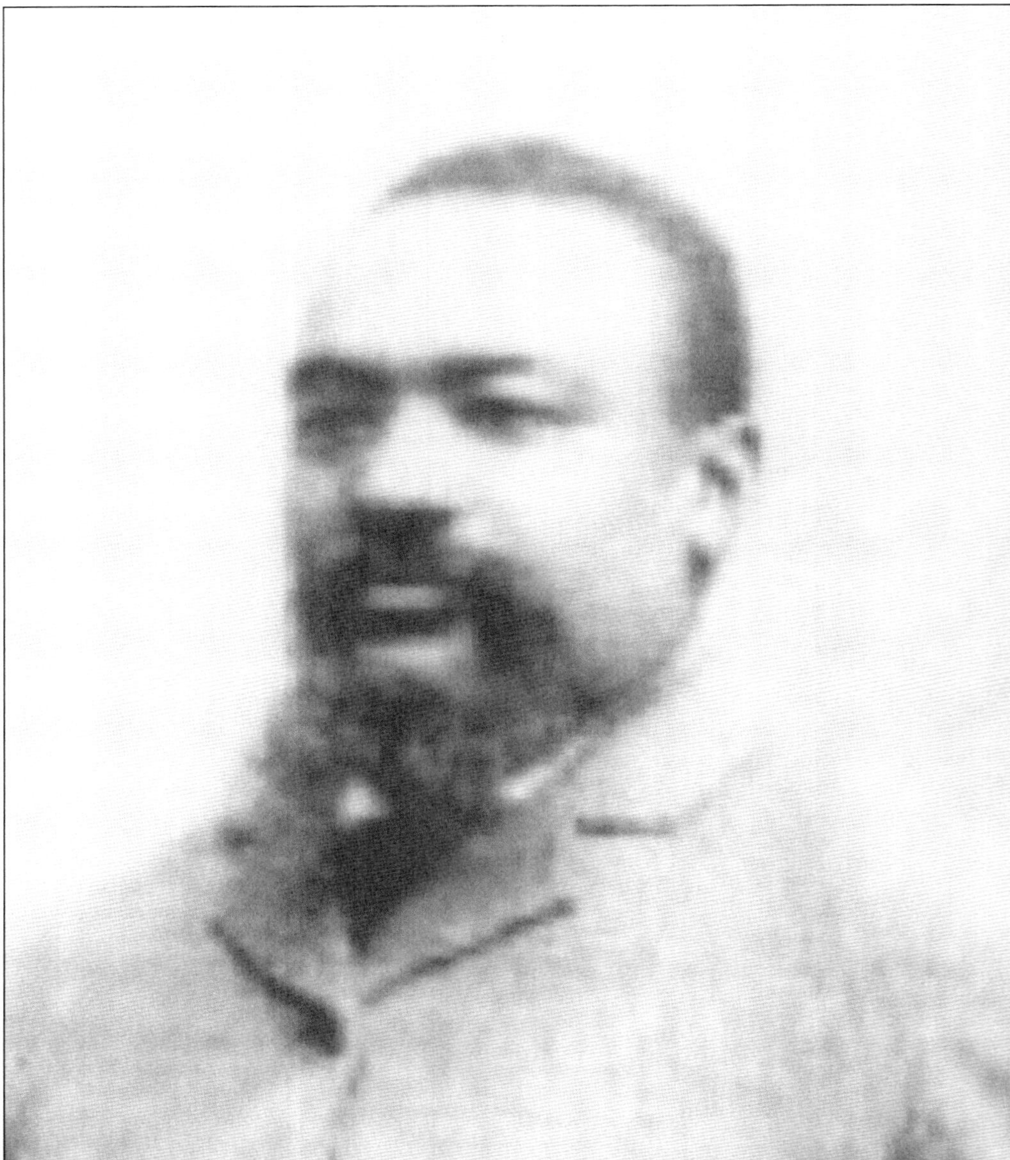

EDWARD D. BROWN, AFRICAN AMERICAN JOCKEY, TRAINER, AND OWNER, 1900. Edward Dudley Brown (1850–May 11, 1906) was an African American born as a slave who rose to become a Belmont Stakes–winning jockey, a Kentucky Derby–winning horse trainer, and an owner of several of the top racehorses during the last decade of the 19th century. These accomplishments earned him induction into the United States Racing Hall of Fame. Born in Lexington, Kentucky, Brown was sold at age seven to Robert A. Alexander, proprietor of the famous Woodburn Stud near Midway, Kentucky. He worked as a groom and grew up developing a keen understanding of horse breeding and how to condition horses for racing. His small stature and knowledge of horses afforded him the opportunity to become a jockey. Following his emancipation after the Civil War, Brown remained as Alexander's employee and rode a number of his horses to victories in important races.

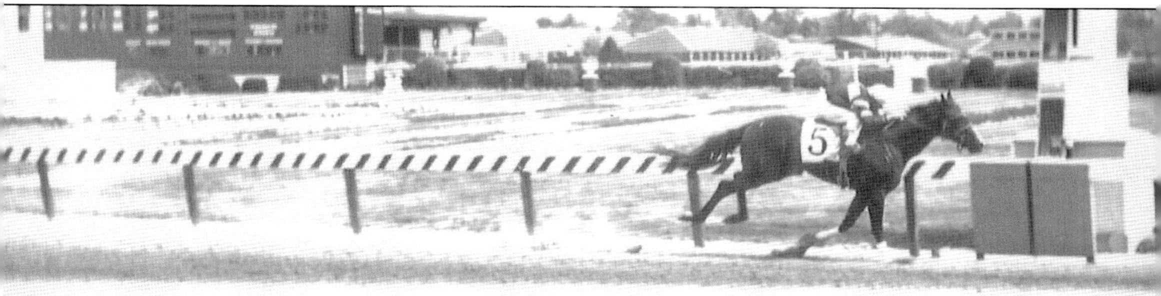

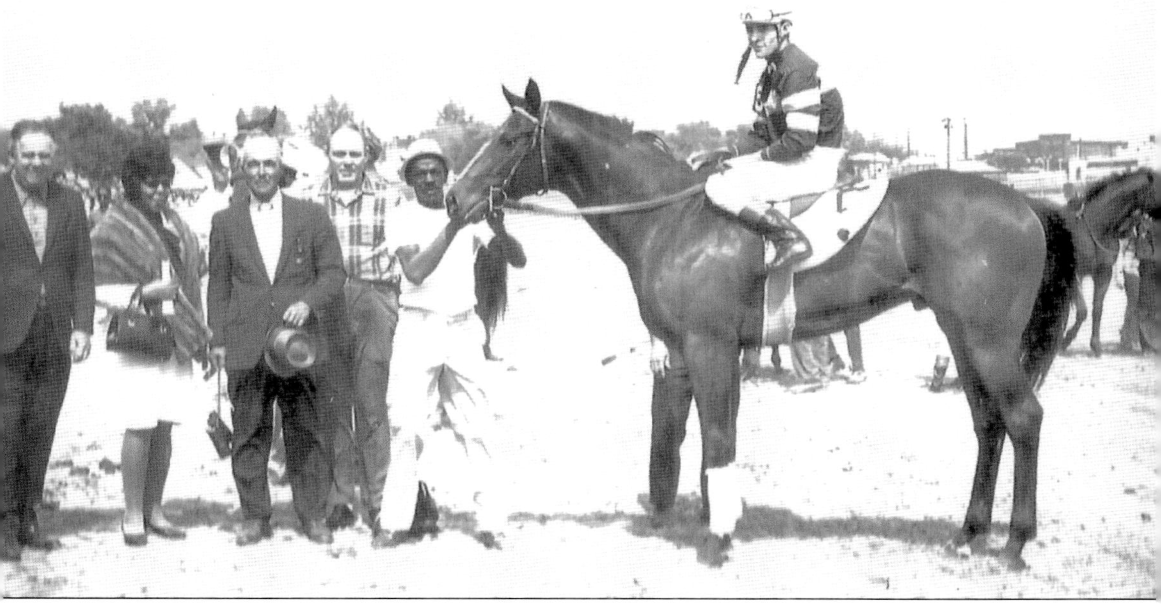

Triple Schnap, Churchill Downs, May 4, 1971. Triple Schnap ran six furlongs in 1:10 with jockey L.G. Rivera on behalf of, from far left, owners W.C. Hines and Essie Sitgraves and trainer Carl Sitgraves. Earlier Kentucky Derby history mentions Babe Hurd, an African American jockey who rode Apollo to a half-length win in the 1882 race. Hurd also was renowned as a steeplechase rider. He died at Longridge Farm on Paris Pike near Lexington, Kentucky, on December 7, 1928. Another jockey, Erskine Henderson became the sixth African American to ride a Derby winner when he rallied Joe Cotton to victory in 1885. George Garret Lewis rode Fonso to victory in the 1880 Derby despite a claim of foul play, the first in race history.

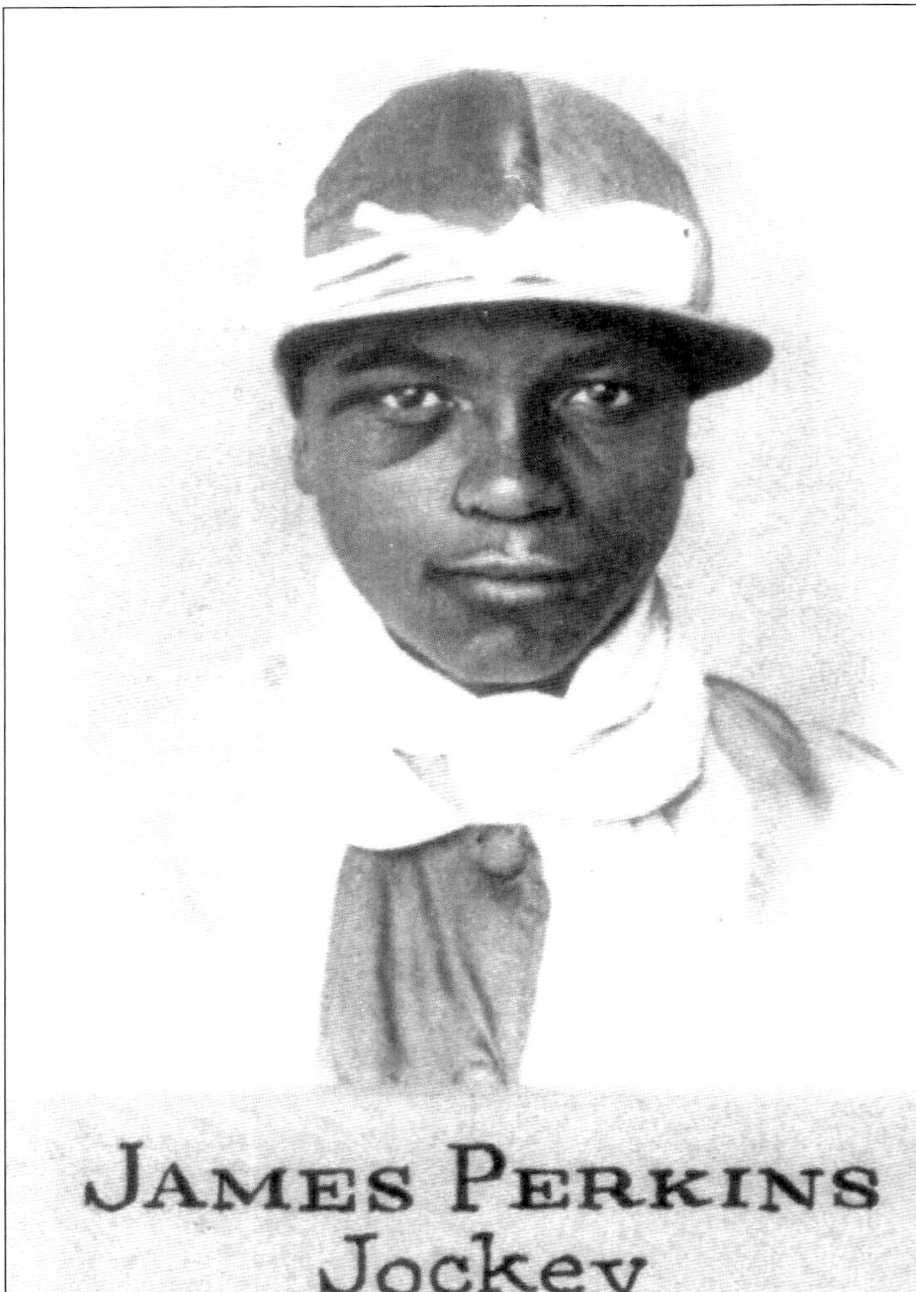

James "Soup" Perkins, Jockey. At age 15, Perkins rode Halma in the 1895 Kentucky Derby, joining his young comrade, African American jockey Alonzo Clayton, as the youngest winning riders of the event. Perkins, whose nickname came for his love of soup, began his riding career in 1891 at the age of 11. His first win was at Kentucky's Latonia racetrack that same year. William Perkins, James's brother, was a prominent trainer who entered six horses in the Derby during his career. Soup died in August 1911 while attending races at Hamilton, Ontario.

Six

"Southeast on Third"

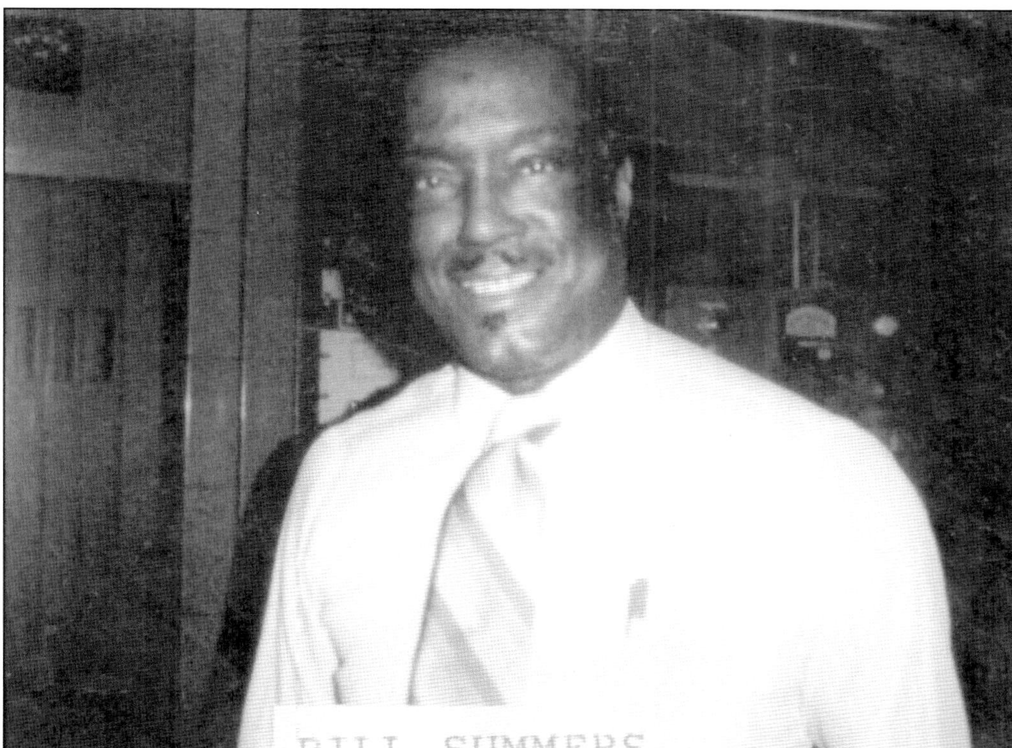

William "Bill" Summers III. WLOU went on the air in October 1948, licensed to Mrs. John E. Messervy. Between 1948 and 1951, several formats were tested until Robert W. Rounsaville of Atlanta, Georgia, became owner in September 1951. Summers, the first black owner of a radio station in Kentucky, came to WLOU in 1952 as an announcer and bought the station in 1972.

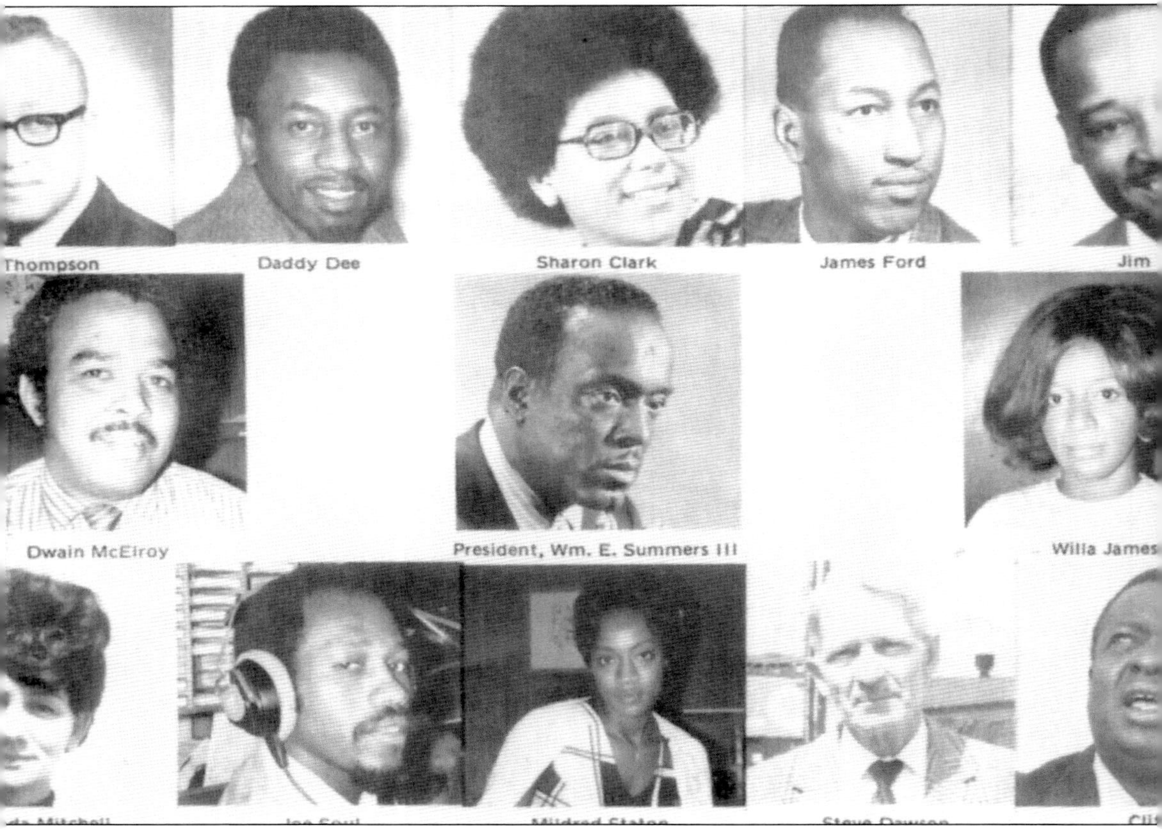

WLOU Staff, 1970s. Pictured here are, from left to right, (first row) Wanda Mitchell, Joe Soul, Mildred Staton, Steve Dawson, and Cliff Butler; (second row) Dwain McElroy, William E. Summers III (president), and Willa James; (third row) Skip Thompson, Daddy Dee, Sharon Clark, James Ford, and Jim Dandy.

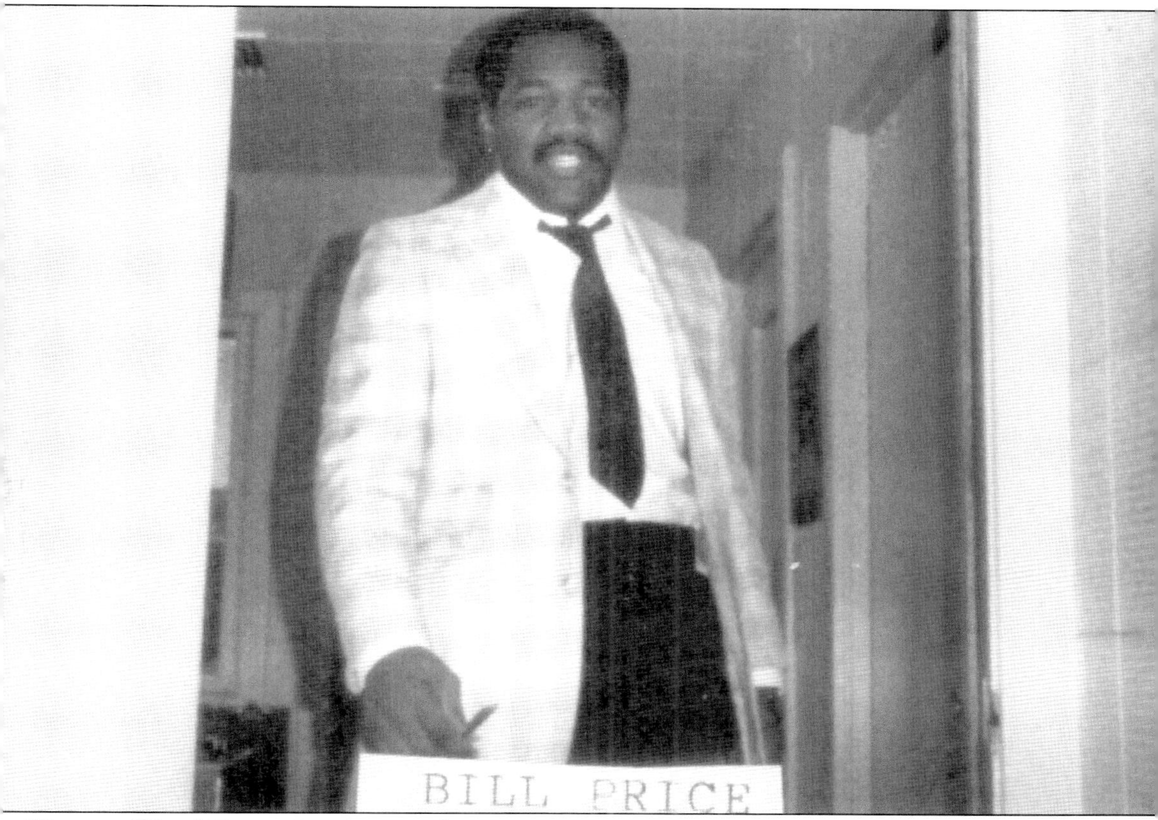

WILLIAM "BILL" PRICE. Price's career began in 1977 as a morning show host at WLOU radio, owned by William E. Summers III. In 1983, WLOU became the No. 1 radio station in the market, and a Top 10 nationally rated station, with Price serving as program director. Price has also held the position as sales manager and is an award-winning broadcaster and 2008 Stellar Award nominee. Currently, he is the general manager of WLOU and WLLV radio stations. Bill's vision, as related by LouisvilleGospel.com: "We're refocusing on servicing core listeners, adults who have grown up listening to the stations, and on becoming more interactive with churches to address their immediate broadcasting needs. Additionally, we will be reestablishing strong community ties, with an emphasis on nonprofit organizations that do great work, like the Urban League, the NAACP, and the Lincoln Foundation. Look for the return of major summer events."

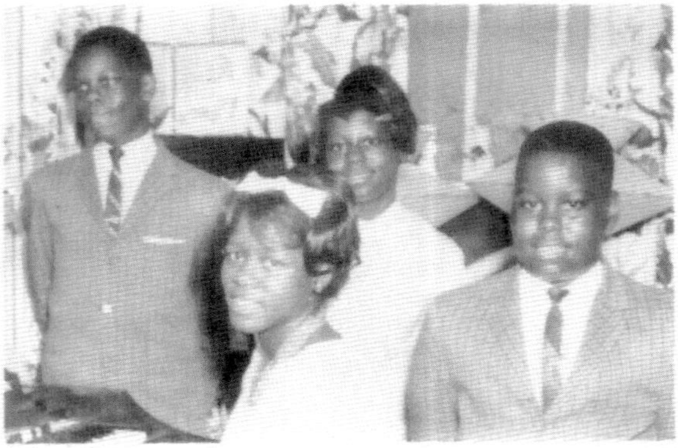

THE SINGING BROWN FAMIL

L to R:

Ricky Maurice 13, Marlyn Gloria 1
Thomas Johnson 10, and Beatri
Sandra, 14 (seated), musician and le
singer. Also serves as organist f
their church.

This exceptionally talented young family group belongs to the Mt. Zion Baptist Church, 1472 Dixie Highway in Louisville. Their pastor, Rev. B. S. Ransom and the congregation is very proud and thankful for these young people and consider them a great asset to the church.

For three and one-half years, the Brown family has brought joy and inspiration to hundreds throughout the Louisville area with their soul-stirring renditions.

For further information or engagements with the Brown family, you may contact their mother, Mrs. Irene at 778-3064.

The Singing Brown Family, 1964. Pictured here are, from left to right, Ricky Maurice, 13; Marilyn Gloria, 12; Thomas Johnson, 10; and Beatrice Sandra (musician and lead singer), 14. Beatrice also served as an organist for their church. This is an advertisement in the 1964 WLOU Gospel Souvenir book. As local talent winners, these young singers were allowed to sing on the first half of the Gospel Extravaganzas held at the armory with such personalities as Mahalia Jackson and Rev. James Cleveland. They were also members of the Louisville's Choral Union and sang under the direction of the late Thomas A. Dorsey in his Gospel Workshops. Their mother, Irene Brown, was their manager.

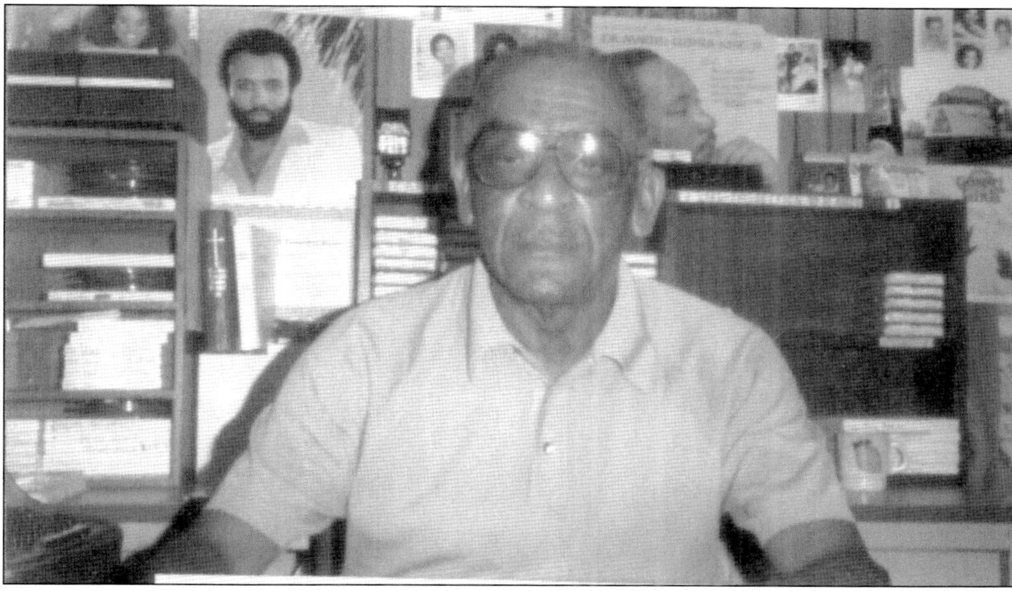

R.G. Lilly. Lilly acted as the first gospel announcer from 1952 to 1960.

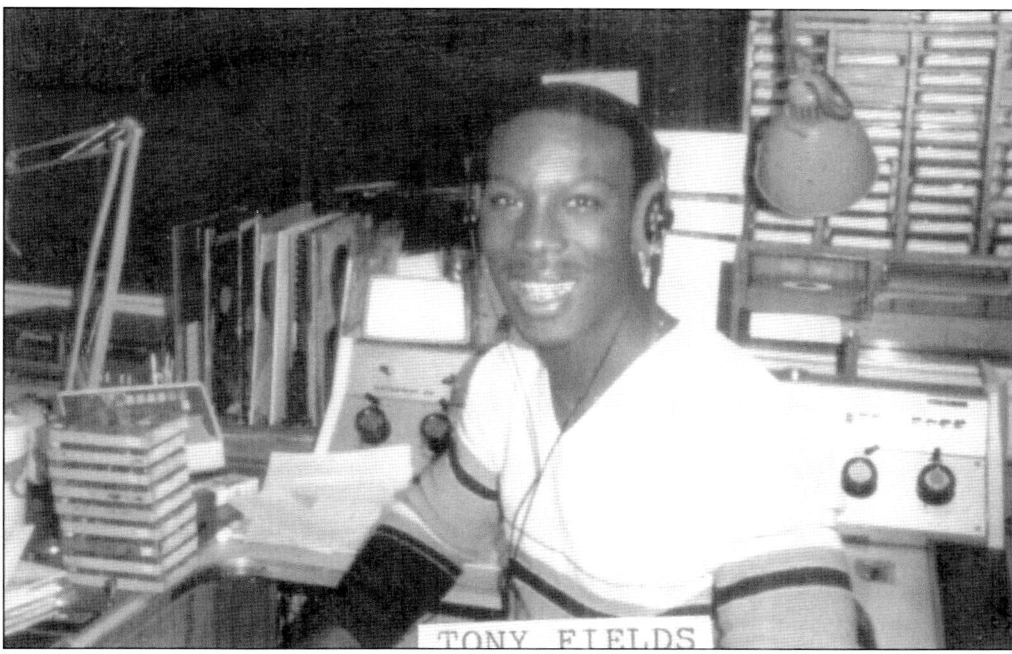

Tony Fields. Fields was the music director at WLOU throughout the 1980s. "About WLOU," a 1983 station anniversary tribute, states: "Gospel and spiritual music has been a part of the format since the earliest days of our history. Among the announcers that have carried the gospel torch are Johnny Martin, R.G. Lilly, Bill Summers III, Cliff Butler (deceased), James Ford (now with WDGS), Vivian Walls, and currently David Anderson, who came to us from Houston, Texas, in 1964." Fields worked alongside colleagues John H. Johnson (president), William E. Summers III (management consultant), David Anderson (religious program director and commercial production manager), Brenda Banks (announcer), and Ange Canessa (announcer).

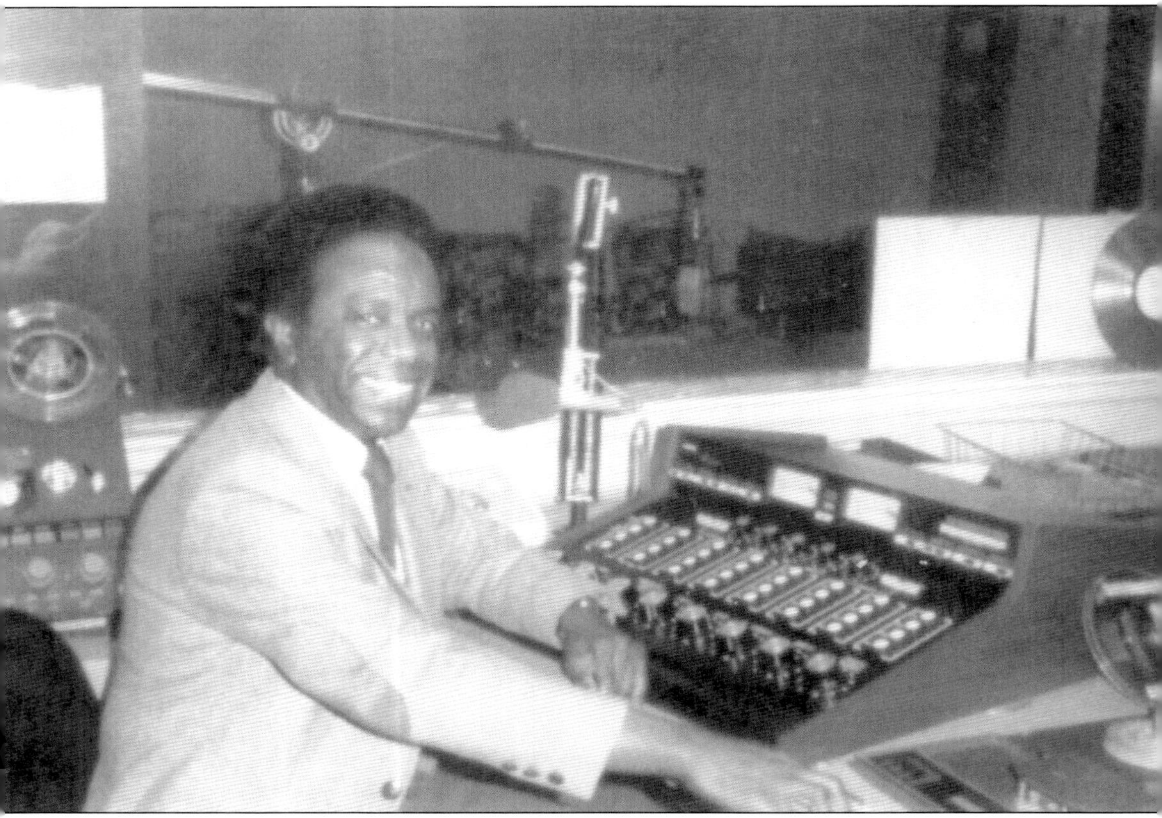

"LITTLE DAVID" ANDERSON. Anderson came with an unusual talent for gospel programming, which became an instant hit with the Louisville community, according to "About WLOU." Anderson knew that tradition, having grown up as a minister's son in Houston. He found his career when his father, Rev. David Anderson Sr., began a radio broadcast with his son during announcements. "That was fun," Anderson said. The budding disc jockey honed his skills at the feet of other announcers, then worked for stations in Dallas and Jackson, Mississippi, before coming to WLOU in January 1964. "Gospel was right in the middle of it," Anderson said, "and I was doing the programming." "He made a real difference," says James "Jay" Ford, current program director at WLLV/WLOU. "Anderson did things a 'new way.' " Rochelle Riley, in " 'Little David' is a Goliath of Gospel Music in Louisville," writes, "Little David had such a fantastic way how he brought this whole thing of gospel music about that made it interesting."

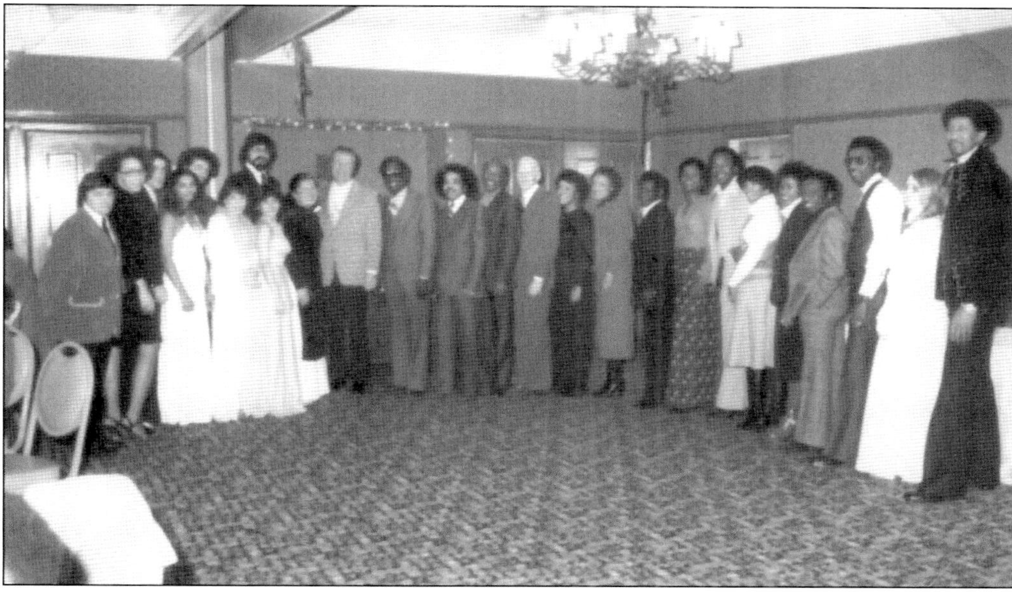

On the Air. "About WLOU" notes: "An innumerable caravan of outstanding churches, ministers, and singing groups have broadcast programs on WLOU through the years. Among them: Reverend Ike, A.A. Allen, David Pitts, H.M. Humphrey Sr., Ben Higgins, G.T. Allen, Lauretta McMurry and the Louisville Quartette Union, Price King, H.G. Hollins, and Geneva Cooper Rich."

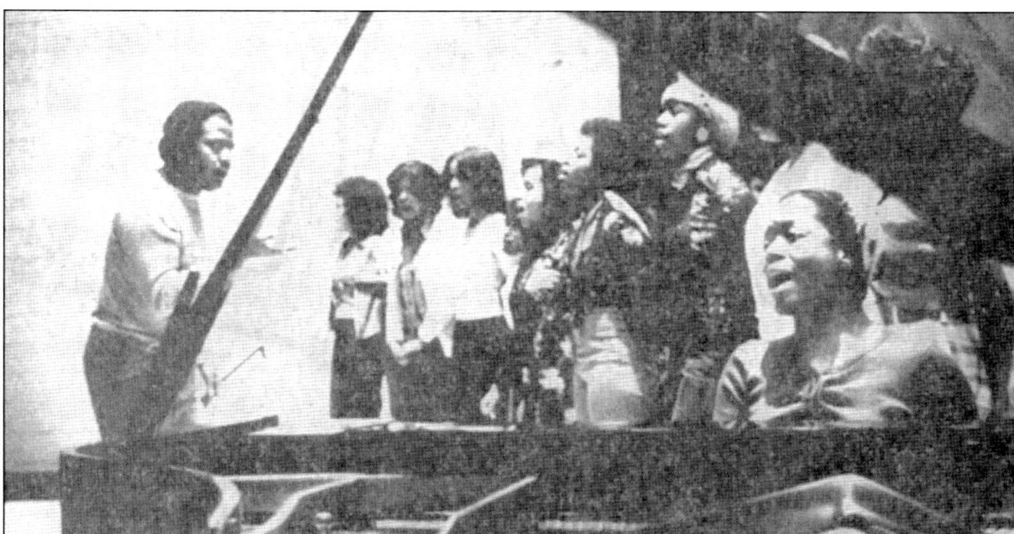

The Black Diamond Choir. Beatrice Brown, choir director, plays and sings as Carl Smith (left) directs the Black Diamonds in 1975. The Black Diamond Choir was founded in November 1969, when Beatrice S. Brown, a University of Louisville music major and 19 at the time, started a choir from her class. She named the choir Black Diamond for the resilience and strength of a people who had endured much. She saw their strength and tenacity as a diamond, and the black represents the people. Other assistants in the Black Diamond Choir were Marilyn Brown and Sherman Bush. Beatrice was then teaching a Black Music Appreciation course.

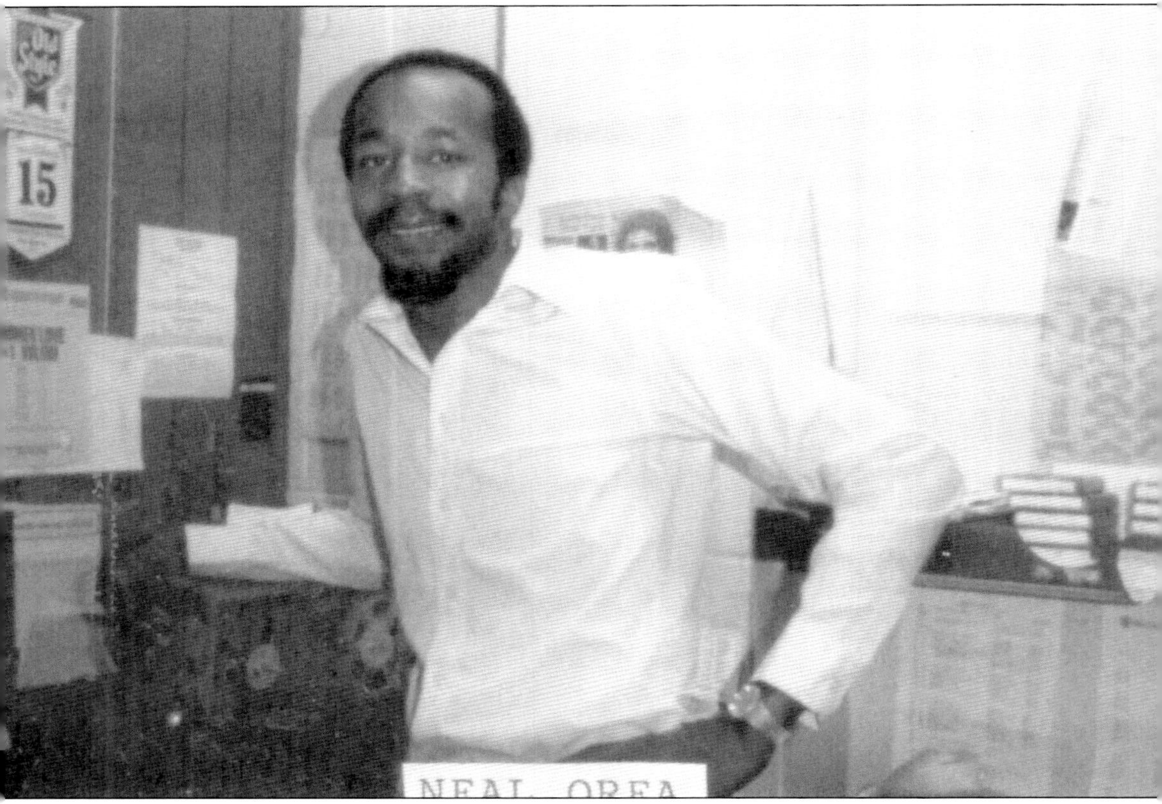

NEAL O'REA. Announcer and chief engineer O'Rea is shown here in 1984. He worked closely with other WLOU employees, including Mildred Staton, business manager; Tony Stroud, account executive; Gery Talbott, account executive; Bruce Branch, sports director; Yvonne Coleman, announcer; Felicia Dixon, announcer; Mary Beth McCormick, news; Helen Phipps, announcer; Gary Rogers, announcer; Jon Rogers, announcer; and Vivian Walls, public affairs director.

Seven

RUSSELL

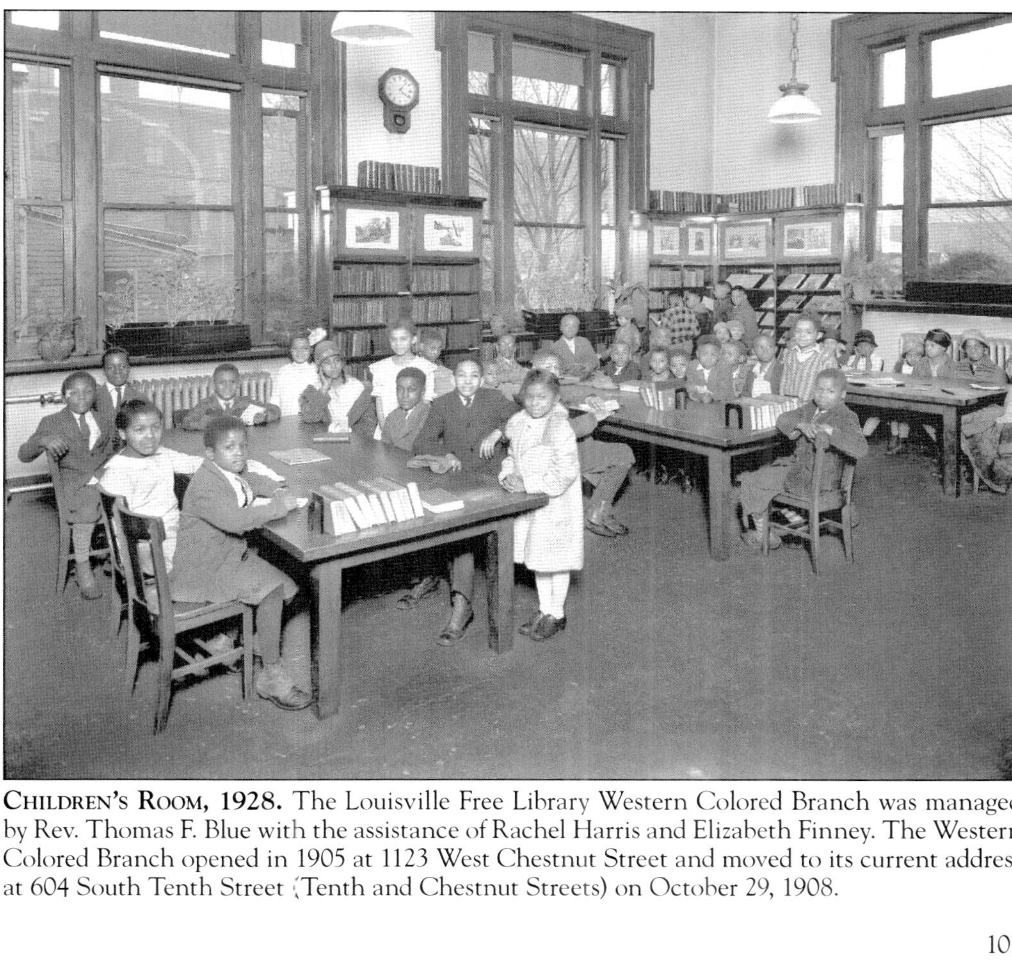

CHILDREN'S ROOM, 1928. The Louisville Free Library Western Colored Branch was managed by Rev. Thomas F. Blue with the assistance of Rachel Harris and Elizabeth Finney. The Western Colored Branch opened in 1905 at 1123 West Chestnut Street and moved to its current address at 604 South Tenth Street (Tenth and Chestnut Streets) on October 29, 1908.

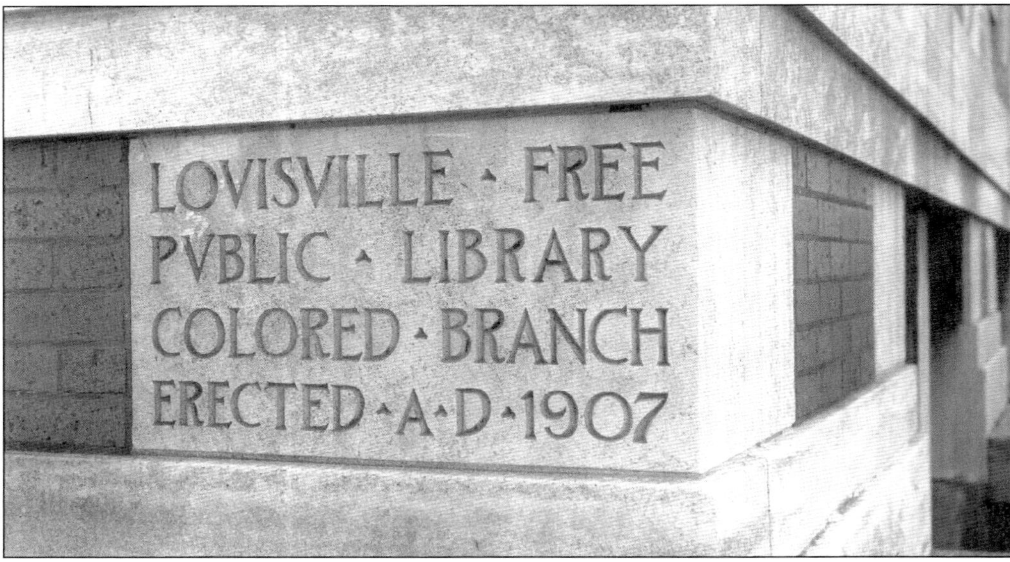

CORNERSTONE, 1907. After the Civil War, there was no place for African Americans to go and participate in extracting information from book collections for educational advancement. The Colored Branch began its legacy in 1905 in a house at 1023 West Chestnut, and the Free Public Library Western Colored Branch was built in 1907.

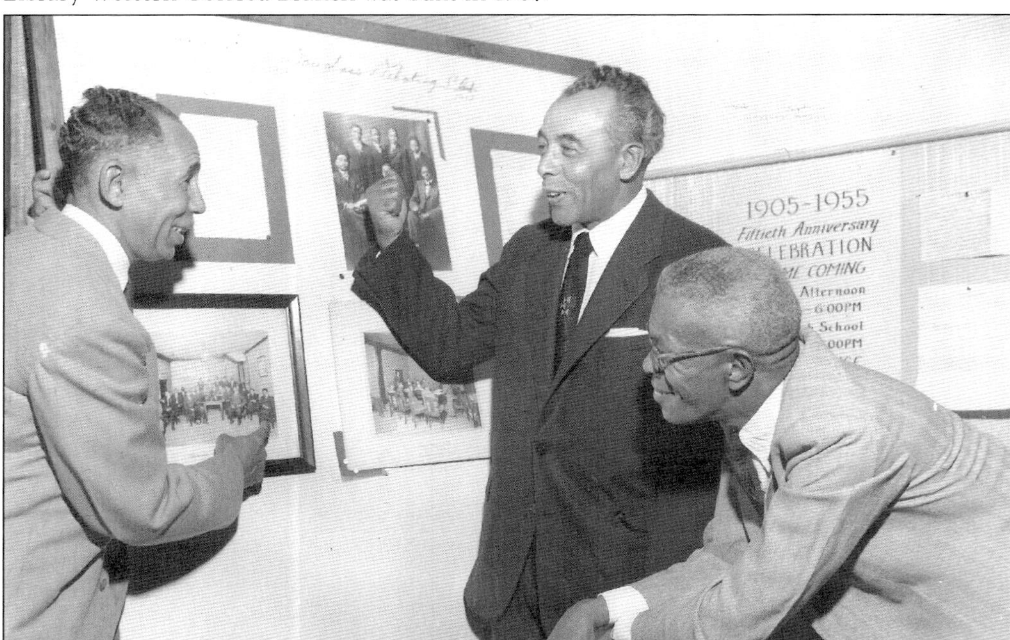

FREDERICK DOUGLASS DEBATING SOCIETY, 50TH ANNIVERSARY, 1955. The Western Colored Branch celebrates its 50th anniversary, and members of the Frederick Douglass Debating Society commemorate their experiences. On September 24, 1883, the great orator Frederick Douglass addressed the National Convention of Colored Men in Louisville, Kentucky, and explained why African Americans needed to fight for their rights: "Liberty given is never so precious as liberty sought for and fought for."

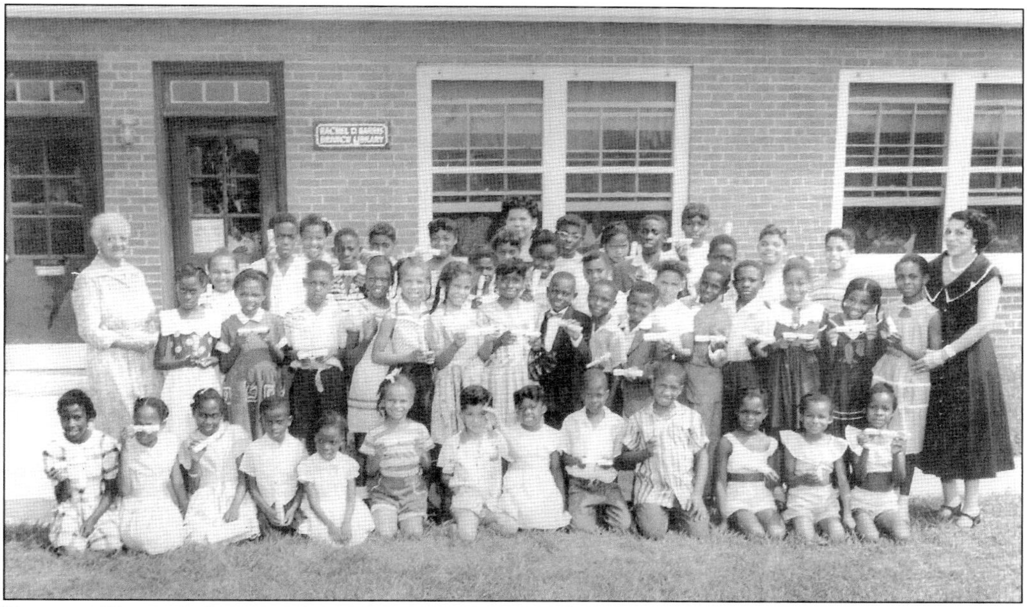

Rachel Harris's Summer Reading, 1956. Pictured here is Russell's Western Colored Branch of the Louisville Free Public Library. Rachel Harris was the assistant librarian to Rev. Thomas F. Blue, chief librarian and branch manager. Russell, a neighborhood west of downtown Louisville, was named after the renowned African American educator Harvey Clarence Russell Sr., a Bloomfield, Kentucky, native.

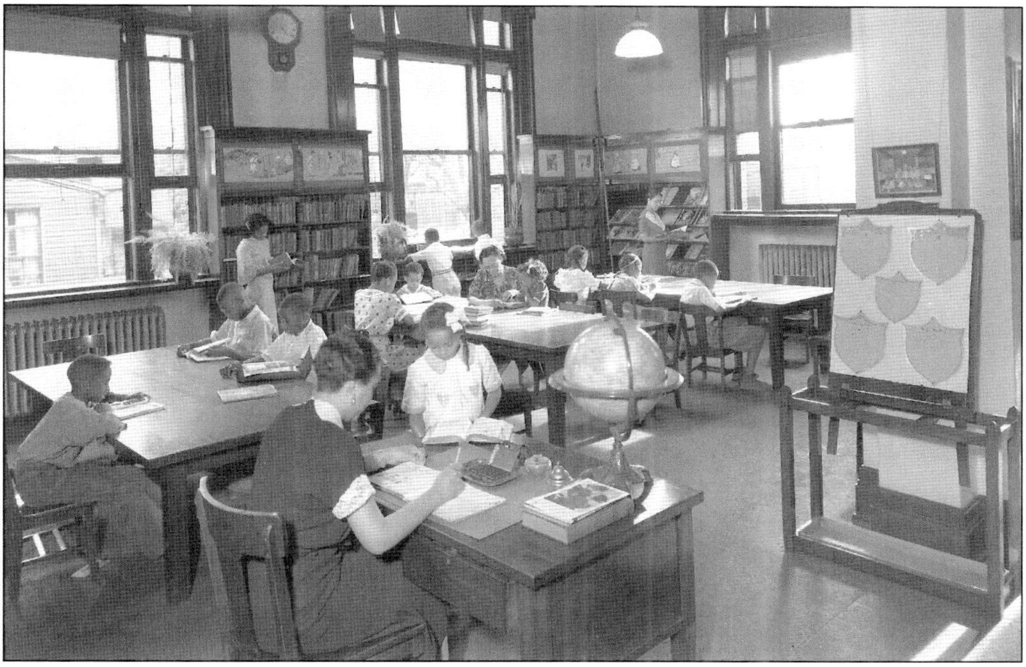

The Children's Room, 1936. This area of the library was used for children to come and study their school assignments as well as sit and read a book from the library's children's collection. Russell neighborhood development began in the 1870s as streetcar lines were extended to the area.

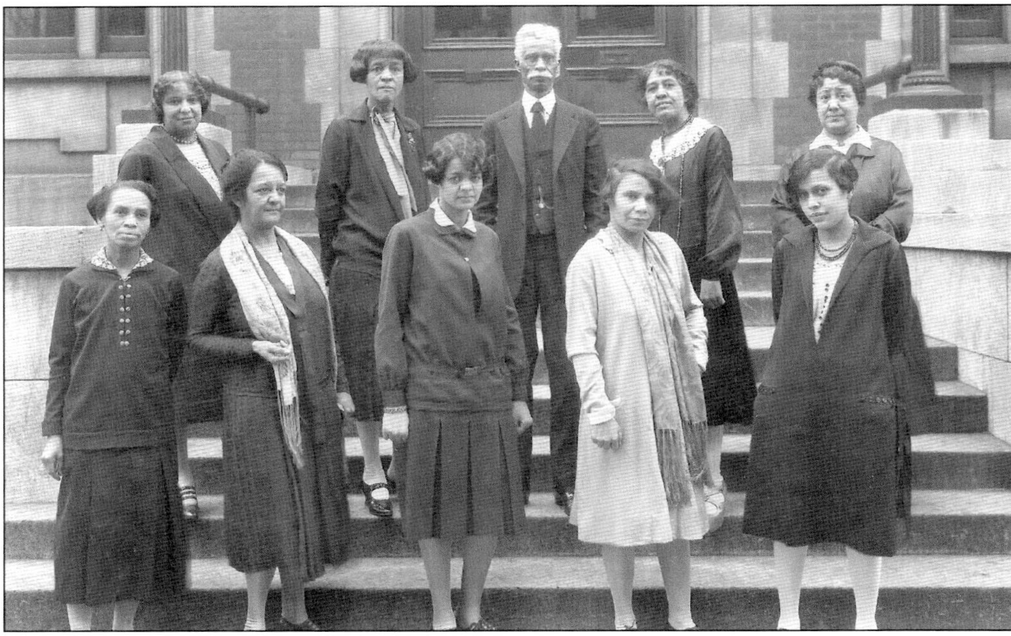

WESTERN COLORED BRANCH STAFF, 1927. In the center is the Rev. Thomas F. Blue, an educator, ordained minister, and the branch's chief librarian and manager. Also in this image are Rev. Blue's assistants, Rachel Harris and Elizabeth Finney. This photograph was taken in front of the Western Branch at 604 South Tenth Street.

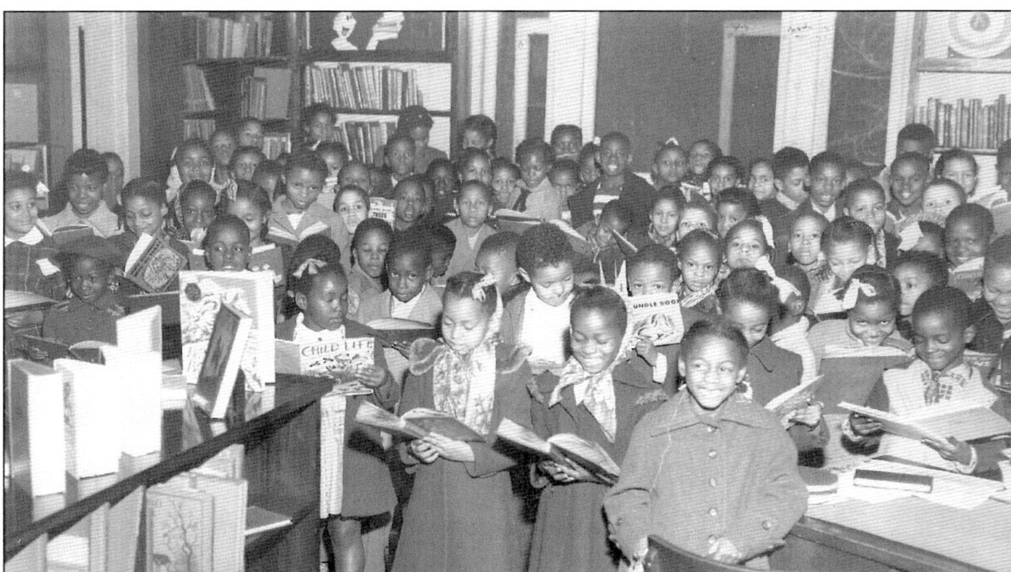

STORY HOUR, RUSSELL'S WESTERN COLORED BRANCH LIBRARY CHILDREN'S ROOM, 1940. The Reverend Thomas Fountain Blue, a native of Virginia, who had been educated as a theologian at Virginia Union University, was chosen branch librarian. The nation's first African American to head a public library, Blue created a high-quality operation, which the community and the library authorities declared was a success from the beginning.

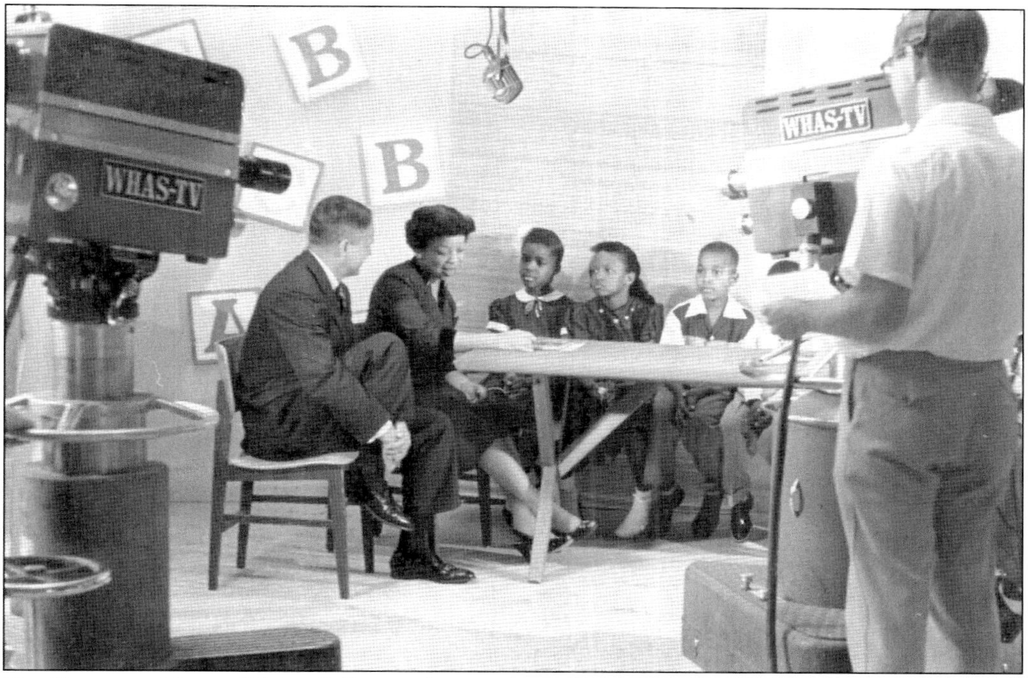

THE BARBARA MILLER *T-BAR-V RANCH* SHOW, 1955. WHAS-TV broadcast Barbara Miller's story hour as a live, weekly television show. Miller, as African American educator, was the director of the children's department at the Main Library, located at 301 York Street in Louisville. She directed the children's department for both white-designated branches as well as for African American children at the Eastern and Western branches.

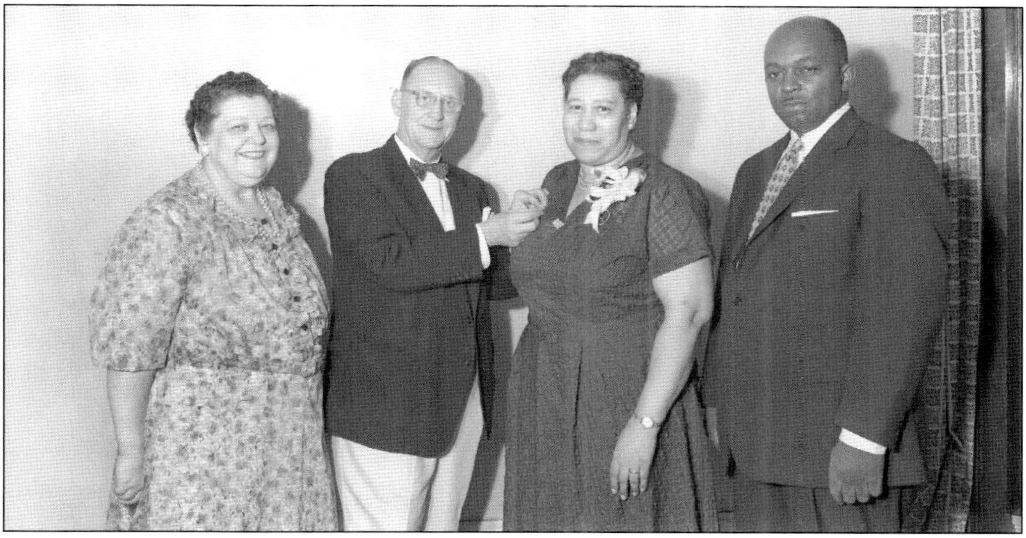

SOUTHERN BELL TELEPHONE COMPANY PIN AWARDS, 1955. A Southern Bell representative is photographed presenting a retirement pin to an African American woman. The Russell area was considered one of Louisville's most fashionable in its early years, with many affluent white families building elegant mansion homes on Walnut, Chestnut, and Jefferson Streets, while working-class blacks and whites lived in shotgun houses on adjacent streets.

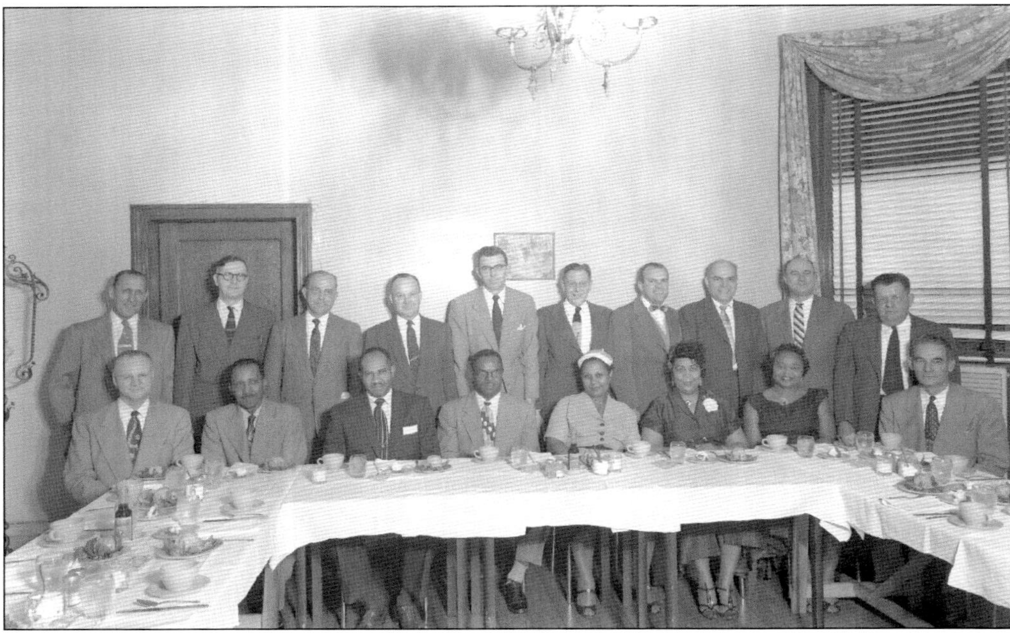

Southern Bell Telephone Company Night, February 10, 1955. Men and women, including African Americans, are gathered at a table for a Southern Bell dinner at Sarah's Tea Room. The Southern Bell Telephone and Telegraph Company was the Bell Operating Company serving the states of Georgia, Florida, North Carolina, and South Carolina.

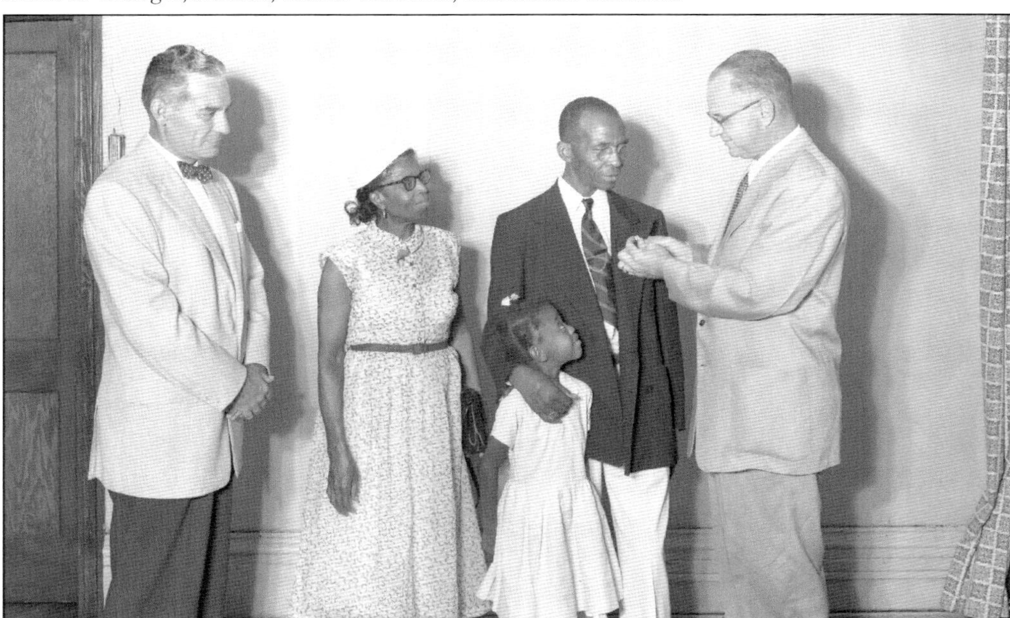

Retirement Party at Sara's Tea Room, August 8, 1955. An African American man, shown with his wife and daughter, receives a pin during a Southern Bell retirement party. By the 1890s, many white families began leaving the area for what would become Old Louisville and the east end, and both middle- and working-class blacks quickly moved into the area.

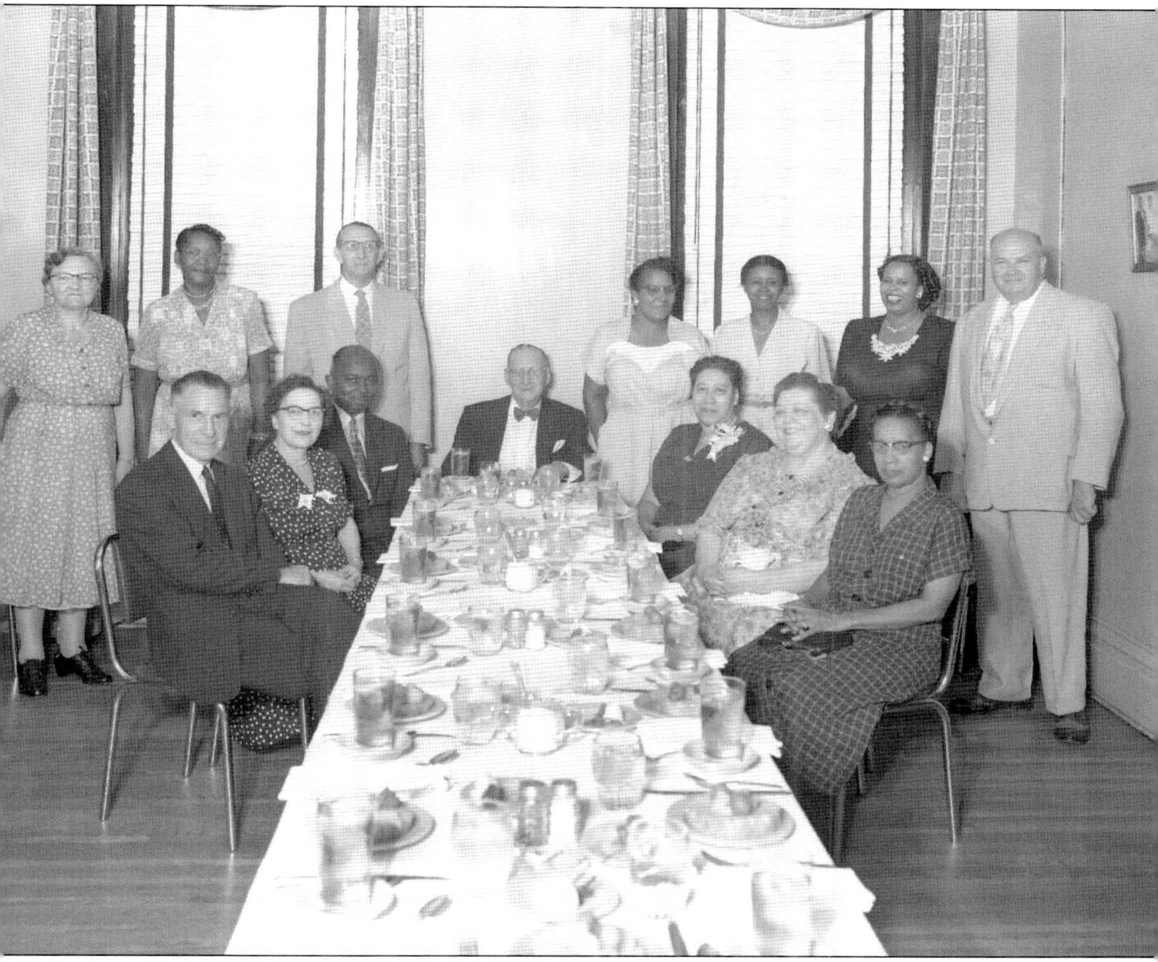

Southern Bell Telephone Company. Southern Bell's employees of both African American and Caucasian descent enjoy a celebrated evening together. Southern Bell began in 1879 as the Atlanta Telephonic Exchange and was based in Atlanta and later changed its name to Southern Bell. On December 20, 1967, Southern Bell Telephone and Telegraph Company formed South Central Bell Telephone Company to operate in five of its nine states: Alabama, Kentucky, Louisiana, Mississippi, and Tennessee.

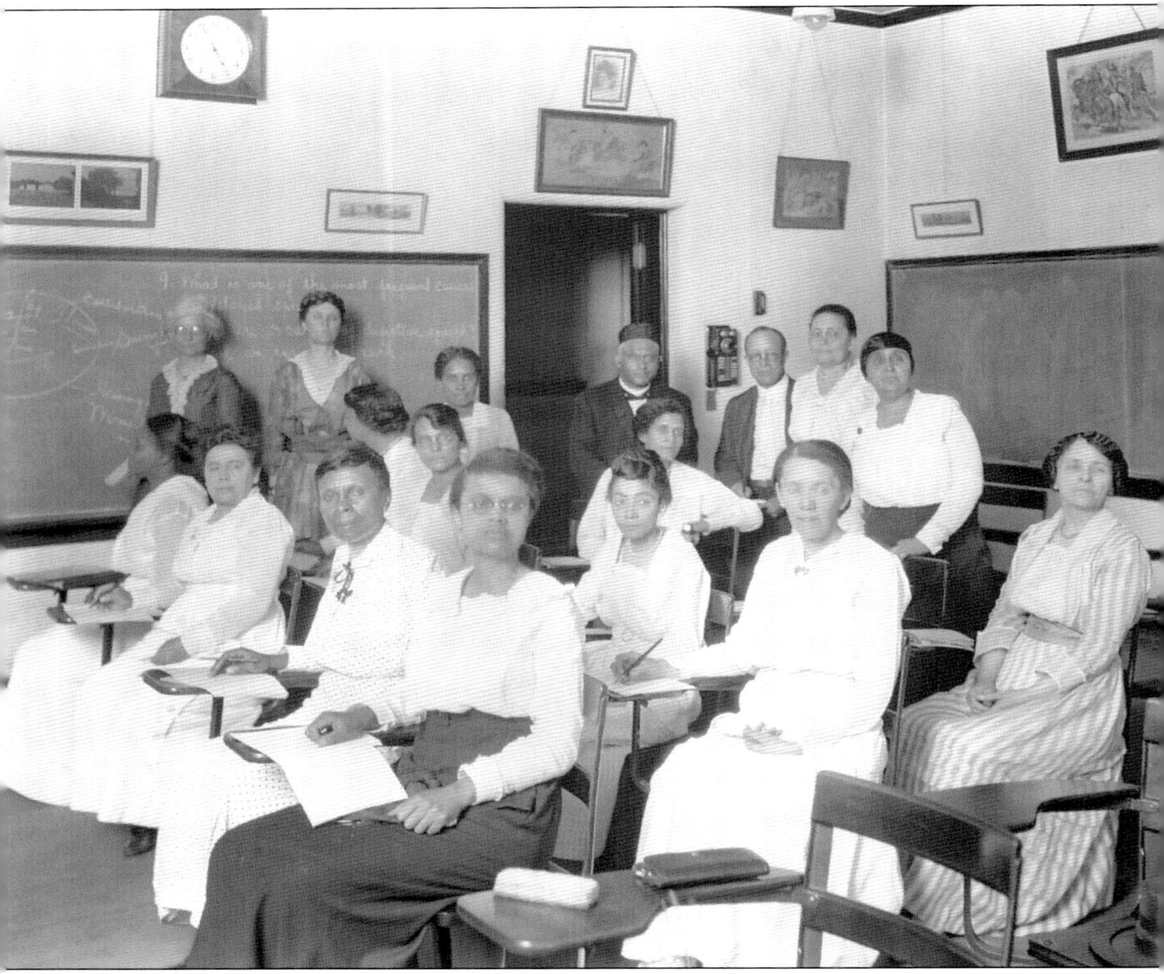

ADULT LEARNERS AT THE CENTRAL COLORED SCHOOL, 1920. The Central Colored School was located at 908 Magazine Street in Louisville. These adult women and a couple of men are taking a night school class at the school. By the 1940s, Russell had become "Louisville's Harlem" as African American theaters, restaurants, and nightclubs lined area streets.

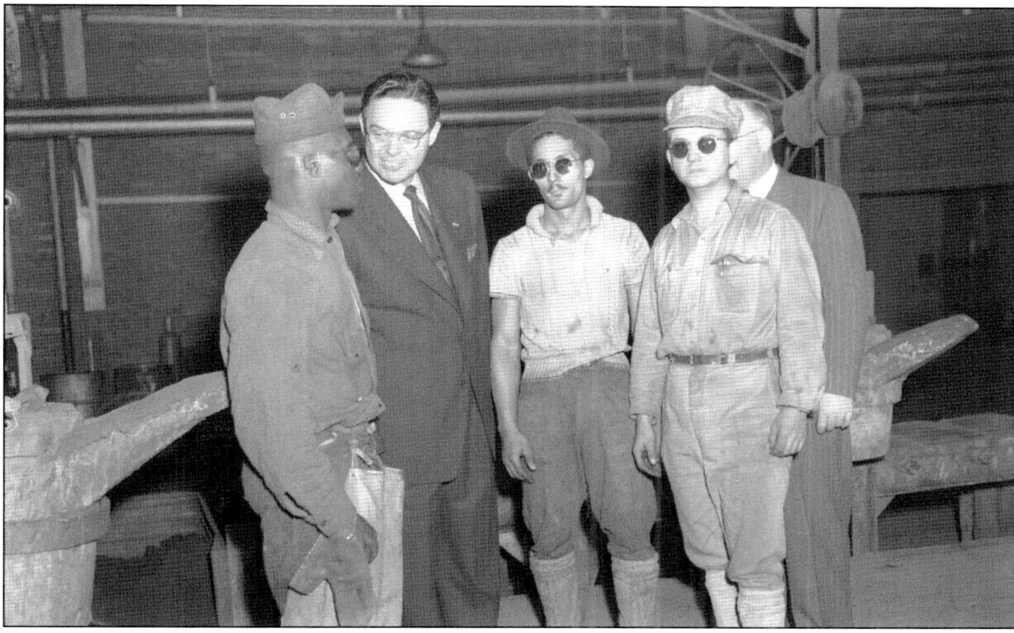

James Melton at Armory, April 2, 1950. Singer James Melton (1904–1961) is seen posing with employees at the Jefferson County Armory in one of a series of promotional photographs.

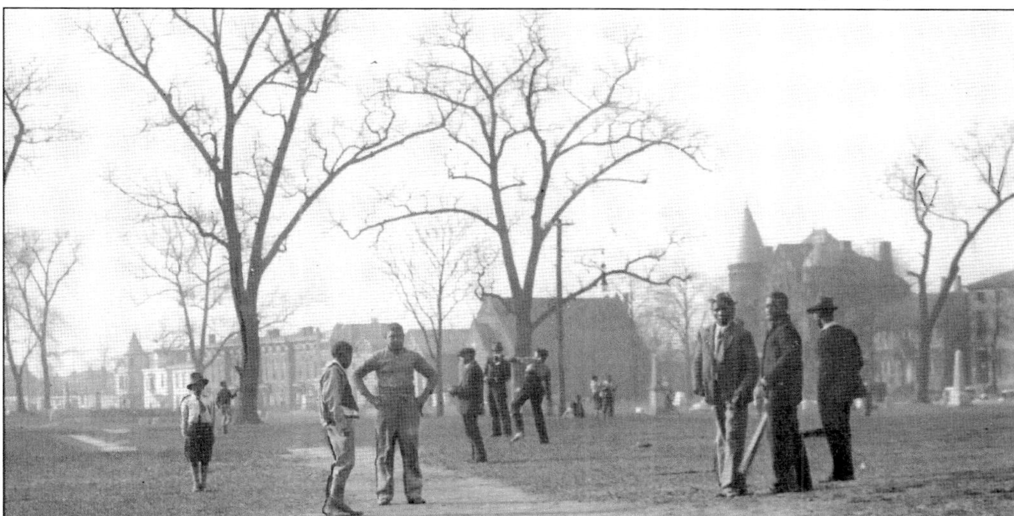

Playing Ball. African American men and boys with baseball equipment are standing in a large clearing in Pioneer Cemetery in Louisville, currently called Western Cemetery, between Fourteenth and Sixteenth Streets on Jefferson Street in the Russell neighborhood. In the *Caron's 1906 Louisville City Directory*, only Greenwood Colored Cemetery and Louisville Colored Cemetery are designated for African Americans. After World War II, the Russell community's middle-class blacks left for newer, integrated neighborhoods in the south and east areas. In the 1960s, urban renewal razed the business districts and built public housing units. America's first public library open to African Americans was in the Russell area. The Western Colored Branch of the Louisville Free Public Library opened in 1905 at 1023 West Chestnut Street.

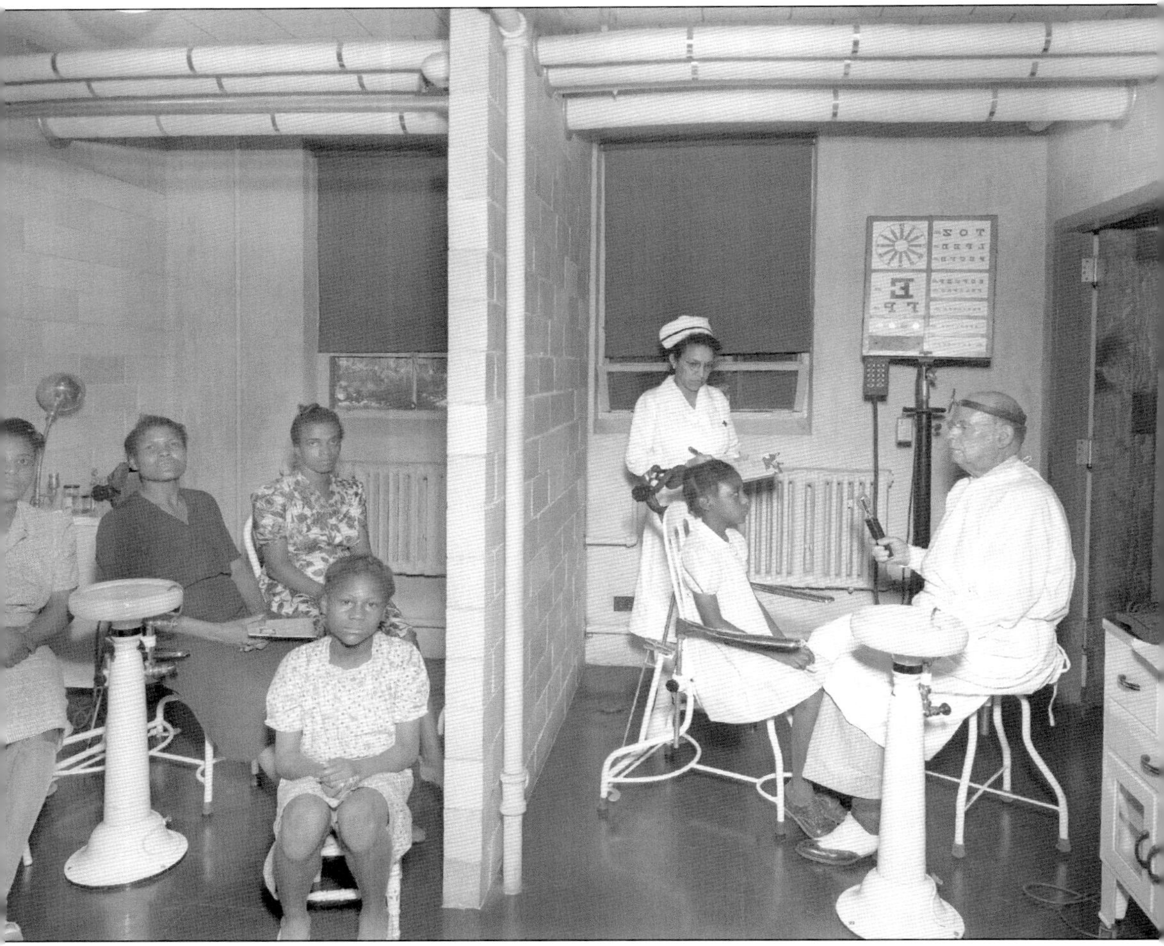

MUNICIPAL HOUSING ADMINISTRATION CLINIC AT BEECHER TERRACE, MAY 26, 1943. A doctor and nurse examine an African American girl while three African American women and another girl sit on the opposite side of a wall at a clinic at Beecher Terrace, located between Ninth and Twelfth Streets on Walnut Street (currently Muhammad Ali Boulevard). In 1940, the Beecher Terrace federal development was completed, and its doors soon opened. Initially, Beecher Terrace was built for defense workers during World War II, but it later became housing for low-income families. By 1943, the Municipal Housing Administration had opened a health care facility and clinic for African American families.

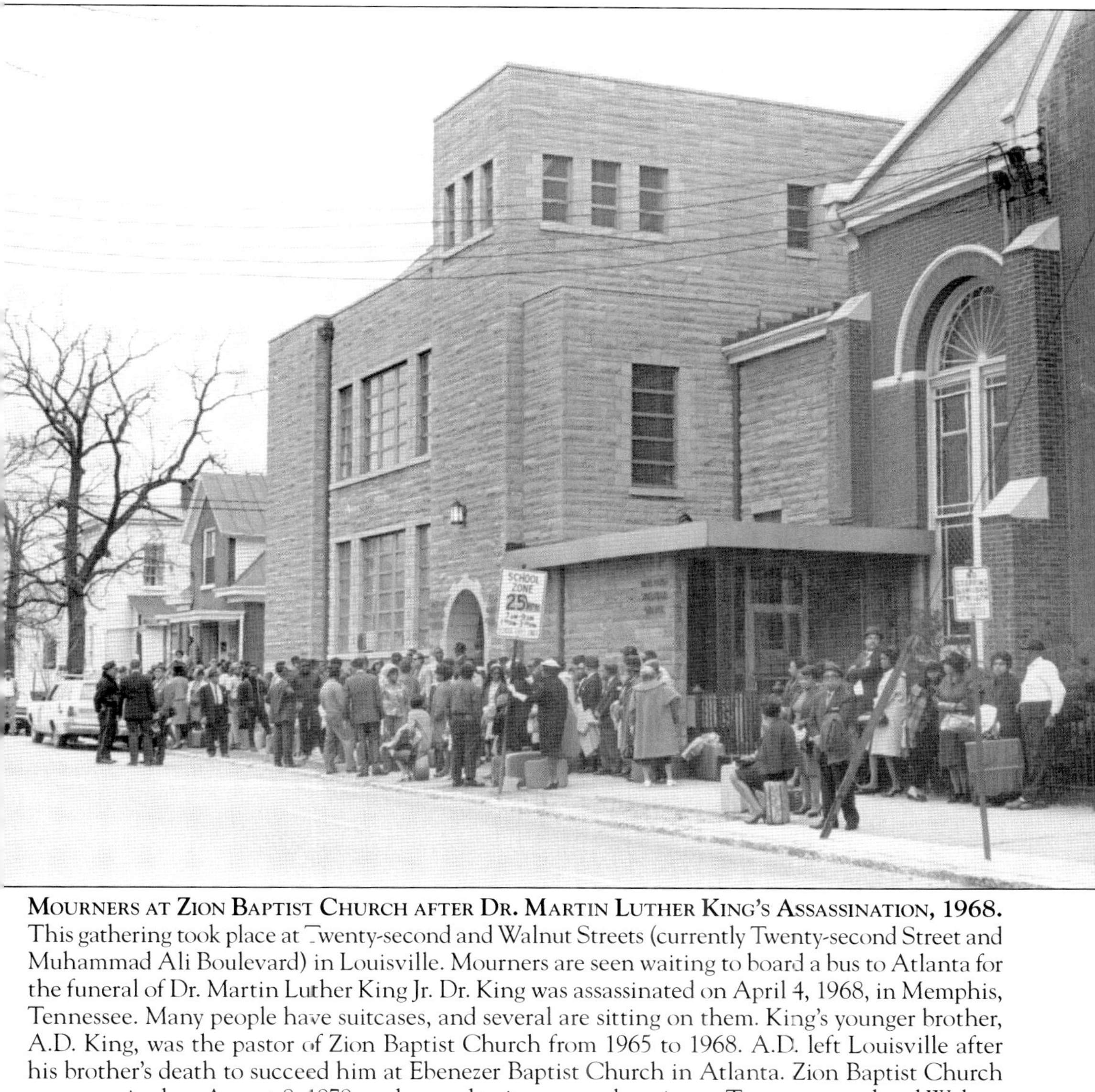

MOURNERS AT ZION BAPTIST CHURCH AFTER DR. MARTIN LUTHER KING'S ASSASSINATION, 1968. This gathering took place at Twenty-second and Walnut Streets (currently Twenty-second Street and Muhammad Ali Boulevard) in Louisville. Mourners are seen waiting to board a bus to Atlanta for the funeral of Dr. Martin Luther King Jr. Dr. King was assassinated on April 4, 1968, in Memphis, Tennessee. Many people have suitcases, and several are sitting on them. King's younger brother, A.D. King, was the pastor of Zion Baptist Church from 1965 to 1968. A.D. left Louisville after his brother's death to succeed him at Ebenezer Baptist Church in Atlanta. Zion Baptist Church was organized on August 8, 1878, and moved to its present location at Twenty-second and Walnut Streets on December 9, 1928. The church was a base for local and state civil rights activities. The Kentucky Christian Leadership Conference office was in the church's adjoining building. Zion Baptist Church's pastors have included Rev. W.H. Craighead, from 1893 to 1942; Rev. D.E. King from 1946 to 1964; Rev. A.D.W. King from 1965 to 1968; pastor emeritus Rev. H.D. Cockerham from 1969 to 2005; and Rev. Gerald Joiner, the current pastor.

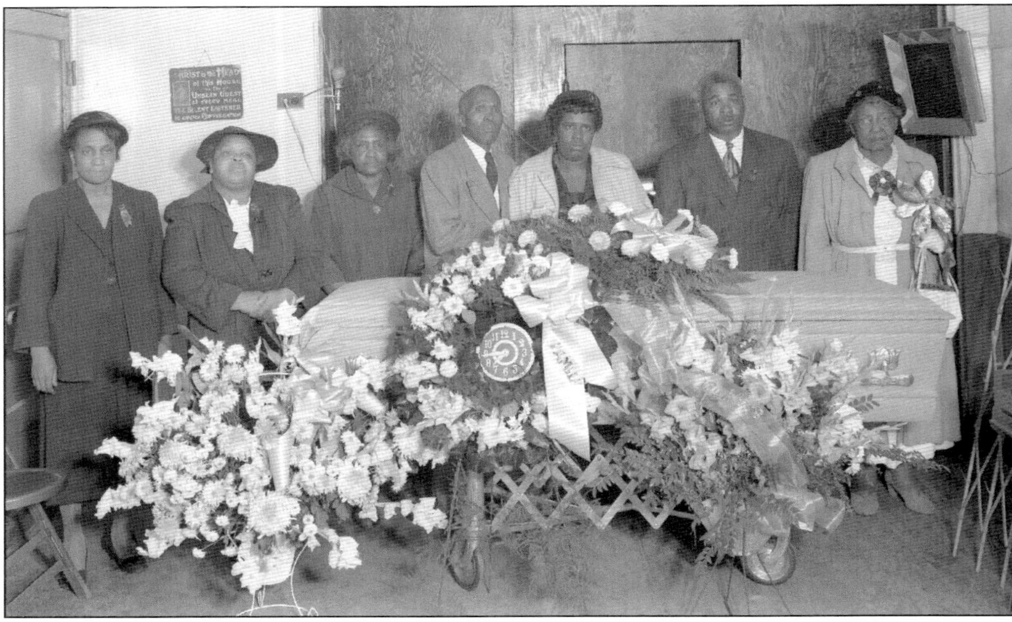

MAY AND SONS FUNERAL HOME, OCTOBER 18, 1955. African American men and women stand in a row behind a casket at May and Sons funeral home. Robert George May opened his funeral home in 1900. It was the first black-owned-and-operated funeral home in Louisville. The second black-owned-and-operated funeral home was Hathaway and Clark in 1901, followed by A.D. Porter and Sons in 1907.

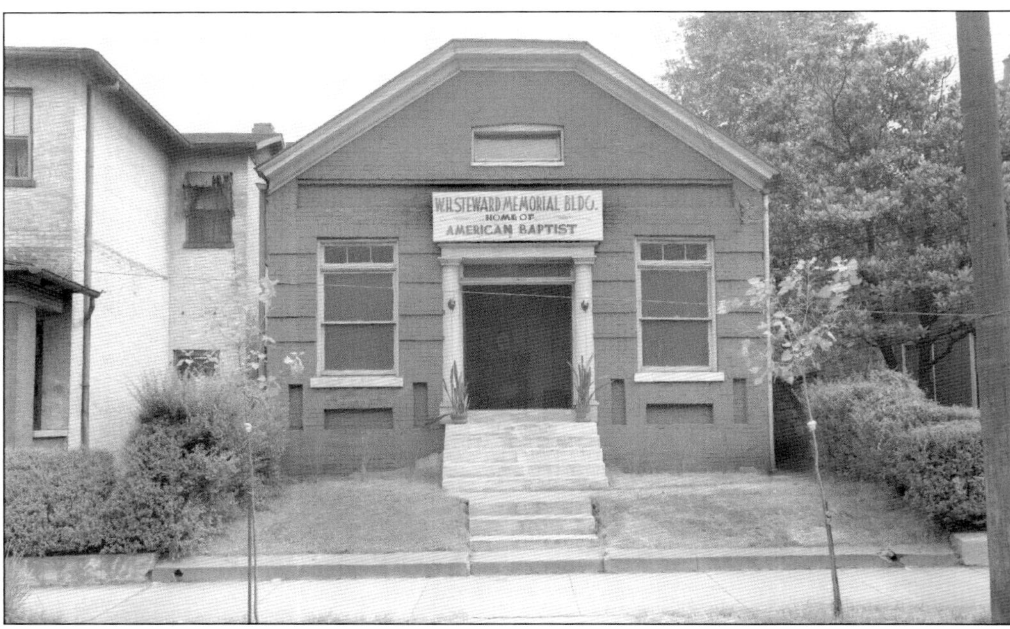

AMERICAN BAPTIST NEWSPAPER BUILDING, JULY 19, 1943. Located at 930 West Walnut Street in Louisville, this small brick building with a sign reading "W.H. Steward Memorial Bldg. Home of American Baptist" above the door was home to the *American Baptist* newspaper.

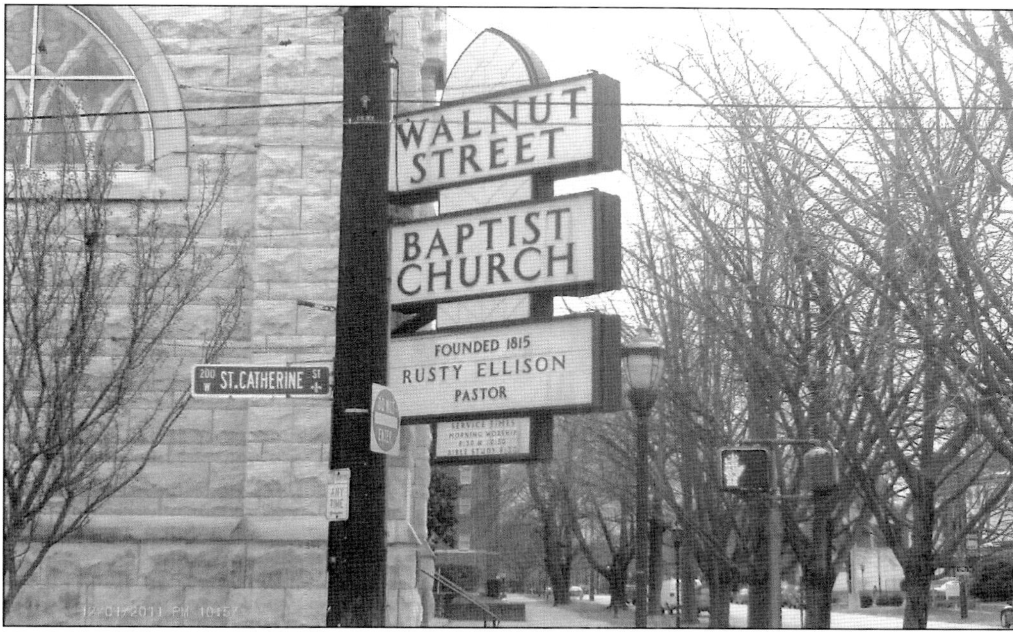

Walnut Street Baptist Church and Fifth Street Baptist Church. Fifth Street Baptist Church's original name was the First Baptist African Mission, under the auspices of First Baptist Church, founded 1815, currently known as Walnut Street Baptist Church. In 1829, members of First Baptist African Mission were given letters and granted the privilege of worshipping as a separate congregation from First Baptist Church. The location of this newly formed church was at Eighth and Market Streets in the Russell neighborhood. The church's first pastor was Rev. Henry Adams, a highly educated black man from Georgia. In 1833, a white friend named Benjamin Stansburg deeded a lot at Fifth and York Streets to the congregation. This was the location owned by and first building to be erected by African Americans in the city of Louisville. Rev. Adams organized and taught the first school for Negroes in the city of Louisville at the First Baptist African Mission. The school opened on December 7, 1841. In 1937, Rev. W. Augustus Jones became pastor; and in 1949, he brought the congregation to its present location at 1901 West Jefferson Street.

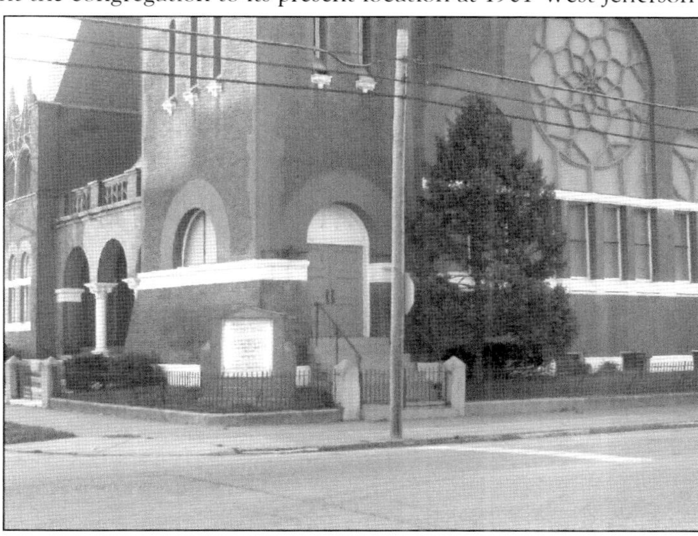

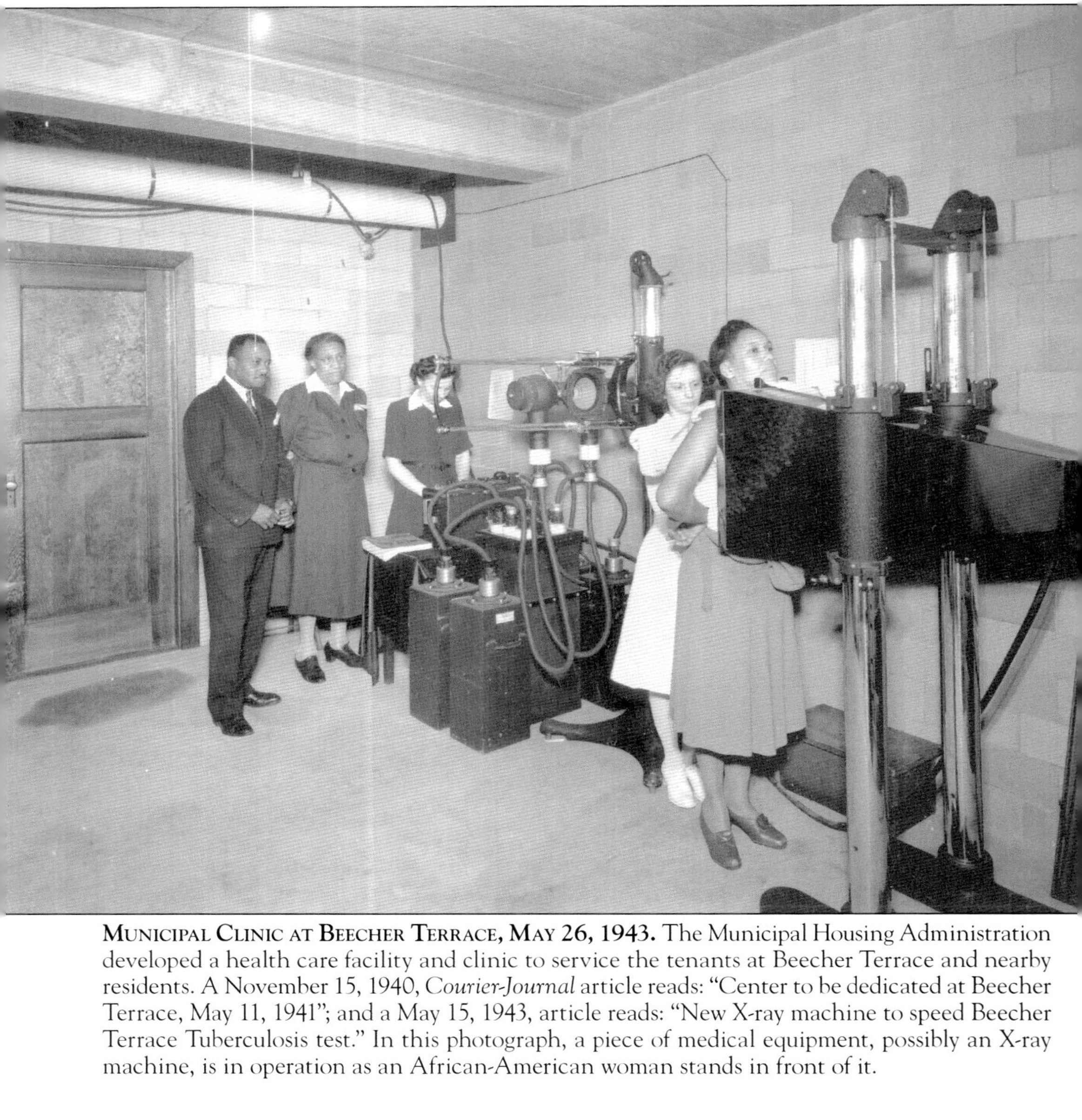

MUNICIPAL CLINIC AT BEECHER TERRACE, MAY 26, 1943. The Municipal Housing Administration developed a health care facility and clinic to service the tenants at Beecher Terrace and nearby residents. A November 15, 1940, *Courier-Journal* article reads: "Center to be dedicated at Beecher Terrace, May 11, 1941"; and a May 15, 1943, article reads: "New X-ray machine to speed Beecher Terrace Tuberculosis test." In this photograph, a piece of medical equipment, possibly an X-ray machine, is in operation as an African-American woman stands in front of it.

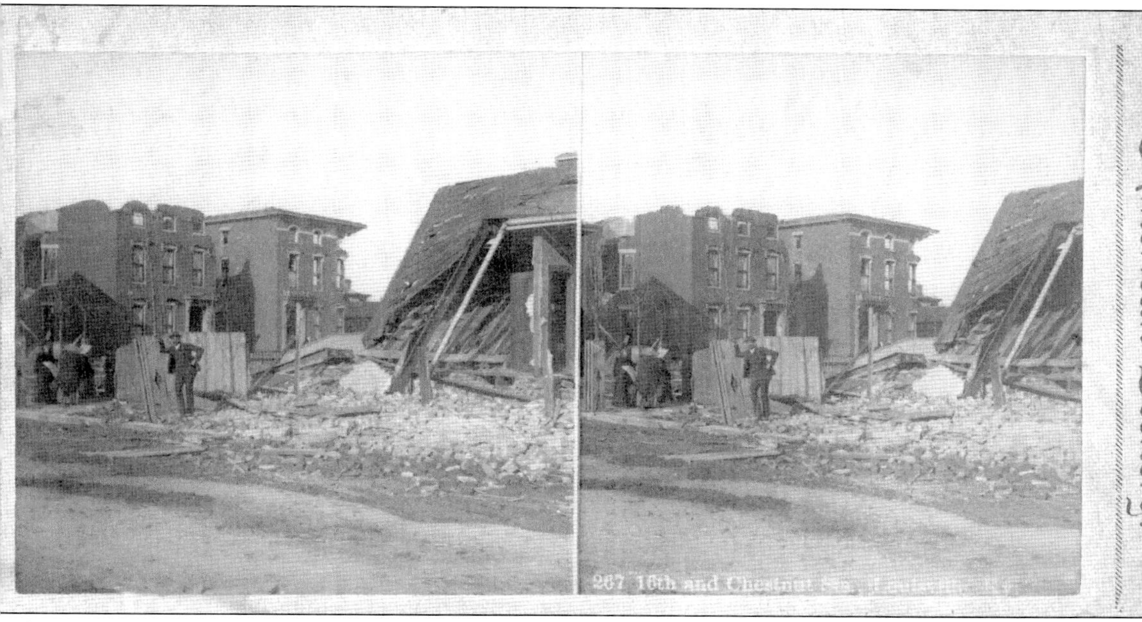

MID-MISSISSIPPI VALLEY TORNADO OUTBREAK. An African American man is leaning against a piece of fence standing between structures that have been completely destroyed by the tornado that hit Louisville on March 27, 1890. Other damaged buildings are in the background in the vicinity of Sixteenth and Chestnut Streets during the Mid-Mississippi Valley Tornado Outbreak. This outbreak was one of the deadliest in United States history, with 24 tornadoes recorded. The most notable of the tornadoes that hit Louisville is estimated to have been an F4 on the Fujita scale. It carved a path from the Parkland neighborhood to Crescent Hill, destroyed 766 buildings ($2.5 million worth in property), and killed an estimated 74 to 120 people; 55 of those deaths occurred when the Falls City Hall collapsed, making it the highest death toll from a single building collapse in Louisville history.

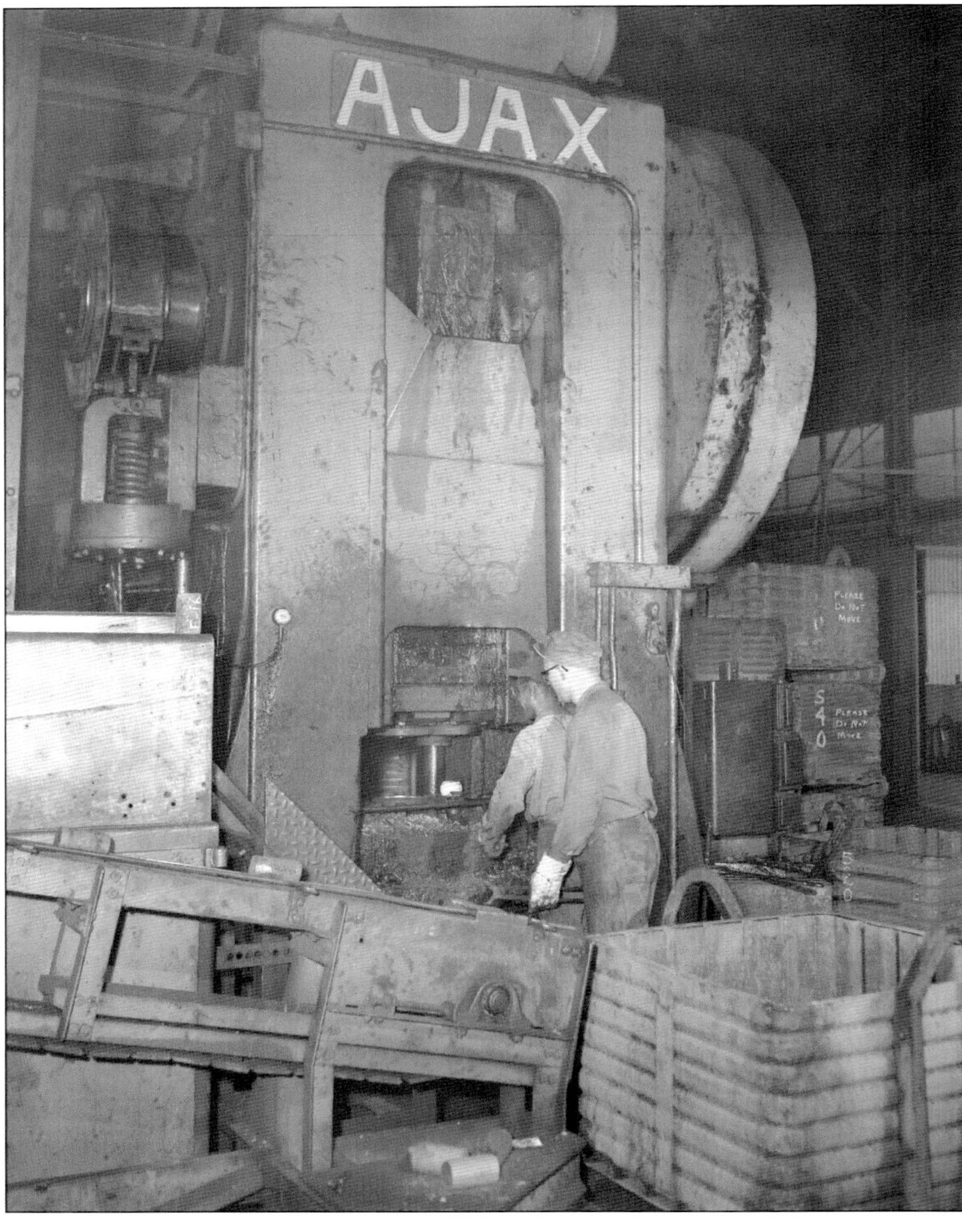

CONSOLIDATED AJAX, JANUARY 18, 1961. African American and Caucasian men work at various machines and equipment at International Harvester in what is now in the Russell neighborhood. The roots of International Harvester run to the 1830s, when Cyrus Hall McCormick, an inventor from Virginia, finalized his version of a horse-drawn reaper, which he field demonstrated through 1831 and for which he received a patent in 1834. Together with his brother, Leander (1819–1900), McCormick moved to Chicago in 1848 and started the McCormick Harvesting Machine Company. The McCormick reaper sold well, partially as a result of savvy and innovative business practices. The products came onto the market just as the development of railroads offered wide distribution to distant areas. Cyrus developed marketing and sales techniques, with a vast network of trained salesmen able to demonstrate operation of the machines in the field.

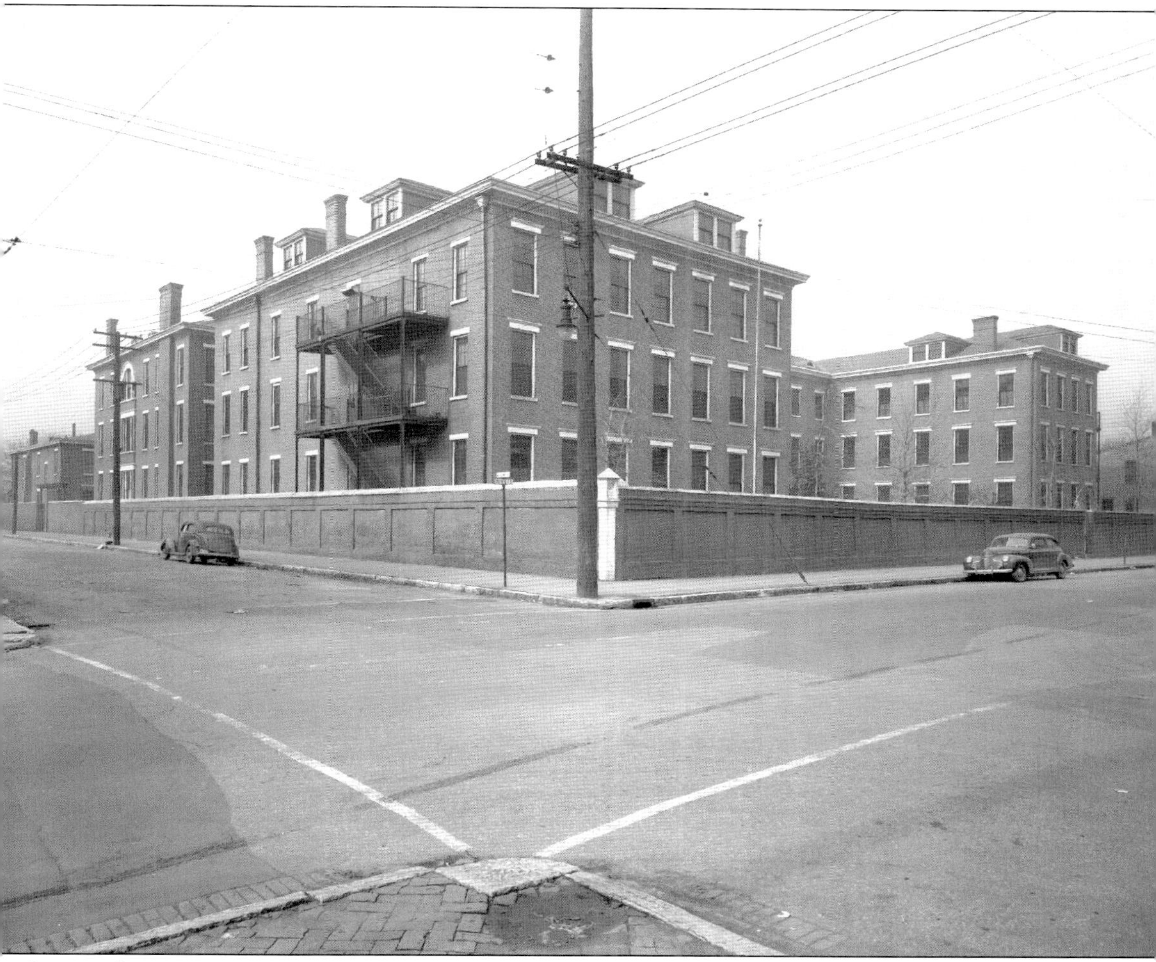

LITTLE SISTERS OF THE POOR ON TENTH AND MAGAZINE STREETS, RUSSELL NEIGHBORHOOD. This exterior view of Little Sisters of the Poor, a three-story brick residential building, was taken on February 4, 1950. This organization began with the charitable work of Jeanne Jugan, born at Cancale, France, on May 15, 1793. According to the Catholic Encyclopedia online article about the order, Jugan, acquainted with others caring for an elderly blind woman, "was soon eager to share in the charitable work, and on October 15, 1840, Marie Jamet and Virginie Tredaniel with their charge, went to live in [Jeanne Jugan's] house. The three young women went out daily to their work, bringing home their earnings for their common support and for the poor blind woman. In time, they were joined by Madeleine Bourges and gave shelter to other helpless old people. The zeal displayed by Jeanne Jugan in securing the means to support those in their care has caused her to be regarded as the real foundress of the order."

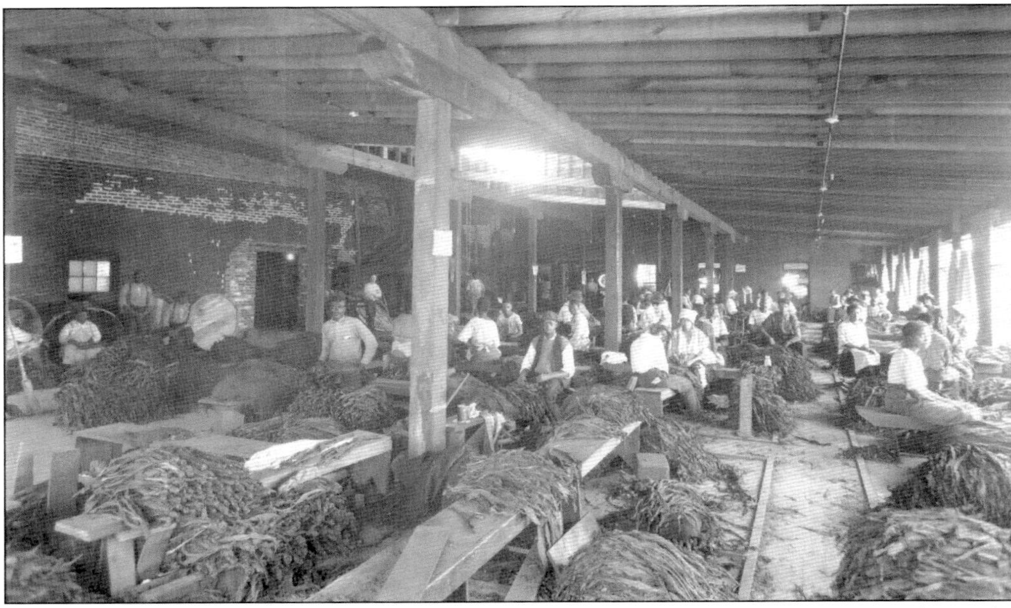

Campbell Company Employees, September 4, 1920. The Campbell Company was located at 1114 West Liberty Street in Louisville. Tobacco leaves are spread on wooden benches in a dimly lit workroom. With the exception of one man standing at the edge of the room who is Caucasian, all the workers are African Americans. Some of the men wear hats, and some of the women wear bonnets. The factory workers' expressions are almost universally somber.

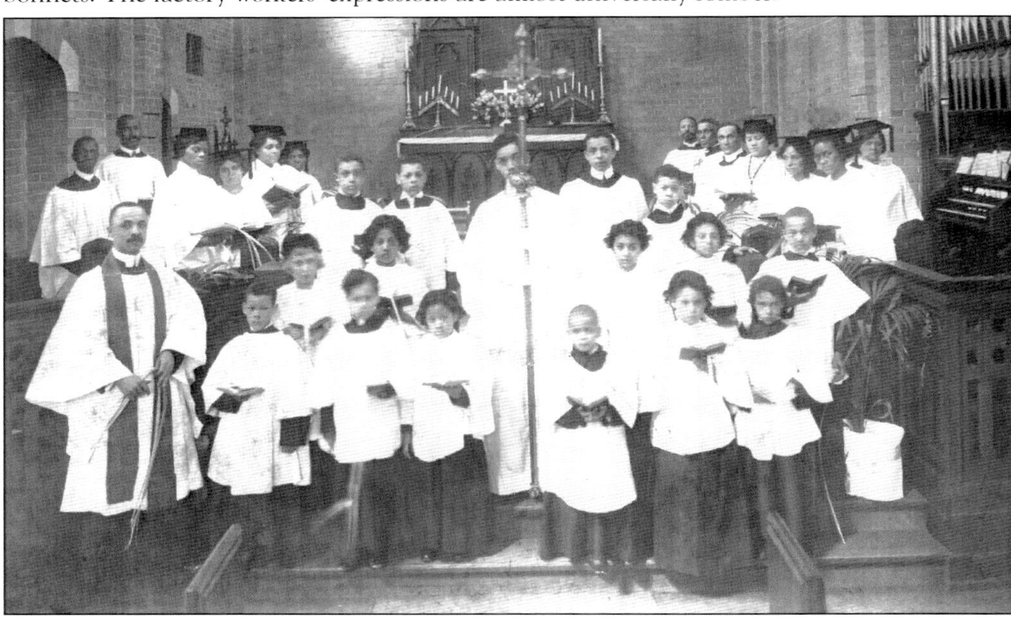

African American Church Choir, 1939. The church has long played a vital role in the African American community and continues to do so today. The church offers hope and for many years, when schools were not available for African Americans, was the center for training and education in the community. The music of the church was and is inspirational and strengthening, enhancing every soul it encounters.

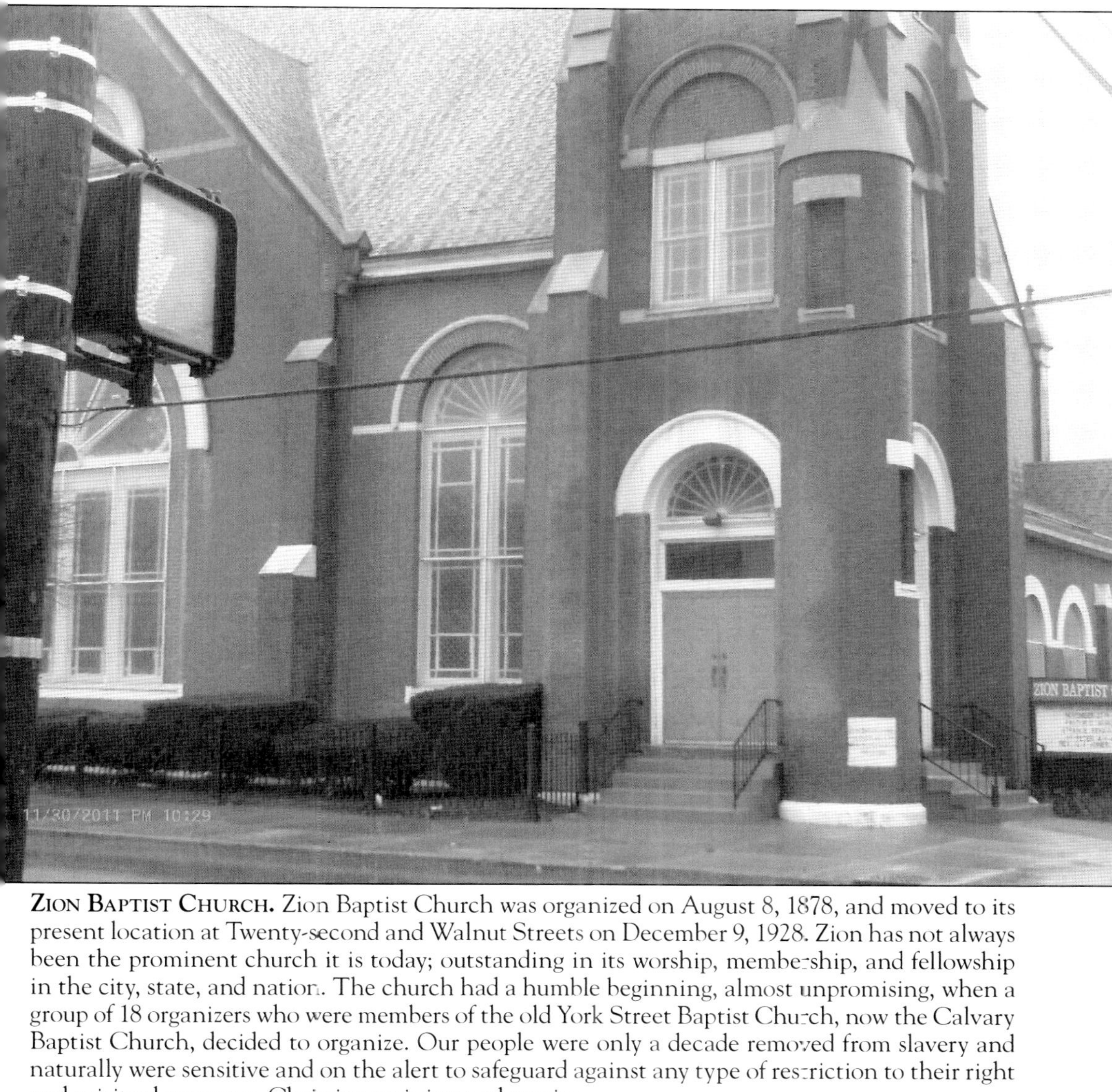

Zion Baptist Church. Zion Baptist Church was organized on August 8, 1878, and moved to its present location at Twenty-second and Walnut Streets on December 9, 1928. Zion has not always been the prominent church it is today; outstanding in its worship, membership, and fellowship in the city, state, and nation. The church had a humble beginning, almost unpromising, when a group of 18 organizers who were members of the old York Street Baptist Church, now the Calvary Baptist Church, decided to organize. Our people were only a decade removed from slavery and naturally were sensitive and on the alert to safeguard against any type of restriction to their right and spiritual response, Christian training and service.

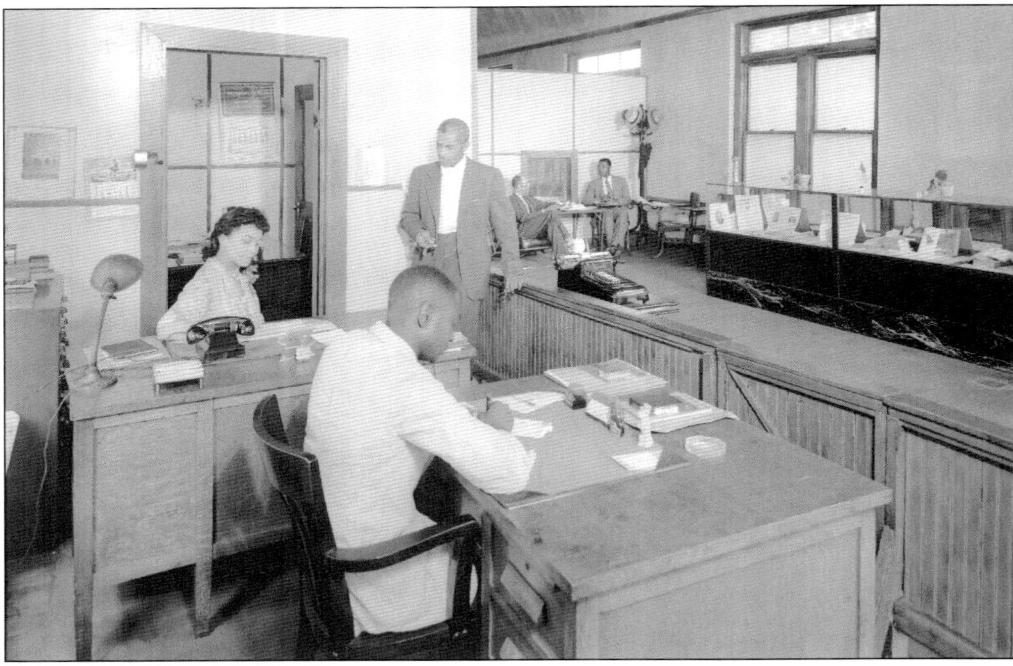

AMERICAN BAPTIST NEWSPAPER, JULY 19, 1943. Pictured here is the interior office space at the newspaper's former address, 930 West Walnut Street. The General Association American Baptist Newspaper is currently at 1715 West Chestnut Street. The company was established in 1878 and incorporated in Kentucky. The newspaper is a multipurpose business: printing notices of job positions that are available in churches and important events throughout the community, and publishing the paper.

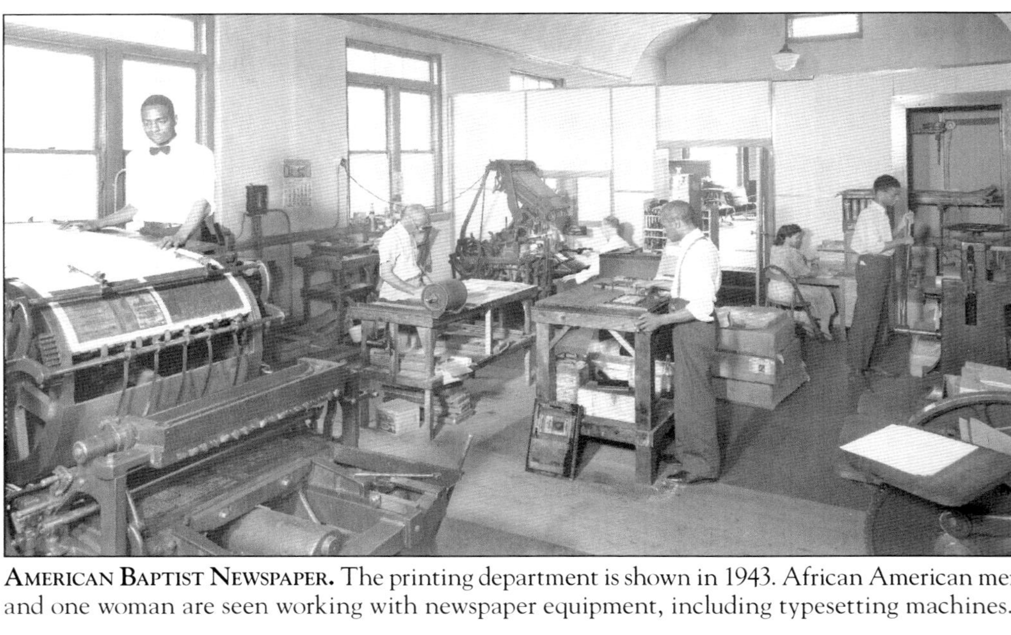

AMERICAN BAPTIST NEWSPAPER. The printing department is shown in 1943. African American men and one woman are seen working with newspaper equipment, including typesetting machines.

Eight

The Lincoln Institute

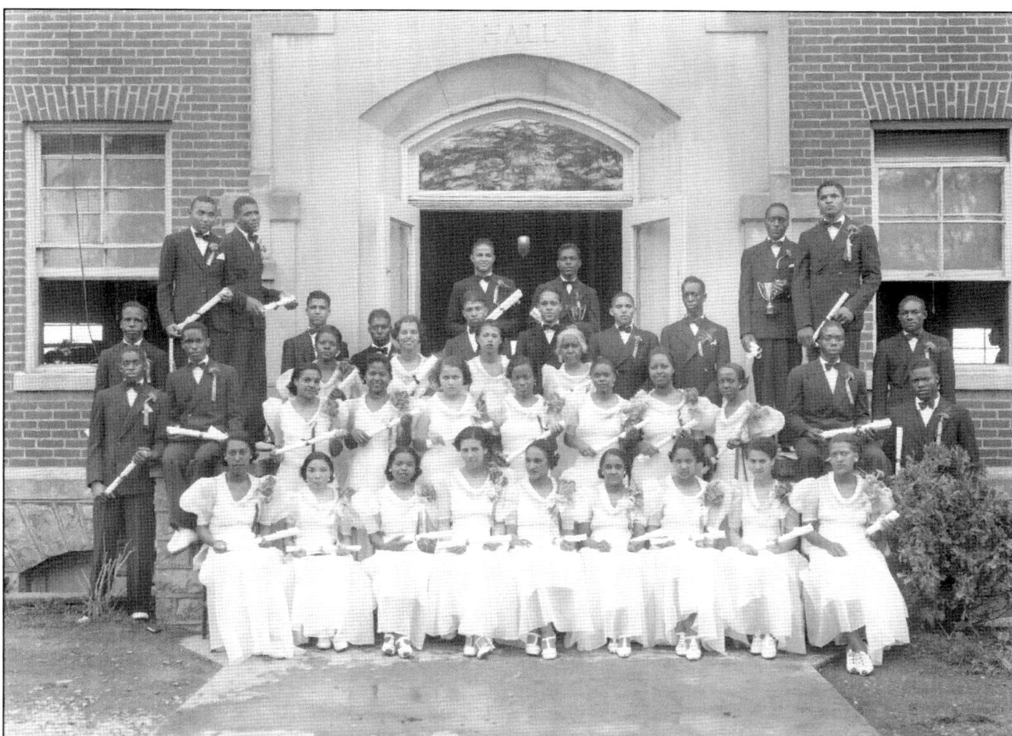

Lincoln Institute Graduation, Simpsonville, Kentucky, June 1937. Approximately 40 men and women pose at the Lincoln Institute. They are holding diplomas from their graduation and are wearing corsages on their shoulders. The men are wearing dark suits with light shirts and black bow ties, while the women are wearing long white dresses. A couple of the men are holding trophies.

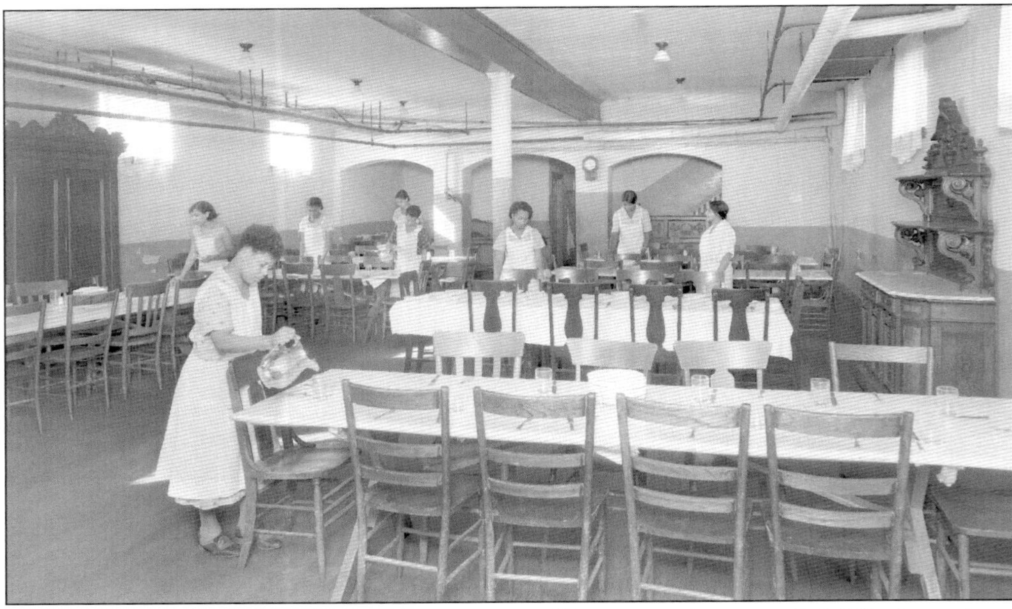

Lincoln Institute Dining Room, Simpsonville, Kentucky, October 7, 1932. A number of young African American women are photographed setting the tables at the Lincoln Institute dining room. Each woman is wearing a white apron over her clothes. The tables are covered with white paper or cloth, and wooden chairs are pulled up. Silverware is laid out, and glasses are being filled from silver-colored pitchers. A stack of plates waits to be spread out.

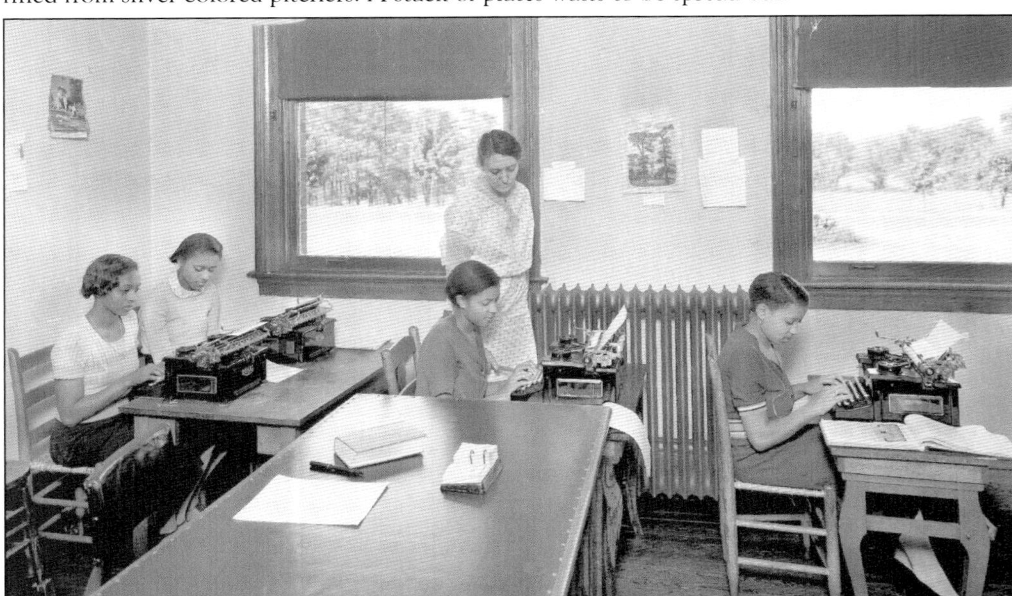

Lincoln Institute Typing Class, Simpsonville, Kentucky, October 7, 1932. A woman watches a young lady typing. Three others are also practicing at their typewriters. Each short desk has one or two typewriters, and a larger table has a book, pen, paper, and calendar on it. A radiator sits between two windows, through which lawn and trees are visible.

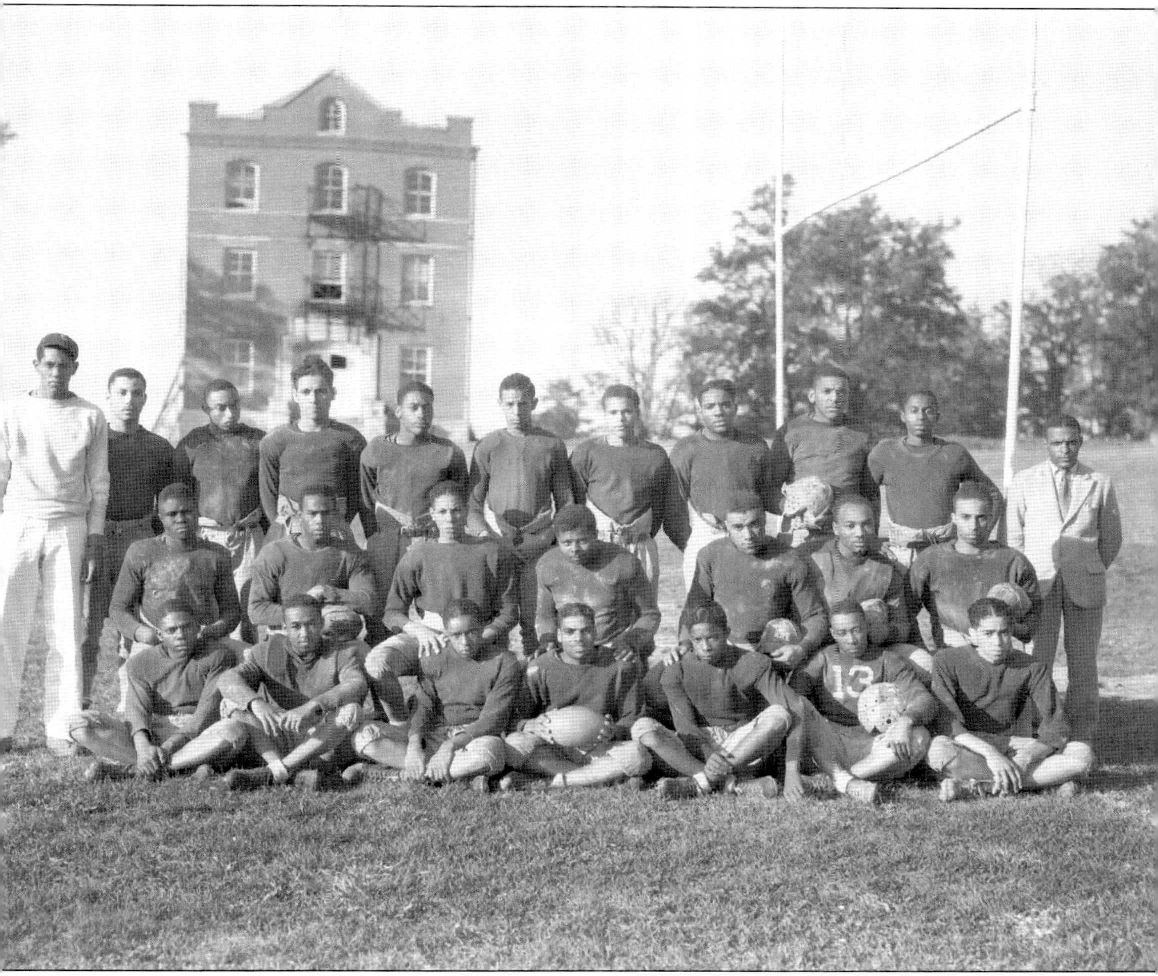

LINCOLN INSTITUTE FOOTBALL TEAM, SIMPSONVILLE, KENTUCKY, OCTOBER 7, 1932. A group of mostly African American men poses for a photograph next to a goalpost. Most are wearing dark, long-sleeved tops and knee-length, light-colored pants. Some are holding helmets, and others have footballs in their hands. To the sides are two men who may be coaches.

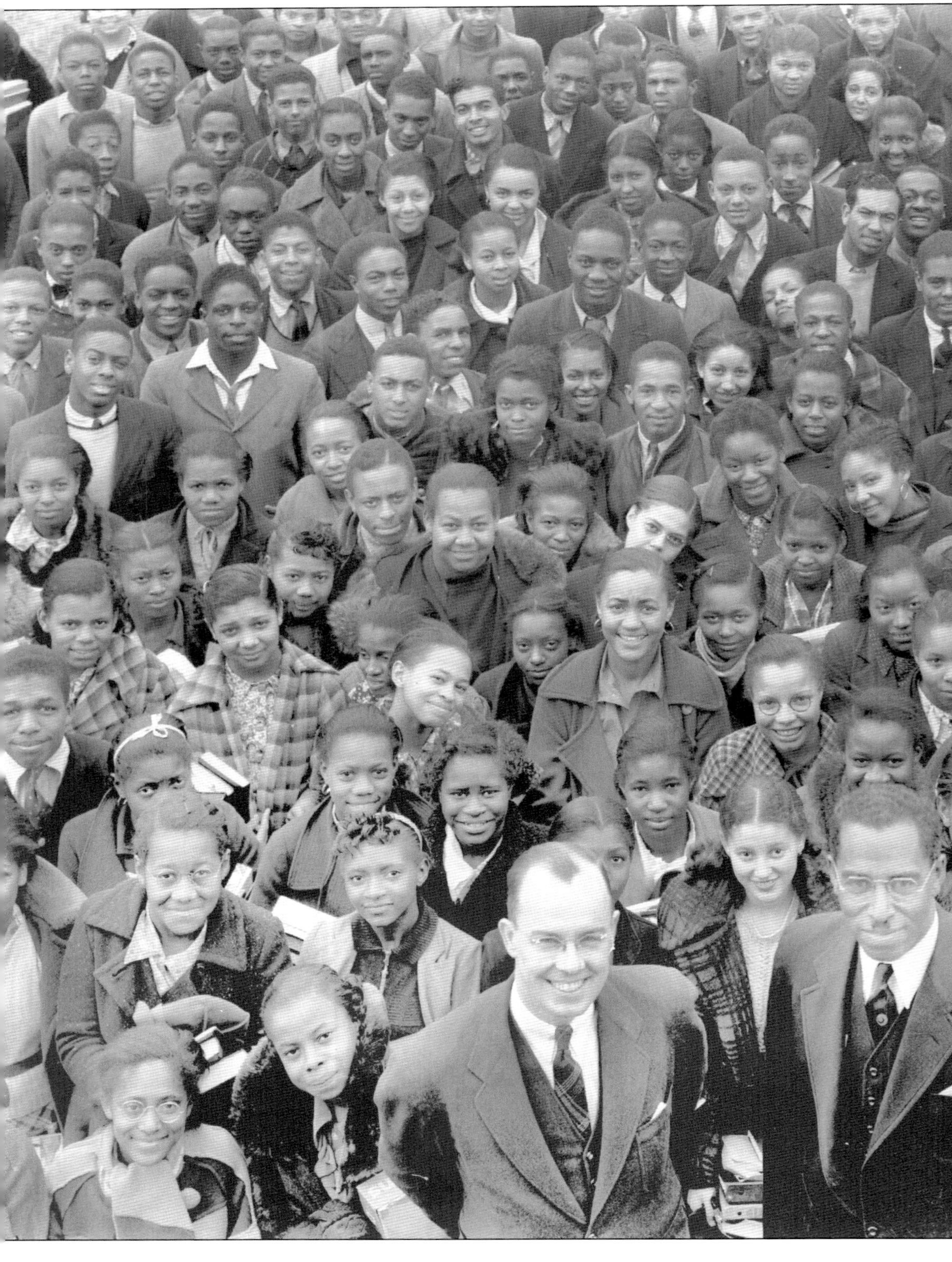

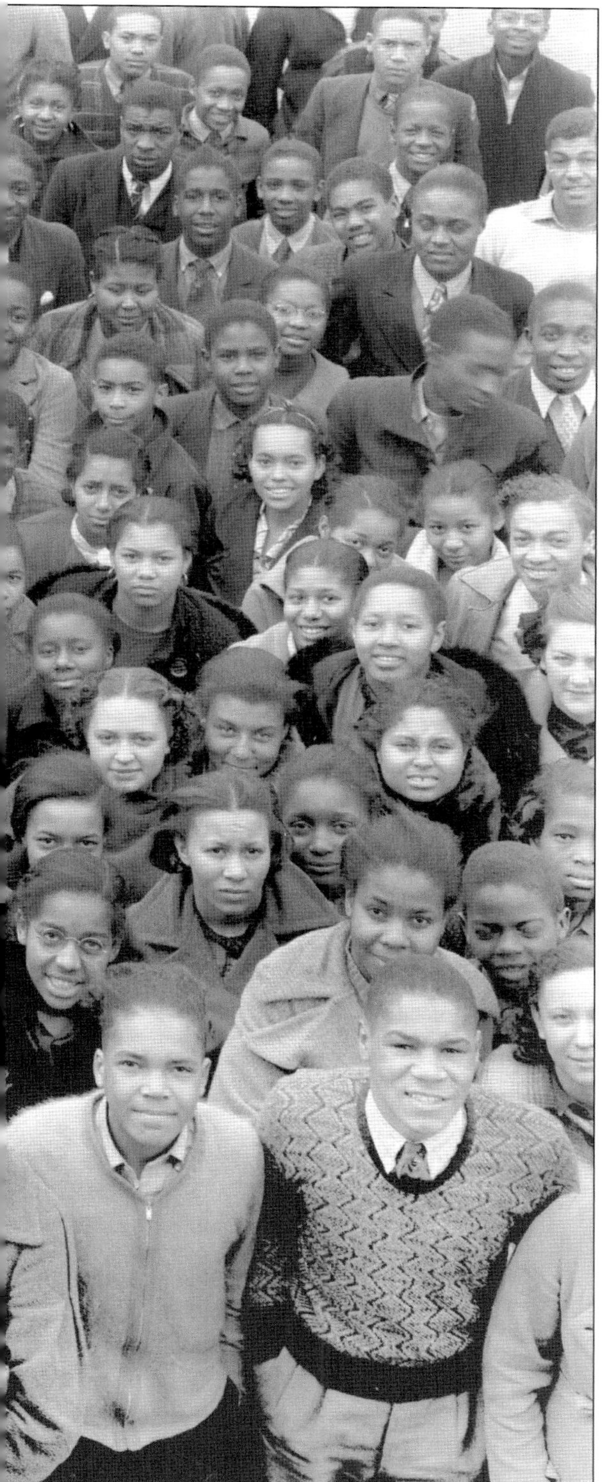

LINCOLN INSTITUTE STUDENTS, SIMPSONVILLE, KENTUCKY, NOVEMBER 11, 1937. Several hundred students from the Lincoln Institute are photographed standing and smiling at the camera. Two men in suits are in the center of the front row. They are probably teachers or administrators of the Lincoln Institute. The children are wearing coats and sweaters, and some of them are holding armfuls of books. In 1906, the president and board of trustees of Berea College, along with Dr. James Bond and Kirke Smith, African American alumni, began fund-raising for a new private school for blacks and by 1909, thanks to a $200,000 donation by Andrew Carnegie, the money was raised. In 1910, the Lincoln Foundation was commissioned to oversee the assets of the new institution, and construction began the following year. Under the direction of its first president, A. Eugene Thomas, the Lincoln Institute opened On October 1, 1912. The institute's enrollment was racially mixed. An African American educational institution, the institute was 20 miles east of Louisville. In 1903, state representative Carl Day, from Breathitt County, visited the campus of Berea College, which during that time was Kentucky's only integrated college. Day was disturbed by the intermingling of blacks and whites. In response, he sponsored the bill that later bore his name, Day Law, which passed the Kentucky legislature in 1904. The bill mandated both public and private schools be segregated. Berea College's officials fought the decision, taking it to the United States Supreme Court, but they lost the case in 1908. Though Berea lost the case, it continue to hold its commitment for equal rights in education for all. (*The Encyclopedia of Louisville.*)

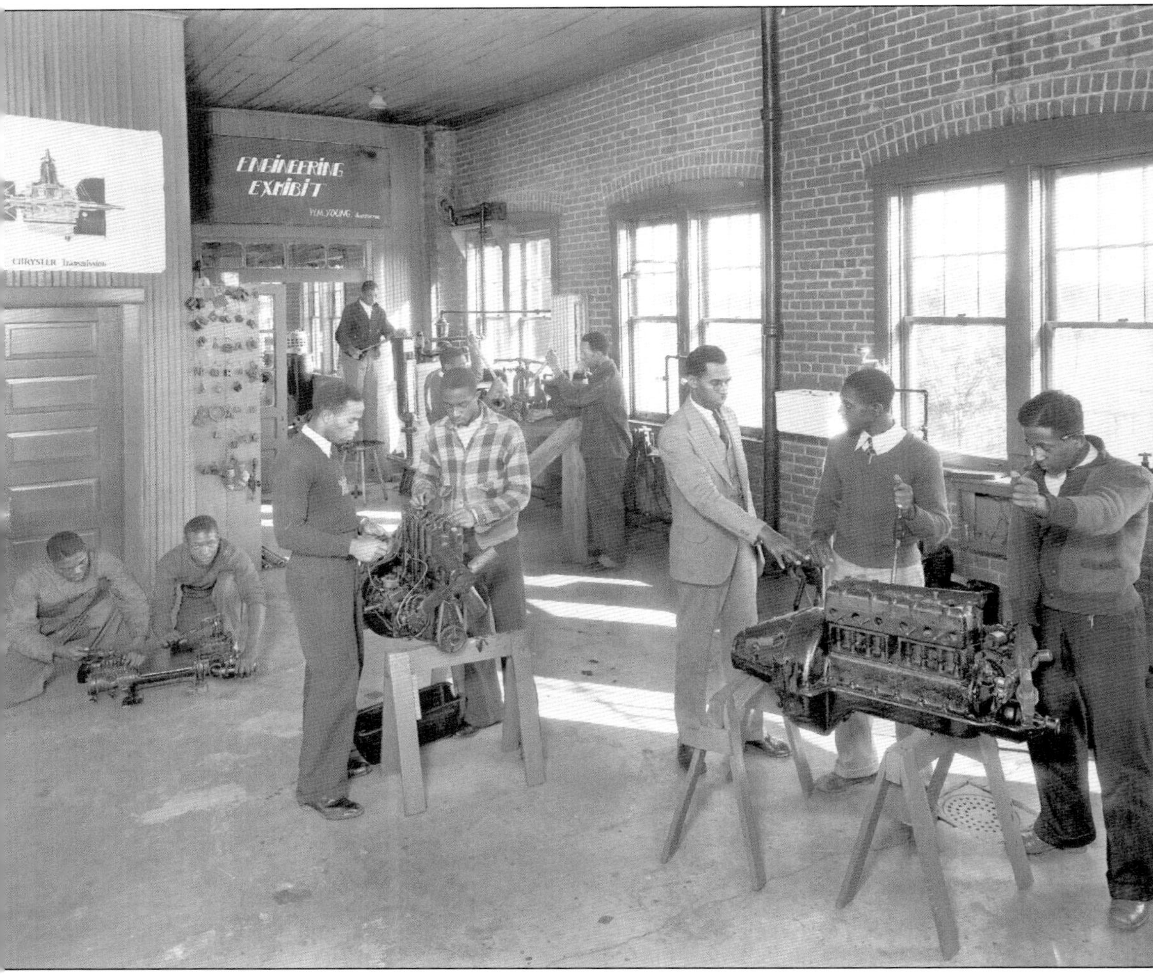

LINCOLN INSTITUTE AUTOMOTIVE CLASS, SIMPSONVILLE, KENTUCKY, OCTOBER 7, 1932. Several groups of African American men are working on engines in a brick room with large windows. One man is wearing a suit and is probably the instructor, while the others are wearing sweaters and slacks. One sign on the wall shows a Chrysler transmission, and another advertises an engineering exhibit.

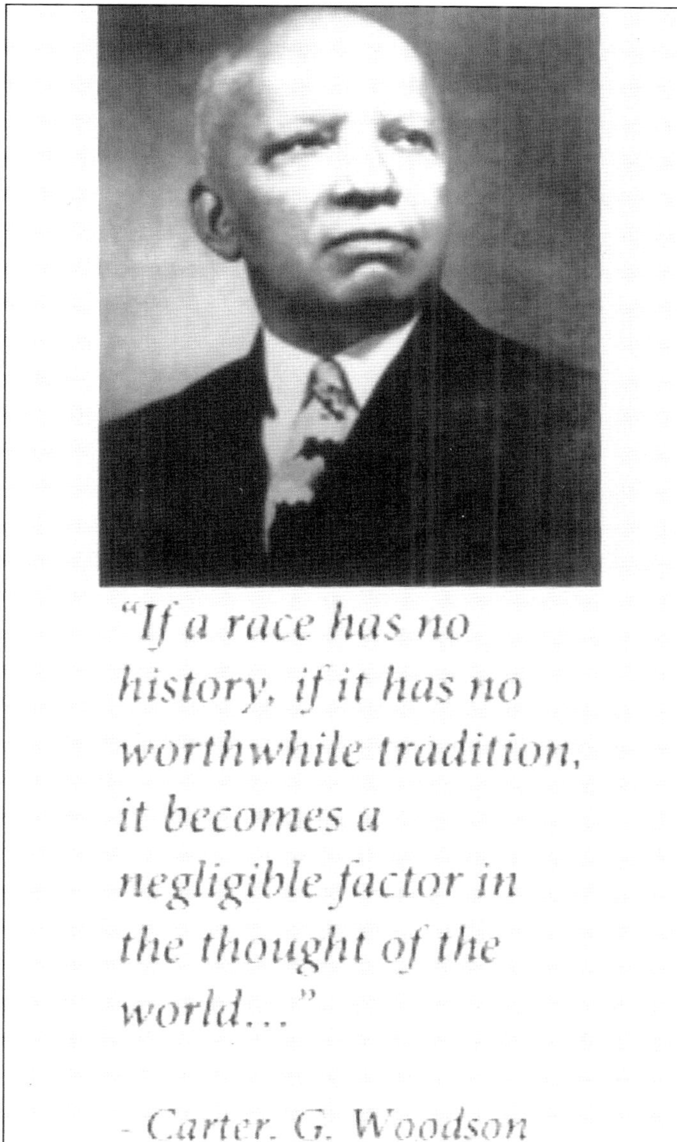

CARTER GODWIN WOODSON (DECEMBER 19, 1875–APRIL 3, 1950). The caption on this image is a quote by Dr. Carter G. Woodson: "If a race has no history, if it has no worthwhile tradition, it becomes a negligible factor in the thought of the world . . ." Woodson was an African American historian, author, journalist, and the founder of the Association for the Study of African American Life and History. He was a founder of the *Journal of Negro History*, now titled *The Journal of African American History*. Woodson has been cited as the father of black history. He was the son of former enslaved Africans James and Eliza Riddle Woodson. From 1903 to 1907, Woodson was a school supervisor in the Philippines. Later, he attended the University of Chicago, where he was awarded a BA in 1907 and an MA in 1908. He was a member of the first black fraternity, Sigma Pi Phi, and a member of Omega Psi Phi. In 1912, he completed his doctorate in history at Harvard University, where he was the second African American (after W.E.B. DuBois) to earn a doctoral degree.

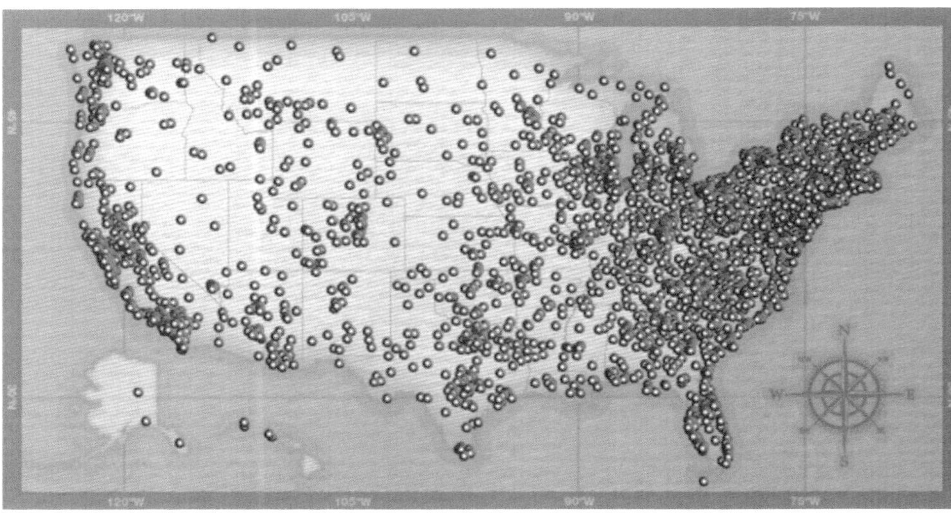